T0305058

Benchmarking and Regulation in Transport

Benchmarking and Regulation in Transport

European Perspectives

Edited by

Chris Nash

Research Professor, Institute for Transport Studies, University of Leeds, UK and Visiting Professor, Masaryk University, Czech Republic

Ginevra Bruzzone

Senior Fellow, Luiss School of European Political Economy, Italy

Edward Elgar
PUBLISHING

Cheltenham, UK • Northampton, MA, USA

Cover image Johny Goerend on Unsplash

Published by
Edward Elgar Publishing Limited
The Lypiatts
15 Lansdown Road
Cheltenham
Glos GL50 2JA
UK

Edward Elgar Publishing, Inc.
William Pratt House
9 Dewey Court
Northampton
Massachusetts 01060
USA

A catalogue record for this book
is available from the British Library

Library of Congress Control Number: 2021943688

This book is available electronically in the **Elgar**online
Economics subject collection
http://dx.doi.org/10.4337/9781800374348

ISBN 978 1 80037 433 1 (cased)
ISBN 978 1 80037 434 8 (eBook)

Printed and bound by CPI Group (UK) Ltd, Croydon, CR0 4YY

Contents

Figures

Tables

Contributors

Ginevra Bruzzone is Senior Fellow, School of European Political Economy, Luiss Guido Carli, Rome, Italy.

Carlo Cambini is Professor, Politecnico di Torino, Italy.

Giovanni Fraquelli is Professor, UPO – Università del Piemonte Orientale, Italy.

Chris Nash is Research Professor, Institute for Transport Studies, University of Leeds and Visiting Professor, Masaryk University, Czech Republic.

Andrew Smith is Professor of Transport Performance and Economics, Institute for Transport Studies and Business School, University of Leeds and Visiting Professor, Masaryk University, Czech Republic.

Eddy Van de Voorde is Professor, University of Antwerp (TPR and C-MAT).

Foreword by Andrea Camanzi

The invitation of the editors to provide this foreword, in my capacity as President of the Italian Transport Regulation Authority in its first years of operation, came as a seal to the completion of my mandate. Yet, my pleasure in responding to it goes beyond my connection with the institution, for technology and emerging patterns of mobility disclose novel paths for the application of benchmarking in transport regulation, which compel ongoing research.

Although, over the past few years, some European countries have established or redefined the competencies of independent economic regulators with functions similar to those entrusted to the Italian authority, certain tasks pertaining to the regulation of access to infrastructure and services and the setting of levels of quality and rights of users remain unique to it. At their core lies a duty to guarantee that the conditions placed on companies to access rail, port, airport and motorway networks as well as to operate transport and mobility services for goods and passengers, are fair and non-discriminatory and that they are defined based on methodologies which create incentives for fostering competition, production efficiency and containment of costs to the benefit of users, companies and consumers. Thereby, the authority has been entrusted with the mandate to deal with major horizontal economic issues concerning all modes of transport.

In the pursuit of this task, the governing body of the authority decided from the outset to set up an Advisory Board to be composed of academics and experts from various European countries whose area of interest included modelling the frontiers of efficiency to be reached by transport companies: a sector that, both in Italy and elsewhere, remains widely characterised by competition for the market and concentration, and that, against a background of progressive opening and liberalisation under EU law, also remains intensely national. Among the members of the board have been the authors of this book.

However, the work presented in this volume reaches beyond that of the Advisory Board. It provides perspective for readers, academics and practitioners alike, with a unique stocktaking exercise of the application of benchmarking in transport in Italy and other European countries and with wide-ranging empirical evidence. The latter substantiates, among others, the need for measuring the impact of individual policy decisions over the economics of concessions and public service contracts. While such decisions pertain to the executive and awarding authorities, providing a metric for production efficiency and containment of costs rests with economic regulators.

Today, the digital economy, which is global in nature and disintermediates production processes, confronts regulators with new challenges. In transport, the reorganisation of the demand–supply relationship in mobility services that is under way, and which is underpinned by platforms and web applications, while creating positive externalities for network infrastructures, also modifies the traditional role and strategic choices of companies, which increasingly diversify and adapt their operations.

Such developments enhance the need for regulators to avail themselves of advanced and dynamic methods for measuring costs and benefits and their distribution among the actors of the new value chain, while ensuring protection of intermediate users and guaranteeing the freedom of customers to make their choices. In this perspective, existing benchmarking methodologies provide a fundamental basis from which to pursue further research and testing. Data-driven regulation relying on artificial intelligence and the Internet of Things, which generate online structured flows of data and are able to feed demand forecasts in ways which are unprecedented, opens up new avenues for the application of benchmarking in transport.

Andrea Camanzi
President of the Italian Transport Regulation Authority,
2013–2020
Rome, November 2020

Preface

The idea of this book came to the authors while some of them were members of the International Advisory Board of the Italian Transport Regulatory Authority, during the period 2017–20. In this context, we had the opportunity to discuss the international experience of the methods and applications of benchmarking in transport regulation. We found this a very interesting subject, as we believe benchmarking has a very important role in price regulation, target setting and contract design, but found a surprisingly small literature specifically related to benchmarking in the transport sector. Thus, we continued our joint research activity and our discussions and concluded that the results of our work might be of interest to a wider audience.

We would like to thank Andrea Camanzi, who was President of the Authority in this period, for encouraging the production of this book. We would also like to express our gratitude to Marco Ponti, who contributed greatly to our early discussions on this issue. A special thanks goes to Margherita Desideri, who assisted us in the preparation of the volume, for her helpfulness and efficiency.

Ginevra Bruzzone
Chris Nash

PART I

Background

1. The role of benchmarking in efficiency-enhancing strategies

Chris Nash and Ginevra Bruzzone

1.1 INTRODUCTION

One of the main features of the transport sector, across its various modes, is the coexistence of competitive markets and markets which have the features of natural monopolies. For infrastructure, the coexistence of several competitors may not be sustainable because of economies of scale which make it inefficient to duplicate the assets serving the same market. The clearest example is rail infrastructure. There are also particular issues concerning public transport, in that an important aspect of service quality received by users depends on frequency and on connections between services, which in turn depend on the range of services provided by different operators. Thus, there may be economies associated with the integrated provision of services by a single undertaking, which should be compared to a scenario of coordination between several companies.

Even in markets not showing the features of natural monopolies, competitive dynamics may be weakened when an undertaking holds a dominant position, i.e. a significant and lasting market power or, alternatively, the market is prone to collusion. Still, even in highly concentrated markets it is still possible to observe a lively competition. For the provision of public transport services, contracts may be awarded directly by the public administration or as a result of a bidding process, entailing "competition for the market".

Depending on which of these situations prevails, undertakings face different incentives to improve efficiency, reduce prices, increase quality and innovate and there is a different need for policy measures aimed at aligning their incentives to the general interest.

Competition in the market, when it is feasible, is a formidable mechanism leading undertakings, in a context of imperfect information, to look for efficiency and better products (through innovation and imitation) and to contain prices to the ultimate advantage of consumers. The process works on a continuous basis. During the process undertakings may make mistakes: they may invest too much, or not enough, or in fruitless directions; they may propose unsuccessful products; or they may set prices at the wrong level. However, the mechanisms for the correction of such mistakes are embedded in the system, since firms would face reduced market shares and profits and, ultimately, may go bankrupt.

Competition "for the market" may provide similar incentives. It depends on bidders being invited to bid for the contract to provide a specific set of services (or to build and manage an infrastructure) for a certain number of years. If the tender is properly designed, potential competitors will reveal information on the best price/quality combination they are able to offer at the time of the tender (in the language of public procurement law, the "most advantageous economic offer"). The bid can take the form of a required level of subsidy or a premium to be paid for the right to run the services.

Provided that the bidder bears both cost and revenue risk, this provides the bidder with incentives to produce efficiently, to reduce cost over time and to attract additional traffic and revenue. But clearly this process also provides the bidder with a monopoly for the period in question, so unless prices are controlled as part of the contract, or there are very closely competing products (for instance other transport modes), monopoly pricing is likely to ensue. Similarly, the monopoly position of the firm may mean there are inadequate incentives to provide high quality services and to invest. So the contract may need to control price, quality of service and investment.

Moreover, requiring firms to also bear risks they cannot control (e.g. oil prices, or changes in traffic and revenue resulting from changes in the state of the economy) may discourage bids, lead to the building of high risk premiums into bids or lead to financial failure of franchises. So, it may be better to try to share risks, with the State bearing those risks the bidder cannot control.

Ultimately, if the State controls service levels and price and bears exogenous revenue risk, it may be regarded as simpler for the State to bear all revenue risk and award a gross cost contract. But then the contract must contain provisions to ensure appropriate quality of service, such as financial premiums or penalties.

Thus it will be seen that competition for the market is far from straightforward, and is demanding in terms of the skills required of the authority administering the contracts. The simplicity of competition in the market dictates that it is to be preferred unless there are good reasons for the different approach, but as indicated in the transport sector there often are such reasons. Direct award of the contract to the incumbent may be seen as much simpler than competitive tendering, but obviously removes all the above incentives to efficiency which must then be provided in another way.

One key issue in determining the efficiency of competition for the market is the reaction of the authority in question if the winner of the competition gets into financial difficulties. If the difficulties arise from a genuinely unforeseea-ble change of circumstances, then the authority may be inclined to renegotiate the contract to provide additional funding; moreover this is often the simplest and indeed cheapest way of securing continuity of service. But if the authority is sufficiently ready to do this so as to lead bidders to believe that they will always be rescued if they get into trouble, then the efficiency of competition for the market fails; bidders may put in optimistic bids which they cannot deliver and the incentive to produce efficiently is removed.

Given these complications of competition for the market, and the costs of changing supplier when the contract comes to an end or the supplier fails, there may be circumstances in which it is considered more efficient to retain a public or private sector monopoly. In this case, the achievement of an efficient outcome depends on how that monopoly is regulated.

Which of the three scenarios (competition in the market, competition for the market or regulation in the absence of competition) should be pursued in a specific case requires an in-depth analysis of the economic features of the relevant market. In the European Union, the legislative framework sets some constraints on the choices of the Member States. Liberalisation directives gradually opened up several services, such as air transport and road haulage, to competition (for an overview of EU regulatory reforms in transport, see Finger and Holvad (2013)). Currently, Directive 2014/23/EU on concessions regulates the award and duration of concessions for toll highways, whereas local public transport services by bus and rail should comply with Regulation (EC) 1370/2007, as recently amended by Regulation (EU) 2016/2338. For ports, Regulation (EU) 2017/352 set common rules on the provision of some port services and the financial transparency of ports, applicable to the ports of the Trans-European Transport Network (TEN-T). For airports, national frameworks should comply with the common rules on airport charges set by Directive 2009/12, which complements the EU rules on the provision of air navigation services and ground handling services.

Benchmarking, which is the process of comparing the performance of different decision-making units to determine what is an efficient level of costs (or more generally an efficient performance) for the process concerned, can play a role in each of these settings. In the absence of competition, since the regulator needs to know what would be the costs of an efficient operator for the service in question, benchmarking is central. However, benchmarking may also be valuable in testing whether competition in or for the market is working effectively, and in designing competitive tendering arrangements.

1.2 BENCHMARKING AND COMPETITION IN THE MARKET

With competition in the market, it is in the interest of the companies to take into account what more efficient competitors do, e.g. price/quality combinations, and adapt their business strategy to meet the competitive challenge.

Comparison of the different offers may even be used by companies as a marketing tool: comparative advertising is legitimate pursuant to EU law (Directive 2006/114/EC) if it is based on objective criteria. On the other hand, it may be in the interest of purchasers to develop instruments aimed at facilitating the comparisons of the different offers thus reducing transaction costs (e.g. price comparison tools).

Thus, when several companies are competing in a market, there is no need for policymakers to promote benchmarking, because of market-led benchmarking, i.e. the task is already carried out by the market.

Within this general framework, there are two exceptions which must be taken into account:

(a) if companies collude, the virtuous competitive mechanism is blocked;
(b) if a company, although not a monopolist, has a dominant position, i.e. such a market power that it is not significantly constrained by actual or potential competitors, there may remain a role for public policy.

The prohibition of anticompetitive agreements, enforced by the European Commission and national competition authorities, aims to avoid collusion distorting the market process. In practice, policymakers should always pay particular attention to whether there are signals of collusion in a given market.

As to dominant positions, which are frequently met in the transport sector, there are different tools which may be used to mitigate the problem. Competition advocacy may be used to promote more effective actual or potential competition, for instance reducing barriers to entry and exit from the market. In case of high and lasting market power, since the step to formal regulation is a strong one, monitoring and benchmarking may be used as a soft tool to align the incentives of the incumbent to best practices.

In the presence of structural obstacles to the competitive process (e.g. a natural monopoly on a lasting basis), *ex ante* regulation is usually more appropriate than antitrust intervention. However, in particular cases in which for any reason regulation is either non-existent or insufficient, competition authorities in the EU are empowered to prohibit the abusive exploitation of a dominant position, such as, for instance, the application of excessive prices (Art. 102(a) Treaty on the Functioning of the European Union (TFEU)). The prohibition of exploitative abuses is seldom used by competition authorities because their main role is not regulating the market, but to protect the market process; however, this power, when needed, is available.

1.3   BENCHMARKING AND COMPETITION FOR THE MARKET

As to competition for the market, first of all, the analysis of costs, including the assessment of economies of scale, density and scope, is useful to properly design the tender. Concessions need to be large enough to exploit such economies, but there is a need to avoid "oversized" concessions that does not depend only on reasons of static efficiency. The coexistence of several concessionaires helps maintain sufficient experienced bidders for future competitions to work, whilst also making it possible to compare their performance and thus develop forms of competition by comparison.

In addition, public decision makers may use benchmarking in order to set the proper incentives for the company in terms of both price and quality (efficiency and effectiveness), by means of a proper definition of the contract with the supplier of the service.

Collusion may also be a problem with competition for the market, since it may eliminate the incentives to present competitive bids and therefore the information and efficiency-enhancing role of tenders. Notably, fighting collusion in public procurement is one of the priorities of competition authorities worldwide.

1.4   BENCHMARKING IN THE ABSENCE OF COMPETITION EITHER IN OR FOR THE MARKET

In the absence of competition, either in or for the market, for public decision makers the task of collecting information in order to avoid inefficiencies and undue exploitation of market power in terms of poor quality or excessive prices/subsidies is crucial, because no information or incentive to this aim results from the operation of the market.

Hence, benchmarking methodologies are needed by policymakers to identify the conditions which might be attained by an efficient company in terms of costs, prices, and contribution of taxpayers, and take them as a target. Moreover, in the absence of competition, some benchmarking may also be needed to ensure proper incentives as to the provision of quality (CBP Bureau for Economic Policy Analysis (2000)).[1]

This, in turn, allows them to write a proper contract in the case of an in-house relationship or direct award of contracts, and to properly regulate the undertaking.

Benchmarking is also relevant for State aid law: as indicated by the European Court of Justice in the *Altmark* judgment (case C-280/00), in the absence of a tender, public authorities may still exclude overcompensation of public service obligations by determining the level of compensation on the basis of an analysis of the costs of "a typical well run and adequately equipped undertaking in the sector concerned" (see Chapter 10).

Yardstick competition, as designed by Shleifer (1985), is a specific form of regulation which requires collecting information on cost conditions of comparable companies and linking the remuneration of the regulated under-taking to the costs of other companies, so as to incentivise it to become at least as efficient as comparable companies. The more efficient the company is compared to competitors, the higher is its profit. It is just one of the reg-ulatory instruments which are based on benchmarking. Whether some form of yardstick competition or the use of another of the available tools is more appropriate in a given situation should be assessed on a case-by-case basis, taking all pros and cons into account. Thus, a yardstick competition approach should be compared, for instance, with the mere publishing of the results of a benchmarking process.

1.5 BENCHMARKING AS A REGULATORY TOOL: THE MAIN CHALLENGES

Looking at the potential use of benchmarking as a tool in an efficiency-enhancing strategy, there are some significant challenges to be considered. In general, it is essential to acknowledge that inefficiency can take different forms depend-ing on the goals of the undertakings involved. In particular, whereas private monopolies usually pursue high profits, the main feature of publicly owned monopolies may be high costs of production.

A first challenge consists in finding comparable situations. The problem arises in all cases of benchmarking; it is particularly serious when benchmark-ing is used as a basis for regulatory decisions which may be challenged before the courts by companies arguing that the regulator did not make reference to an appropriate benchmark. Technical instruments may be used to deal with the problem of heterogeneity (see Chapter 2), but the issue of whether a meaning-ful benchmark can be found may be a serious problem in some markets.

The second challenge is the risk of collusion, not only within a market but also across markets. If companies collude not to strive for efficiency (for instance by not challenging inefficient working practices), any benchmark based on the observation of their conduct will not be effective. Although from an institutional viewpoint the competence to enforce the prohibition of anticompetitive agreements is within competition authorities, an issue to be addressed is how competition authorities can more effectively obtain the relevant information to challenge these practices. This is an area for potential cooperation between sectoral authorities and competition authorities. Another issue is how policymakers may check for collusion before using market information in order to develop benchmarks. In the economic literature a number of studies can be found which focus on how to design regulation so as to reduce the risk of collusion (see, for instance, Tangeras (2002)).

A third challenge which has been pointed out by the literature on yardstick competition is ensuring that the rules aimed at enhancing efficiency do not have an adverse impact on incentives to invest because of their focus on (short-run) cost minimisation (Dalen (1998); Guthrie (2006)).

In a political economy perspective, a further challenge is represented by the risk of regulatory capture, which may be particularly serious in the absence of competition (Cramton et al. (2017)), whereas the links between public administrations and undertakings which may give rise to capture are weakened with competition in the market and, at least to some extent, also with competition for the market. As to the latter, with the periodic tendering of concessions, the winners tend to rotate, and the tendering administration will be incentivised to try to extract the best services at a minimum cost, with limited time or opportunity for lobbying to play a role. In the tendering scenario, the main risk of capture arises after the contract is awarded, when the winner may try to renegotiate it.

In the case of yardstick competition the risk of regulatory capture is different since the proper incentives depend only on the action of public administrations: the administration will either compare the performance of the existing regulated company with other ones, or create an "internal" yardstick competition by unbundling the incumbent company, along the lines of "minimum efficient dimensions". Two problems arise: information (for instance on costs), which has to be guaranteed by an external agent, and effective sanctions against the non-performing subjects (or, vice versa, rewards for performance). Information that the tendering process usually provides will not be observable, and sanctions/rewards need to be effective in changing the behaviour of the regulated companies. If capture persists, the administration may have little incentive to sanction, if not formally. Also the incentive to show a strong attitude in defending the public interest against an "external, profit-minded" subject suffers, unless in the presence of a strictly binding budget constraint, and this not overall, but aimed at that specific company. In light of the above, with yardstick competition, the best defence against regulatory capture is entrusting the regulatory tasks to an independent authority with a strong reputation and adequate powers.

1.6 STRUCTURE OF THIS BOOK

This book is divided into five parts. The first part addresses general analytical issues: in addition to this introductory chapter, it contains a review of alternative statistical approaches to benchmarking, their strengths and weaknesses (Chapter 2) and discusses the issue of data needed for benchmarking exercises (Chapter 3).

The second part considers benchmarking and regulation in the different transport modes. Chapter 4 reviews studies and regulatory experiences with benchmarking in the provision of roads and highways, with a focus on the Italian experience in the regulation of tolled highways. Chapter 5 considers benchmarking in the rail sector, in particular the studies undertaken by the UIC (Union internationale des chemins de fer) and the British rail regulator, and studies on European train operators and rail systems as a whole. Chapter 6 reviews studies on benchmarking in local public transport in different countries, and key problems in doing so, such as allowing for differences in quality of service. Chapter 7 discusses the relevance of benchmarking in the case of ports and airports, which are generally more competitive sectors than highway and rail infrastructure and therefore less tightly regulated, and the key comparability problems that arise.

The third part of the volume picks up two case studies which embody interesting experience. Chapter 8 focuses on the experience of regulation of the rail sector in Britain. Britain has undertaken the most extensive rail reforms in Europe, and is widely regarded as a model in terms of its approach to regulation. This chapter reviews the methods used in seeking to ensure an efficient rail transport system, through comprehensive franchising of passenger operations and through regulation of the rail infrastructure manager, highlighting the role of benchmarking in these processes. Chapter 9 considers two particular cases concerning, respectively, the application of rules on State aid to the port of Antwerp and the economic regulation of the Brussels airport company. This chapter highlights debates over the need for benchmarking and regulation and comparability issues when the method is used.

Part IV of the volume considers the interplay of regulation and competition policy, with a focus on benchmarking. Public funding is still widespread in the transport sector, both for the construction and operation of infrastructure and for the provision of public transport services. Chapter 10 discusses the interaction of economic regulation and the control of State aid and whether there is room for streamlining the use of these different policy tools. Chapter 11 focuses on the use of benchmarking in EU antitrust law, particularly in the assessment of whether a dominant company is imposing "unfair prices", contrary to Article 102 TFEU.

In the final part we present our conclusions.

NOTE

1. An example of benchmarking focusing on the output/quality dimension is provided by the system of performance assessment created by the Laboratorio MeS of the Scuola Superiore Sant'Anna in Pisa. In this case, the system of benchmarking works with the participation of a group of regional public administrations on a voluntary basis. See Nuti (2012).

REFERENCES

CBP Bureau for Economic Policy Analysis, (2000), *Yardstick Competition, Theory, Design and Practice*, Working Paper No. 13, December.

Cramton P., M. Ponti and F. Ramella (2017), "Capture Mechanisms in the Transport Sector", *Transport Research Procedia*, 25, 5174–5184.

Dalen, D. M. (1998), "Yardstick Competition and Investment Incentives", *Journal of Economics and Management Strategy*, 7(1), 105–126.

Finger, M. and T. Holvad (2013), *Regulating Transport in Europe*, Edward Elgar Publishing.

Guthrie, G. (2006), "Regulating Infrastructure: The Impact on Risk and Investment", *Journal of Economic Literature*, 44, 925–972.

Nuti, S. (2012), "Assessment and Improvement of the Italian Healthcare System: First Evidence from a Pilot National Performance Evaluation System", *Journal of Healthcare Management*, 57(3), May–June, 181–199.

Shleifer, A. (1985), "A Theory of Yardstick Competition", *Rand Journal of Economics*, 16(3), 319–327.

Tangeras, T. P. (2002), "Collusion-Proof Yardstick Competition", *Journal of Public Economics*, 83(2), February, 231–254.

2. Methodology

Andrew Smith, Giovanni Fraquelli and Carlo Cambini

2.1 INTRODUCTION

This chapter reviews the available parametric and non-parametric methods that can be used for benchmarking purposes and indeed have been used in empirical and regulatory studies, as noted in the other parts of this volume.

It starts by explaining why simple comparisons of unit costs or partial productivity measures may not be sufficient and more advanced methods are needed (section 2.2). Productivity indexes are covered in section 2.3, whereas section 2.4 focuses on data envelopment analysis (DEA) and bootstrapping and section 2.5 illustrates parametric frontier techniques, including stochastic frontier methods. Section 2.6 discusses the challenges associated with the different approaches and the reasons which may justify the choice of a technique or a set of techniques.

2.2 WHY WE NEED A BENCHMARKING METHODOLOGY[1]

Studies of transport efficiency usually have one of two motivations. Firstly they may aim to identify which transport operators and/or infrastructure managers are efficient and which are not, in order to draw lessons as to the level of improvement that may be required. An example of this is the benchmarking studies conducted on behalf of the British rail regulator in deciding on the financial requirements of Network Rail, the infrastructure manager discussed below (see, for example, Smith et al., 2010). Secondly, studies may seek to draw policy conclusions about which policies regarding industry structure, competition and regulation will be most beneficial.

In both cases the importance and motivation of efficiency analysis, and the reforms and policy interventions which may occur based on such analysis, is for the delivery of efficiency savings (and productivity gains more generally) with the ultimate aim of delivering either lower prices to users of transport services, or reduced taxpayer support.

In sectors of the economy in which markets are a reasonable approximation to perfectly competitive, a measure of overall efficiency may simply be the profitability of the firm. Under perfect competition, prices are not influenced by the individual firm and therefore the more profitable the firm, the more it has been able to minimise costs of production and to produce the most valuable combination of goods in the eyes of consumers.

However, transport provision is in many cases a long way from being a perfectly competitive industry. Road and rail infrastructure is typically a monopoly, whilst arguably other transport infrastructure often has a degree of monopoly power. Road and rail public transport is often a monopolistic industry, whilst rail freight, air and sea transport are characterised by an oligopoly market structure. For this and other social reasons, public transport prices are often regulated by governments, which also play a key role in specifying infrastructure requirements and passenger sector outputs. If the aim is to examine the efficiency of management, these factors must be allowed for. To the extent that managers have limited control over their outputs, the key issue is whether they produce them at minimum cost.

Further, in the absence of competition, regulatory pressure is needed to ensure that transport firms operate in an efficient manner. Given the standard problem of asymmetric information – firms know more about their costs than regulators – regulators need to arm themselves with additional information to overcome this asymmetry. Benchmarking – which involves comparing the efficiency performance of the regulated firm with other transport firms – is thus an important, indeed crucial, part of the regulatory process. The data that is used in benchmarking could be drawn from other domestic transport firms, where possible, international benchmarks, which can be more problematic, or internal benchmarks, for example comparing the performance of different regions of an infrastructure manager (Chapter 3 of this volume looks in more detail at data issues in benchmarking).

Economists are used to distinguishing between technical and allocative efficiency. Technical efficiency is measured by whether output is maximised for a given level of inputs (or conversely inputs are minimised for a given output). The standard economic approach to examine this is to estimate a production function using econometric methods, although non-parametric methods – such as data envelopment analysis (DEA) – have also been used. The different approaches are considered further in sections 2.3 to 2.5 of this chapter. Allocative efficiency considers whether the correct mix of inputs is used to minimise cost for a given level and quality of output.

Cost efficiency is the product of technical and allocative efficiency, and thus takes both technical and allocative efficiency into account. Cost efficiency measures are typically obtained by estimating a cost function or frontier, though such measures can also be obtained via DEA.

Arguably cost efficiency is the most relevant concept from a regulatory perspective since it is through cost reductions that prices can be reduced to users, or the burden of subsidies lowered. That said, in situations where it may be unrealistic for firms to optimise the capital input – as may be the case in regulated network industries – and/or where there is a lack of good and comparable data on costs or input prices, technical efficiency could be a more relevant measure.

Before turning to discuss advanced techniques for measuring the relative efficiency of transport firms, it is first worth considering why it is important to go beyond simple partial productivity measures – such as (in a rail context) cost per train-km, cost per passenger-km or cost per route or track-km. In principle, benchmarking could simply proceed by collecting comparable data across firms and using these to compare unit costs across companies – thus raising the question as to whether advanced techniques are needed at all.

However, unit cost measures are only partial measures of efficiency performance and raise multiple questions. Firstly, such measures may not cover all costs and thus would not give an overall assessment of performance. For example, staff costs per train-km could be distorted in comparisons between firms if different firms take different outsourcing decisions. Further, capital substitution possibilities may be ignored. Even if the measure of costs covers all costs, there is then a question as to how to characterise the outputs in multiple output industries, where output may be described in terms of passenger-km, train-km or even represented by the size of the network, making cost per track-km another candidate measure. Further disaggregation is also possible as between freight and passenger traffic, or even further traffic-type disaggregation within the generic categories.

Typically, unit cost comparisons with different denominators can give very different rankings. Similar problems emerge in other regulated industries, such as the water sector, where unit costs may be calculated per customer or per unit of water delivered or per length of mains, potentially with very different results. It is thus problematic, since it is not always clear which is the preferred measure, and different rankings and efficiency scores result from using different measures.

An approach that simultaneously takes account of multiple denominators/drivers of costs is therefore needed – this being a key advantage of the econometric approach, as multiple cost drivers can be included in the model at the same time. DEA can also handle multiple inputs and outputs, sometimes via a two-stage process. A second key advantage of adopting an econometric framework (and to some extent also a DEA approach), as compared to simple unit cost measures, can be illustrated in Figure 2.1 below.

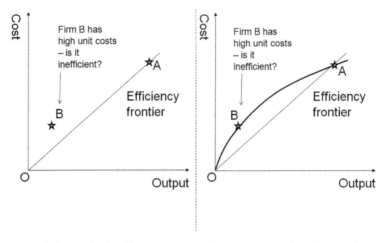

Figure 2.1   Scale effects versus inefficiency: a graphical example

Simple unit cost comparisons make an implicit assumption of constant returns to scale, which is very unlikely to hold in transport applications. Thus, in the left hand panel of Figure 2.1, firm A appears to be inefficient because it has higher unit costs. However, once the presence of increasing returns to scale is permitted – as represented by the right hand panel of Figure 2.1 – it becomes apparent that the reasons for firm A's higher unit costs is that it operates at small scale. Given its scale – which will usually not be under the control of management – firm A turns out to be operating on the cost frontier and is thus an efficient operator.

By using an econometric model, the shape of the cost frontier can be esti-mated as part of the modelling framework. Indeed, the assumption of constant returns to scale can be tested directly. Likewise, DEA methods can be adapted to take account of the possibility of non-constant returns. Having controlled for the underlying technology, efficiency comparisons can then be more accu-rately assessed.

Before proceeding to look at the methods that can be used to operationalise a benchmarking framework, it is worth noting another set of important factors that are needed in a benchmarking framework and which more advanced methods – that is, going beyond simple unit cost measures of key performance indicators – can deal with, at least to some extent. This requires accounting for:

- variations in service quality between firms and over time;
- observed (or unobserved) heterogeneity between firms that impacts on costs, but is not related to management performance – these are likely to be persistent features that do not vary over time, and may relate to factors

such as the weather conditions or topography of the country or region being benchmarked;

- the natural cycle of asset replacement and enhancements to assets, which can cause expenditure to vary substantially from year to year, such that unit cost measures at a point in time may be highly misleading.

In the subsequent sections of this chapter we document further the methods that have been developed to undertake benchmarking – setting out the essence of the methods whilst also reflecting the state of the art and explaining how the combination of methods, data and regulatory judgement can combine to deliver a powerful benchmarking framework with wide social benefits.

2.3 BENCHMARKING BY PRODUCTIVITY INDEXES

2.3.1 The Concept of Productivity

The concept of productivity concerns both efficiency and technological change in production. Efficiency relates to the quantity of output obtained from the inputs in the production process, given the technology available (the effect of time is neglected). Technical efficiency improvements imply movements of the observed unit towards "best practice" or the reduction of organisational inefficiencies (Diewert and Lawrence, 1999). If we introduce time varying effects, allowing for the change of the productive combination, we can also measure technological change. Technological change can arise through disembodied forms concerning new scientific results and organisational techniques or through forms embodied in new products or services. In Figure 2.2, the approach of firm A to the best production function reflects an efficiency improvement, while a technological change allowing a higher amount of output with the same set of observable inputs produces a shifting up of the production frontier.

A correct analysis of productivity trends requires isolating output variations due to an increase of inputs (and any associated economies or diseconomies of scale or density) from those connected to technological change. It is possible to see the change in productivity in the Solow (1957) formulation of a production function. Given Hicks' neutral technical progress (the ratio of marginal product of capital to the marginal product of labour remains unchanged at constant capital labour ratio) and a production function:

$$Y_t = A_t f\left(K_t, L_t, M_t\right) \tag{2.1}$$

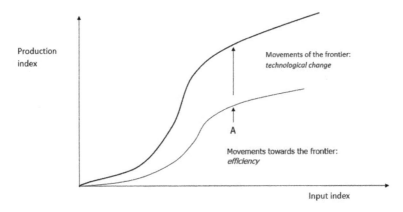

Production index

Movements of the frontier:
technological change

A

Movements towards the frontier:
efficiency

Input index

Figure 2.2   Efficiency and technological change in production

where Y_t is output, $f(\cdot)$ is a function of observable inputs capital K_t, labour L_t, materials M_t, and A_t is the factor-neutral index of technical progress (increasing function of t that measures cumulated effects of shift over time), productivity change could be investigated by A_t. The coefficient A_t represents the efficiency, time varying, while dA_t represents the variation of efficiency and therefore it proxies technical progress.

Denoting $dA_t = \dfrac{dA_t}{dt}$ and $f_t = \dfrac{df(\cdot)}{dt}$, the change over time of total product Y is determined by totally differentiating the production function A_t, i.e.,

$$dY_t = dA\left[f\left(K_t, L_t, M_t\right)\right] + A_t\left[df_t\right] \tag{2.2}$$

with:

- $dA\left[f\left(K_t, L_t, M_t\right)\right]$ denoting the change of output from technical progress and,

- $A_t\left(df_t\right) = A_t\left[\dfrac{\partial Y}{\partial K}dK + \dfrac{\partial Y}{\partial L}dL + \dfrac{\partial Y}{\partial M}dM\right]$ denoting the change of output due to a change in the use of observable factor inputs, keeping A_t constant.

2.3.2   Different Productivity Measures

The measures and indexes used in productivity analysis are numerous. For instance, we can refer to single factor productivity measures (output compared to a single measure of input, e.g. labour or capital) or multifactor productivity measures (output compared to a set of input measures e.g. labour–capital–energy–materials).

Once the productivity measures have been identified, several methodological approaches can be followed in the implementation phase. From this viewpoint, the main distinction is between parametric and non-parametric estimates.

Relying on econometric (parametric) techniques, we can determine productivity by estimating the parameters of a production or cost function. When we rely on non-parametric approaches, instead, some properties of the production function are used to identify empirical measures, such as index number, or efficiency scores, such as those obtained through data envelopment analysis ("The growth accounting approach to productivity measurement is a prominent example for non-parametric techniques"; OECD, 2001, p. 13).

2.3.3   Total Factor Productivity Indexes

Measuring actual production data

The main economic activity of a firm consists in transforming a set of inputs into one or more outputs. Given a set of inputs, a more efficient technology allows the production of a larger quantity of output. Moreover, as different inputs have different costs, the efficiency assessment turns into a cost minimisation problem: one firm is considered more efficient than another one if it is able to obtain the same output by using a cheaper set of inputs.

There are, indeed, different methods that might be used to obtain the same output; for example, in the local public transport industry we can see different combinations per vehicle-kilometre of work forces, fuel, maintenance materials and transportation equipment.

The nature and the required quantity of each input depend on several factors, such as the home country economic situation, the relative price of inputs, the particular business links between firms and the different legislation in each country. Regulation may be considered as part of this latter factor and influences the economic decisions of firms.

When we try to construct productivity measures from firm production data, we have to address a number of problems. The first one relates to the degree of homogeneity among outputs. Given the same number of passengers transported, we can have a different quality of service. Quality is expensive and should be valued. At the same time, we have to pay attention to the negative outputs such as the level of pollution linked to the production process: investments in the bus service sector can be devoted to reducing harmful emissions, moving towards the use of cleaner energy sources. Further, firms' data sometimes do not contain measures of output quantities. Revenues could be observed from the firms' reports but, as inflation rates affect the values of sales, erroneous increases in efficiency might result from analyses based on nominal values. A correct analysis should refer to real values, hence considering constant prices by properly choosing a reference year.

The second set of problems concerns the inputs. The correct measurement of inputs is crucial because an underestimation of their value results in an untrue improvement in productivity. As regards the labour inputs, we can use the number of employees or the hours worked, or alternative measures such as the annual cost, properly deflated. The last measure has the advantage of highlighting the quality of the resource used in relation to the marginal productivity of the different units of work employed. However, labour quality can be embodied in the productivity measure, as stated in the following statement:

> Attempts to capture labour quality differences in labour measures rather than productivity are the impetus behind using the wage bill to measure labour inputs rather than the number of employees or employee-hours. The notion is that market wages reflect variations in workers' contributions to production; firms with more productive workers will have a higher wage bill per employee. Of course, there are problems with this approach: wage variation might reflect the realities of local labour markets, or causation could be in the other direction, if more productive producers earn rents that are shared with or captured by employees. (Syverson, 2011, p. 340)

The evaluation of physical capital appears even more problematic. Capital could be measured using the firm's book value of its capital stock or depreciations. There are some doubts about these measures as a correct proxy of the service of capital and about the need to deflate such variables with appropriate methodologies (which we shall discuss further below). For materials and services, problems are similar to those highlighted for the output, because usually we have the amount of the expenses and not the quantity of inputs.

The third set of problems concerns the type of multifactor productivity indexes to be used. The construction of the indexes needs to weight properly the individual outputs and inputs. The weights are closely related to the index used and the nature of the underlying production function. In the next paragraph we shall examine the most used and appreciated indexes.

2.3.4 Which Indexes? Which Periods to Compare? Chained or Direct Comparisons?

The most commonly used methods for the assessment of total factor productivity are the Laspeyres, Paasche, Divisia, Fisher and Törnqvist indexes. The choice should not be random. Economic theory indicates the different capacity of each index in correctly approximating the technology outlined by the production or the cost functions (Diewert, 1981). Some indexes, basically, assume a particular production technology. When few observations are available and it is not possible to make econometric estimates, the choice of the index becomes difficult, but the literature often suggests the use of Törnqvist or Fisher index number.

The Fisher index is a geometric average of the Laspeyres and Paasche indexes and the Törnqvist index is a weighted geometric average of outputs and inputs. Törnqvist and Fisher indexes, being exact for a flexible functional form, are called "superlative" index numbers (Diewert, 1976).

> For example, the Törnqvist index is exact for the translog flexible functional form (... it can be directly derived for the translog flexible functional form ...) – a widely used specification in empirical economics. Thus, if one accepts a translog form as an approximation to a production function, and uses standard assumptions about producer behaviour, the Törnqvist quantity index provides an exact formulation for inputs and outputs. (OECD, 2001, p. 88)

> Törnqvist index is superlative in considerably more general sense than shown by Diewert. We are not aware of other indexes that can be shown to be superlative in this more general sense. (Caves et al., 1982, p. 1411)

Once a specific index has been chosen, we have to decide which periods to compare. Later on in this chapter we shall deepen this theme by examining the model of Malmquist (see section 2.4.3). Here it is important to recall that comparisons could be made over several periods or with respect to two specific periods (for example: period 0 and period 4). We can choose the first or the last observation as the base, or adopt the chain approach. A change in the relative prices of single outputs or inputs gives too much (or too little) weight to goods characterised by a fall (or a rise) in the relative prices. Chain weighted indices are less sensitive to a substitution bias. "The economics literature as well as the SNA 93 are quite unanimous in this respect: for inter-temporal comparisons, changes over longer periods should be obtained by chaining: *i.e.* by linking the year-to-year movements" (OECD, 2001, p. 83).

2.3.5   Laspeyres and Törnqvist Indexes[2]

Laspeyres and Törnqvist indexes, briefly described below, are the most used indexes.

The Laspeyres index is represented by a quantity index, which relates outputs and inputs valued at constant prices. The productivity ratio between period t and $t = 0$ by Laspeyres formula is:

$$TFP_L = \frac{\left(\dfrac{\sum_i Y_i^t p_i^0}{\sum_i Y_i^0 p_i^0} \right)}{\left(\dfrac{\sum_h X_h^t W_h^0}{\sum_h X_h^0 W_h^0} \right)} \tag{2.3}$$

where Y_i indicates the quantity of output i produced, p_i the output price, x_h is the quantity of inputs h used and w_h its unit price, and $t = 0$ is the time basis. As inputs are simply added up, the model implies perfect substitutability.

The Törnqvist index is an approximation in the discrete case of the Divisia index (Diewert, 1981). The latter are derived from Solow's production function, which implies constant returns of scale and neutral technological change (para. 2.3.1). In the situation of one output and two inputs (labour and capital) it can be expressed as follows:

$$Y_t = A_t f \left(L_t, K_t \right) \tag{2.4}$$

where A_t is the neutral technical progress. To model the production function, we can start from a Cobb–Douglas functional form that is linear in logs, homogeneous of degree one and a first-order approximation to any production function of the form $Y_t = A_t L_t^a K_t^b$, with a indicating the relative weight of labour (labour output elasticity) and b indicating the relative weight of capital (capital output elasticity). By taking the logarithm and differentiating with respect to time we get the impact of the variation of the technical progress over time:

$$\frac{dA_t}{A_t} = \frac{dY_t}{Y_t} - \left(a_t * \frac{dL_t}{L_t} + b_t * \frac{dK_t}{K_t} \right) \tag{2.5}$$

We can rewrite the previous equation as: $\dfrac{A_t^*}{A_t} = \dfrac{Y_t^*}{Y_t} - \left(a_t \dfrac{L_t^*}{L_t} + b_t \dfrac{K_t^*}{K_t} \right)$, where the

symbol * means the derivative of that variable respect to time and A_t is the Divisia index of the residual.

Considering the case one good (Y) and g-inputs (X):

$$\frac{A_t^*}{A_t} = \frac{Y_t^*}{Y_t} - \left(\sum_h^g s_{ht}^* \frac{X_t^*}{X_t} \right) \tag{2.6}$$

where s_h is the share of the receipts going to the hth input.

The apparent shift of the function over time $\dfrac{A^*}{A}$ is the growth of the Divisia total factor productivity. (Star and Hall, 1976, p. 258).

To get the index of total factor productivity, we can integrate the previous equation (2.6):

$$\frac{A_T}{A_0} = \frac{Y_T}{Y_0} \exp\left(-\sum_h^g \int_0^T s_{ht} * \frac{X_{ht}^*}{X_{ht}} d_t \right) \tag{2.7}$$

Normalising and assuming $A_0 = 1$, A_T will be the index of productivity at time T.

In empirical work, the calculation of the Divisia index is not easy because we need a correct value of the share s_h over time. Star and Hall (1976, p. 258) suggest a good approximation of the value of share s_h. To calculate the value of the Divisia index at time T, they suggest the use of constant values for the shares ("that give the same index as the true fluctuating shares") using data only from the periods 0 and T.

First, using a constant share, Star and Hall show (p. 258) that:

$$s_{ht} \log\left(\frac{X_{hT}}{X_{h0}} \right) = \int_0^T s_{ht} * \frac{X_{ht}^*}{X_{ht}} d_t \tag{2.8}$$

After substituting in the previous Divisia index of total factor productivity (2.7) we obtain:

$$\frac{A_T}{A_0} = \frac{Y_T}{Y_0} exp\left(-\sum_h^g s_{ht} \, log\left(\frac{X_{hT}}{X_{h0}}\right)\right) \tag{2.9}$$

$$\frac{A_T}{A_0} = \frac{\dfrac{Y_T}{Y_0}}{exp\left(\sum_h^g log\left(\dfrac{X_{hT}}{X_{h0}}\right)^{s_h}\right)} \tag{2.10}$$

$$\frac{A_T}{A_0} = \frac{\dfrac{Y_T}{Y_0}}{exp\left(log\left(\prod_h^g \left(\dfrac{X_{hT}}{X_{h0}}\right)^{s_h}\right)\right)} \tag{2.11}$$

$$A_T = \frac{\dfrac{Y_T}{Y_0}}{\prod_h^g \left(\dfrac{X_{hT}}{X_{h0}}\right)^{s_h}} \tag{2.12}$$

where the approximation of the true s_h could be the simple average of s_{ht} at the beginning and end of the period (p. 259): $s_h = \frac{1}{2}(s_{h0} + s_{hT})$.

The index of inputs of the previous formula "has been advocated as a quantity index by Törnqvist " (Star and Hall, 1976, p. 259).

The Törnqvist discrete approximation index of total factor productivity takes the following form:

$$TFP_{Tt,t-1} = \frac{\dfrac{Y_{it}}{Y_{it-1}}}{\prod_h^g \left(\dfrac{X_{ht}}{X_{ht-1}}\right)^{\frac{1}{2}(s_{ht} + s_{ht-1})}} \tag{2.13}$$

The denominator can be considered as a weighted geometric mean of the input ratios between two subsequent years. The weights can be represented by the average expenditure shares. In fact, if we make the assumption of perfect competition and constant returns to scale, "the elasticities equal the share of revenues paid to each input. This makes constructing the S_h simple. Materials' and labor's shares are typically straightforward to collect with the wage bill and materials expenditures data at hand. Capital's share can be constructed as the residual, obviating the need for capital cost measures." Hence, "cost-share-based TFP index numbers are easy to construct and offer the robustness of being a nonparametric first-order approximation to a general production function" (Syverson, 2011, p. 332).

As the Laspeyres indexes are used with fixed base prices and Törnqvist indexes with variable-base prices, the latter take into account relative price changes; this means that they are sensitive to strategies that reduce the weight of those inputs that have become more expensive.

2.3.6 The Cost of Capital

As to the estimation of the cost of capital, we have to move away from the simple consideration of financial charges since a correct measure of the total cost of capital should include the opportunity cost of equity. We need the value of the amount of capital invested and the cost rate to apply to that value.

The *Weighted Average Cost of Capital* (WACC) is the most used methodology by regulators for the determination of the cost of capital. WACC is applied to the estimation of the assets value of the regulated firms (RAB, *Regulatory Asset Base*).

WACC is the return required by equity and debt financing of a firm's investments. The most commonly used formula is:

$$WACC = (1-g)Re + gRd \tag{2.14}$$

where:

- Re is the cost of the equity (E);
- Rd is the cost of the debt (D);
- g is the *gearing ratio* given by D/(E+D);
- (1 − g) is the weight of the equity on total funding volume, given by E/(E+D).

The gearing ratio and the weight of equity on total assets can be obtained by:

- The book value of debts and equity. If based on historical time series, this approach is not suitable when we need a ratio for future projections.
- The market value of debts and equity. In this way we have the actual value of the firm, but there are problems because of market volatility.
- The "notional" gearing ratio given by an efficient financial structure of a firm. This ratio, often used by public utilities regulators, is based on a benchmarking approach.

The cost of equity is usually determined as sum of the risk-free rate (related to an investment with zero risk) and the equity risk premium. The Capital Asset Pricing Model (CAPM), developed by Sharpe (1964), Lintner (1965) and Mossin (1966) is the standard way to estimate the cost of equity. The model relates to the return of a share paying attention to the relative volatility compared to the average tendency of the stock market.

The cost of the debt is also composed of two elements, the risk-free rate and the debt risk premium, DRP (the lender's compensation for the risks associated with the default probability of the enterprise).

The WACC computed using the formula reported above is often referred to as "vanilla" WACC, since it does not consider the impact of taxes on the average cost of the capital. Adjusting the cost of equity upwards to cover taxes and the expected return of shareholders, the pre-tax WACC will be:

$$WACC = \left(\frac{(1-g)}{(1-\tau)}\right)Re + gRd \tag{2.15}$$

where τ is the company tax rate.

The amount of capital invested and depreciation

The estimation of the total capital invested in the firm can be obtained by subtracting from net assets (at current purchasing power (CPP) method) the amount relative to commercial debt and other current liabilities.

As to depreciation, the calculation of consumption of fixed capital can be obtained by employing two different approaches.

The first one is a simple revaluation of the book value as it is recorded in the profit and loss accounts. It is important to note that this value does not represent a good measure of physical depreciation and economic obsolescence of installations and machinery, as fiscal reasons and inflation rates have a high influence on it and may lead to biased values that are not economically acceptable.

The second approach results from the application of the perpetual inventory method (Blades, 1998; Meinen et al., 1998; OECD, 1998) and is based on a breakdown of the capital stock in classes according to the year of acquisition of the assets. It enables the obtaining of a "real value" of assets for each year. Average depreciation rates drawn from annual reports can be applied to the gross values of fixed assets.

This method takes account of the fact that for each year, the value of fixed assets is the result of a stratification process, with investments and disinvestments respectively increasing and decreasing the amount recorded at the beginning of the year. Starting from a base year, the asset values of which often need to be expressed in terms of market values, additions and subtractions could be calculated at constant prices following the equation below:

$$K_{t+n} = K_{t+n-1} + \frac{I_{t+n}}{IP_{t+n}} - \frac{D_{t+n}}{IP_{t+n-z}} \tag{2.16}$$

where K_{t+n} indicates the value of fixed assets for year $t+n$ at the prices of year t, IP_{t+n} is the price index for year $t + n$, I_{t+n} is the investment done in year $t + n$ and D_{t+n} is the depreciation for year $t + n$. The use of the price index of year $t + n - z$ for deflating withdrawals points out the fact that in general disinvestments are not relative to machinery purchased or constructed during the current year but instead reflect withdrawals and sales of old equipment.

In many cases this approach leads to very high values of gross fixed assets as compared to the book values recorded in the balance sheets; this reflects the fact that accounting systems based on original costs do not take into account the effects of inflation, which could be very relevant, especially with respect to the base year. For applications of Laspeyres and Törnqvist indexes, see Fraquelli and Vannoni (1996).

In many empirical applications in transport, capital expenditure measures are also used to measure the capital input, for example, capturing the amount of rail renewal costs incurred in a given year. This measure avoids some of the problems noted above, but runs the risk of identifying a firm as inefficient if it happens to be carrying out a large volume of renewals in a given year. It might be considered that this measure is a reasonable measure if it is seen to be in "steady state", but there will often be cases where cash constraints reduce renewals to artificially low levels, which later rise to catch up. Thus careful consideration of such issues is required (see for example, Chapter 5).

Table 2.1   *Use of DEA methods in electricity benchmarking in Europe*
                 for Distribution System Operators (DSO) and Transmission
                 System Operators (TSO)

Direct or not direct implementation in regulation	Countries that rely on DEA for benchmarking of DSO	Countries that rely on DEA for benchmarking of TSO
Direct implementation in regulation	Austria, Germany, Norway, Slovenia	Belgium, Denmark, Finland, Germany, Iceland, Netherlands, Norway, Portugal
Not direct implementation in regulation	Belgium, Iceland, Sweden, Switzerland	Austria, Estonia, France, Greece, Italy, Lithuania, Luxemburg, Spain, Sweden, United Kingdom

Note: The table reports both exclusive DEA use and DEA combined with other methods.
Source: Our elaboration from Agrell and Bogetoft (2017), p. 11.

2.4   BENCHMARKING BY DEA APPROACH AND BOOTSTRAPPING

2.4.1   Data Envelopment Analysis (DEA)[3]

DEA is a benchmarking approach based on non-parametric programming techniques to evaluate the efficiency of homogeneous units, in contexts with multiple inputs and multiple outputs. The most efficient firms contribute to form a "best-practice frontier" that will be useful to compare the performance of other firms. As noted by some authors, "DEA's empirical orientation and absence of a priori assumptions have resulted in its use in a number of studies involving efficient or best-practice frontier estimation in the non-profit, regulated, and private sectors" (Cook and Zhu, 2013). Table 2.1 gives an example of the use of the DEA approach in electricity benchmarking in Europe.

The measurement of efficiency based on the comparison of a firm (or more generally, decision making unit – DMU) with its efficient counterpart lying on the technological frontier dates back to Debreu (1951) and Farrell (1957). The basic idea is that the capacity of each unit to transform inputs into outputs cannot be assessed as efficient or inefficient in itself, but only in connection to an external (optimal) benchmark. A firm can be regarded as efficient if it is not possible to identify a benchmark whose processing capacity is better.

The efficiency of a firm can be measured in terms of minimising the use of the inputs given a certain amount of output (input-oriented approach) or, alternatively, in terms of maximising the output given certain input level (output-oriented approach). Of course, the choice between these alternatives depends on the assumption about the firm's behaviour, i.e. the degree of control that individual firms may have in terms of input saving or output expansion.

Charnes et al. (1978) and Banker et al. (1984) subsequently extended the original intuition by Debreu and Farrell by means of a mathematical approach, based on optimisation algorithms, aimed at deriving a technological frontier from a set of observed units. This approach takes the name of data envelopment analysis (DEA). For a comprehensive discussion of DEA models see Cook and Zhu (2014) and Coelli et al. (2005).

Analytically, let $Z = \{(x_n, y_n) \mid n = 1, ..., N\}$ be a set of N firms for which information is available on the amount of K inputs and M outputs (x_n is a K-dimensional input vector and y_n is an M-dimensional output vector). The input-oriented model in case of variable returns to scale (VRS) for the DMU n_0, consists in the following linear programming problem (Banker et al., 1984):

$$\min_{\{\theta_{n_0}, \lambda_n\}} \theta_{n_0}$$

s.t.

$$y_{m,n^0} \leq \sum_n \lambda_n y_{m,n}, \qquad m = 1,...,M$$

$$\theta_{n_0} x_{k,n^0} \geq \sum_n \lambda_n x_{k,n}, \quad k = 1,...,K$$

$$\lambda_n \geq 0, \qquad\qquad n = 1,...,N$$

$$\sum_n \lambda_n = 1 \qquad\qquad (2.17)$$

where λ_n is an N-dimensional vector of weights (or "intensity variable") assigned by the linear programming algorithm to each firm in order to determine input/output linear combinations belonging to the efficient frontier. The solution to the linear programming problem provides the optimal value of the scalar θ_{n0}, such that $0 < \theta_{n0} \leq 1$. This represents a measure of radial projection towards the frontier. A value of the latter coefficient equal to 1 indicates full efficiency, while a value below 1 indicates an inefficiency of $1-\theta_{n0}$. For instance, a score θ_{n0} equal to 0.8 indicates an inefficiency of 0.2, thus suggesting that the firm may reduce its input use by 20 per cent without changing the output. The last equality constraint provides flexibility in terms of scale econ-

omies, allowing the comparison of each unit against a subset of peers characterised by similar size, thus avoiding comparison between units operating at
different returns to scale regimes. The efficiency measure calculated in this
way is thus net of any effect on average productivity due to economies of scale,
and efficiency differential would only reflect managerial factors.

Dropping the last constraint, the efficiency scores are calculated under the
hypothesis of constant returns to scale (CRS), in which the scale and pure managerial effects are not separated. Analytically, the scale efficiency (SE) can be
measured as the ratio of CRS and VRS (variable returns to scale) efficiency
scores:

$$SE = \theta_{n_0 CRS} / \theta_{n_0 VRS} \qquad\qquad (2.18)$$

A value of scale efficiency equal to 1 indicates that the firm operates at the
most productive scale size. Scale efficiency values lower than unity may
be due to undersizing or oversizing problems. By comparing observed and
optimal scale size, the model allows the identification of the presence of local
increasing returns to scale (IRS) or decreasing returns to scale (DRS).

Figure 2.3 illustrates the methodology by means of a simplified one-output
one-input technology. The CRS and VRS frontiers are determined by "envel-
oping" the observed units. The distances B″B and B′B and identify respectively the CRS (overall) and VRS (pure managerial) inefficiency. In contrast,
the distance B″B′ identifies a scale inefficiency associated with oversizing
with respect to the most productive scale size, thus indicating the presence of
local decreasing returns to scale. Analogous measures of (in)efficiency may
be calculated with respect to the unit A. In this case, the scale inefficiency is
due to undersizing and reveals the presence of local increasing returns to scale.

2.4.2   Bootstrapping

DEA efficiency scores are, by construction, biased, since they refer to
a technology that is *estimated* starting from the sample data, and that is an
approximation (and also a subsample) of the true technology, which is unobserved (Simar and Wilson, 1998). The presence of bias can lead to unreliable
efficiency scores and ranking of units. Bootstrap techniques, following Simar
and Wilson (1998, 2000a, 2000b), represent a useful approach to correct the
bias of DEA results. They are also a way to run inference analysis on the estimates. The bootstrap (Efron, 1979) is an approach (usually computer-based)
that relies on repeated resampling with replacement from the original sample,
in order to create random replicates of the latter. Statistics can be computed
for each replica. The number of replicates is usually large, thus allowing the

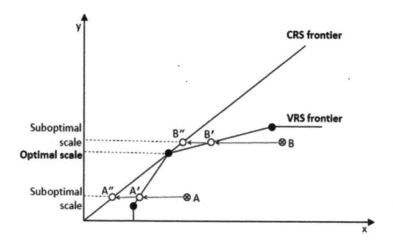

Source: Our adaptation from Erbetta and Fraquelli (2012).

Figure 2.3   CRS and VRS efficient frontier

obtaining of a distribution for the relevant statistics (Bogetoft and Otto, 2010). To give a very simple idea of the application of bootstrapping to DEA, it is important to point out that the resampling occurs after a preliminary efficiency estimate, on the obtained efficiency scores. Each new set of scores obtained through resampling is manipulated to simulate a continuous distribution, while avoiding values larger than 1. Subsequently, the manipulated scores are applied to the original data to modify them in order to obtain a new frontier. Then, new efficiency scores are computed for the original units with respect to this new frontier. The process is repeated many times (e.g. 2000), allowing the obtaining of a distribution for each efficiency score, thus allowing inference and bias correction (Bogetoft and Otto, 2010; Simar and Wilson, 1998, 2000a, 2000b).

2.4.3   Assessing Productivity Changes over Time with DEA

Input distance functions are also used to measure productivity changes between two points in time. To this end, we resort to the Malmquist index (M) proposed by Caves et al. (1982). For each unit of observation, this can be expressed as:

$$M = \left[\frac{\theta^t\left(x^t, y^t\right)}{\theta^t\left(x^{t+1}, y^{t+1}\right)} \cdot \frac{\theta^{t+1}\left(x^t, y^t\right)}{\theta^{t+1}\left(x^{t+1}, y^{t+1}\right)} \right]^{1/2} \tag{2.19}$$

where $\theta^t(x^t, y^t)$ is the input distance function in time period t in relation to the production technology at time t and $\theta^t(x^{t+1}, y^{t+1})$ is the input distance function in time period t in relation to the production technology at time $t+1$; $\theta^{t+1}(x^t, y^t)$ and $\theta^{t+1}(x^{t+1}, y^{t+1})$ are similarly defined.

Malmquist indices can assume values that are smaller or greater than unity. A Malmquist index greater than 1 indicates a productivity growth from year t to year $t+1$; conversely an index M smaller than one indicates a productivity decline.

Moreover, under the assumption of constant returns to scale, a Malmquist index can be decomposed into two components, or possible sources of productivity change: an efficiency change and a technical change (Färe et al., 1994). That is:

$$M = \frac{\theta^t\left(x^t, y^t\right)}{\theta^t\left(x^t, y^t\right)} \cdot \left[\frac{\theta^{t+1}\left(x^{t+1}, y^{t+1}\right)}{\theta^t\left(x^{t+1}, y^{t+1}\right)} \cdot \frac{\theta^{t+1}\left(x^t, y^t\right)}{\theta^t\left(x^t, y^t\right)}\right]^{1/2} \qquad (2.20)$$

The first component represents the efficiency change from year t to year $t+1$ and measures the extent to which a unit has moved closer to the frontier.

The second component is the technical change. For a given sample, a technical change greater than unity indicates an industry-level technological progress and vice versa.

2.4.4   Undesirable Outputs and the Directional Output Distance Function Approach

Previously, we discussed the nature of the outputs used for analysing the activity of transport companies and relevant for benchmarking. The available measures can be numerous, as shown above. As a component of the outputs, quality was also cited, noting that "quality is expensive and should be valued".

Quality can be measured in terms of good or bad outputs, depending on the nature of the available variables and on the issue concerned. A simple example is the maintenance of the road surface. The increase of vehicle-km represents a desirable output, but implies more maintenance. The lack of maintenance is made evident by kilometres of rough road and may generate delays and interruptions of traffic, hydroplaning, breakage of cars and more accidents. Reducing such undesirable outputs may be possible but is expensive. The phenomenon can be regulated by various constraints; however, it is practically impossible to produce complete contracts able to fully avoid any opportunistic behaviour.

A good support to reduce information asymmetries could be represented by a measure of efficiency that includes quality. If the quality level is measured by bad outputs variables, the directional distance function approach (i.e. imposing specific "directions" for optimising with respect to different variables) can be useful: "joint production of good and bad outputs has gained attention in the literature on efficiency and productivity. One can distinguish between two lines of inquiry: (i) how to model joint production of good and bad outputs and (ii) how to account for reductions of bad outputs" (Chung and Färe, 1995, p. 1). The main idea behind this approach is that, in a certain production process, good and bad outputs are produced together. Usually, the latter are not avoidable (it is not possible to reach a "zero-level" of bad outputs); their proportion, however, can be reduced. A directional (output) distance function model allows the measuring of efficiency in terms of good output maximisation and contemporaneous bad output minimisation, for a given level of inputs. It relies on a non-parametric framework similar to standard data envelopment analysis. More flexible approaches, oriented to optimising also (some of the) inputs, can also be considered. As an example, Martini et al. (2013) apply a directional distance function framework to the airport industry.

2.5   PARAMETRIC FRONTIER TECHNIQUES

2.5.1   Introduction

As noted above, the focus by regulators on cost reduction and in turn reductions in user prices or subsidies makes efficiency analysis through the estimation of a cost function advantageous as compared to other possibilities that only address technical efficiency (that is, production or distance functions). There is an additional practical reason, namely, that in many contexts cost data is more reliable and better reflects the inputs of production. In particular, physical measures of inputs such as staff numbers are greatly affected by the degree of contracting out, and measures such as the size of network or number of vehicles do not closely reflect the age, condition or amount of investment that has gone or is going into different networks at different times. It is also not possible to represent all inputs in a physical measure, leaving another input category, "other costs", which either has to be included as a monetary value or in some cases is ignored.

Even for cost data, it should be said, there remain problems of inconsistencies in treatment of costs such as depreciation and interest, particularly in international comparisons. The problem is not simply different assumptions about asset lives. In some cases, where assets are purchased with grants, no depreciation or interest is entered into the accounts. In some cases historic debts have been written off; in other cases interest is still charged on them.

Getting consistent data remains a challenge. Where close working with the industry or regulator is possible, rather than relying on published data, there is a greater possibility for better overcoming these challenges.

However, overall, the cost function approach does at least ensure that all inputs are considered and the allocative efficiency (or inefficiency) associated with using different input combinations is accounted for; and ensures that the capital input is represented in a form that goes beyond mere consideration of the size of the network.

The remainder of this section focuses on the technical aspects of efficiency analysis conducted through econometric methods in the context of a cost function. The same methods can be applied to other functions such as production and distance functions, which are discussed briefly at the end.

2.5.2   Cost Function Estimation

As shown in the microeconomic literature, the cost function relates costs (C) to the level of outputs (Y) and input prices (P) and, where data is available over time, some measure of how costs change over time (t) as a result of technical change. Thus

$$C_{it} = C\left(Y_{it}, P_{it}, t\right) \tag{2.21}$$

It therefore automatically allows for one key issue in comparing costs between companies in different countries, and in a single country over time, namely different input prices.

There has been a vast array of functional forms proposed for the cost function. Notable developments include the constant elasticity of substitution (CES) (Arrow et al., 1961) and generalised Leontief (Diewert, 1971). The most widely employed cost function is the Translog (Christensen et al., 1971). The Translog nests the simpler, and widely used Cobb–Douglas function (see, for example Beattie and Taylor, 1985) as a special (restricted) case; however, it is not derived from any production function using duality theory. Instead the Translog cost function is usually presented as a functional form which is a second order approximation to any cost function rather than being derived directly from economic theory. The general form of the Translog cost function for m outputs and n inputs is represented as:

$$\ln C = \alpha_0 + \sum_{i=1}^{m} \beta_i \ln y_i + \sum_{i=1}^{n} \gamma_i \ln w_i + \frac{1}{2}\sum_{i=1}^{m}\sum_{j=1}^{m} \beta_{ij} \ln y_i \ln y_j$$
$$+ \frac{1}{2}\sum_{i=1}^{n}\sum_{j=1}^{n} \gamma_{ij} \ln w_i \ln w_j + \frac{1}{2}\sum_{i=1}^{m}\sum_{j=1}^{n} \delta_{ij} \ln y_i \ln w_j \tag{2.22}$$

The function includes both first and second order terms in all variables. Importantly, the Translog allows for elasticities and marginal costs to vary flexibly with the level of outputs and prices. In this sense the Translog does have appealing economic characteristics, such as the ability to deal with varying degrees of returns to scale and density as firm size varies.

Finally, the Translog cost function is often estimated along with the factor share equations. Factor share equations are expressions for the proportion of total cost used by each input and are derived using Shephard's (1953) lemma as the partial derivative of the cost function with respect to each input price. Estimation can then proceed using Zellner's (1962) seemingly unrelated regression (SUR) which is more efficient (in terms of estimation) than single equation ordinary least squares.

When it comes to measuring outputs, the need to distinguish between scale and density effects or the choice between different measures of output is only part of the wider issue of how to account for the heterogeneity of outputs that may occur in transport applications (for example passenger versus bus-km or different types of rail freight traffic). One way to deal with the heterogeneity in outputs is to group outputs (denoted y) into m groups and include a further set of r variables which characterise the outputs (denoted q):

$$C\left(y_1,\ldots,y_m,q_1,\ldots,q_r,w_1,\ldots,w_n\right) \tag{2.23}$$

The move from potentially hundreds or thousands of outputs to a more manageable number of m outputs is obviously a simplification. However, the inclusion of output characteristic variables is an attempt to reintroduce heterogeneity in outputs back into the model. Such variables may include revenue measures (such as passenger-km and freight tonnes-hauled) where availability measures such as train-km or vehicle-km are adopted as output and vice versa. As such it can become a little ambiguous as to what variables represent outputs versus output characteristics versus network size.

Wheat and Smith (2015) is an attempt to introduce heterogeneity by means of a hedonic cost function (Spady and Friedlaender, 1978 and Bitzan and Wilson, 2007). Under this approach there is only one output as opposed to n outputs (this is relaxed in some applications). Secondly, the output and output characteristic variables enter into their own function and this then enters into the general cost function. The benefit of this approach is a more parsimonious model. It is perhaps surprising that there have not been too many applications of hedonic cost functions in transportation operations. In Wheat and Smith (2015), the model included three outputs (train hours, route length and number of stations operated) and many characteristic variables relating to the train-hours output. This analysis provided rich insights into the impact of output heterogeneity on economies of scale and density, whilst enabling a less demanding model in terms of variables used.

2.5.3   Stochastic Frontier Methods

The above discussion has focused on the relationship between costs, outputs, output characteristics and input prices. As noted earlier, a key motivation for policymakers is to understand the relative cost efficiency of transport operators. The cost function relationships discussed above can be augmented to allow the relative efficiency of companies to vary and for this degree of variation to be estimated.

The efficiency measurement literature cites three functions which may be estimated, depending on the appropriate behavioural assumption: cost functions, production functions or distance functions (the latter two are focused on technical efficiency as noted above). Cost functions are often used in highly regulated environments such as transport applications (and particularly railway infrastructure), where it may be seen as appropriate to view transport firms as seeking to minimise cost for a given level of output (where the latter is more or less determined by government). In this section we focus on cost function relationships or, more precisely, now that we are introducing inefficiency into the approach, cost frontier relationships.

The simplest econometric approach is to use the method of corrected ordinary least squares (COLS). This method proceeds by ordinary least squares (OLS), but then shifts the regression line down by the amount of the largest negative residual (for the cost function case), thus translating an "average" cost line into a cost frontier. However, like DEA, the COLS method is a deterministic approach which does not distinguish between genuine inefficiency and statistical noise when looking at deviations from the frontier. It is, however, with suitable adjustments, widely used by economic regulators, in part due to its simplicity.

The alternative and more widely used method in the academic literature (and increasingly by economic regulators) is stochastic frontier analysis (SFA). The stochastic cost frontier model can be represented as:

$$C_{it} = f\left(Y_{it}, P_{it}, N_{it}, \tau_t; \beta\right) + v_{it} + u_{it} \tag{2.24}$$

where the first term ($f\left(Y_{it}, P_{it}, N_{it}, \tau_t; \beta\right)$) is the deterministic component, and Y_{it} is a vector of output measures, P_{it} is a vector of input prices, N_{it} is a vector of exogenous network characteristic variables (such as a measure of network length as the area size, or the physical length of a network), τ_t is a vector of time variables which represent technical change and β is a vector of parameters to be estimated. C_{it} represents the cost variable to be explained. The i and t subscripts refer to the number of firms and time periods respectively. Whilst some applications may use only cross-sectional data, most transport applications utilise panel data, and this type of data greatly expands the possibilities for increasing the richness of the analysis in a number of ways, as discussed further below. The v_{it} term is a random component representing unobservable factors that affect the firm's operating environment. This term is distributed symmetrically around zero (more specifically assumed to be normally distributed with zero mean and constant variance). A further one-sided random component is then added to capture inefficiency (u_{it}).

For cross-sectional data, it is necessary to make distributional assumptions concerning the one-side inefficiency term, and the estimation proceeds via maximum likelihood. This is a significant limitation as these assumptions may not be valid. For panel data, there are additional estimation possibilities. Before turning to the panel data approaches it is worth summarising the benefits of the econometric methods for studying the structure of costs and relative efficiency performance.

First, through the development of stochastic frontier analysis, econometric techniques are also able to distinguish between random noise and underlying inefficiency effects. However, econometric approaches do require the choice of an appropriate functional form, and the more flexible forms (such as the Translog) are not always straightforward to implement due to the large number of parameters to be estimated. In addition, the choice of distribution for the inefficiency term in stochastic frontier analysis is arbitrary. The precise method that researchers should use will therefore depend on a range of factors, and in many academic papers more than one method is used in order to provide a cross-check against the other approaches.

Secondly, compared to cost function (or average response function estimation), it is clear that frontier methods are a significant development since they explicitly allow for the possibility of variation in efficiency performance between firms and over time. Compared with the DEA approach, econometric methods provide estimates of the underlying structure of production/costs, for example, the elasticity of costs with respect to different cost drivers, such as traffic volumes – which DEA does not in most applications (though the literature does contain methods for deriving scale elasticities from DEA, but an additional computation is needed). As noted, the study of these elasticities allows us to say something about the scale and density characteristics of the industry. Whilst DEA can be adapted to allow for non-constant returns to scale, it does not in its mostly used form produce estimates of the extent of returns to scale or its variation with firm size (as with a Translog); further, it is more difficult for DEA to deal with economies of scale versus density or indeed other drivers of costs (though this can be addressed to some extent through using a two-stage approach).

This latter point merits further insights. Indeed, the inclusion of an indicator of the size of the network or service along with an output in a parametric analysis on a total cost function allows the distinguishing between economies of scale and economies of density (this idea going back to the work of Caves et al., 1984).

Economies of density, whose definition is close to the traditional definition of economies of scale, are defined as the proportional increase in total cost resulting from a proportional increase in output, holding the network size (N_{it}) of the company fixed (in local bus transportation, for instance, it might be the length of the bus routes). This is equivalent to the inverse of the elasticities of total cost with respect to output:

$$ED = \frac{1}{\dfrac{\partial \ln C_{it}}{\partial \ln y_{it}}} \qquad (2.25)$$

Economies of density are present if ED is greater than 1, and accordingly, diseconomies of density emerge if ED is below 1. In the case of ED = 1, no economies or diseconomies of density exist. Economies of density exist if the average costs of a company decrease as output increases by raising the service within the same network N (i.e. in the local bus transport industry, increasing the frequency of bus services on the existing route). This measure is relevant for deciding whether side-by-side competition or local monopoly is the most efficient form of provision of the final service.

Economies of scale are defined as the proportional increase in total cost brought about by a proportional increase in output (Y) and the size of the network (N). Economies of scale (ES) can thus be defined as:

$$ES = \frac{1}{\dfrac{\partial \ln C_{it}}{\partial \ln y_{it}} + \dfrac{\partial \ln C_{it}}{\partial \ln N_{it}}} \qquad (2.26)$$

Economies of scale are present if ES is greater than 1, and accordingly, we identify diseconomies of scale if ES is below 1. In the case of ES = 1, no economies or diseconomies of scale exist.

Economies of scale are absent if average costs remain constant when a bus company increases the length of the network without changing the traffic intensity on its network. This measure is very important for defining the optimal size of a service area in a transport industry (i.e. regional train, local bus, airports) to be assigned as a franchised monopoly through a competitive tendering process. Further, this measure is relevant for analysing the impact on cost of merging firms providing the service in adjacent markets.

2.5.4   Stochastic Frontier Methods: Panel Data Approaches

The use of panel data, when available, offers a number of important benefits. First of all, by combining cross-sectional and time series observations it provides additional degrees of freedom for estimation. This may be very important, particularly if the number of companies for which data exists is small, as it often is for economic regulators. Secondly, it provides an opportunity to simultaneously investigate inter-firm efficiency disparities, changes in firms' efficiency performance over time, as well as industry-wide technological change over the period of the study. Third, it can for some models permit the estimation of firms' efficiency without recourse to potentially restrictive distributional assumptions. Finally, it offers the prospect of disentangling inefficiency from unobserved factors. This latter benefit may be particularly important for transport applications, where substantial differences exist between transport infrastructure and operations both within and between countries, but where it is hard to capture these differences in a set of variables to be included in the model.

One way of dealing with a panel is to treat each data point as a separate firm. In this case, each observation, including observations for the same firm over multiple time periods, is given a separate efficiency score. In the case of econometric estimation this assumption may not be appropriate, since it assumes that inefficiency is independently distributed across observations, even though it might be expected that an inefficient firm in one period is likely to retain at least some of that inefficiency in the next period. It is, however, a method widely used by economic regulators in the UK owing to its simplicity, and thus transparency, in terms of how the regulator communicates with regulated firms.

The alternative and more usual approach is explicitly to recognise the panel nature of the data set. Within this alternative, there are two further options. Firstly, to estimate the model using traditional panel data methods (fixed effects or random effects); see Schmidt and Sickles (1984). Alternatively, Pitt and Lee (1981) offer a maximum likelihood version of the same approach. In both cases, inefficiency is assumed to be "time-invariant" and each firm is given one efficiency score for the whole period, rather than one score per firm for each period as in the simple pooled approach. The advantage of the traditional panel approach (fixed and random effects) is that it does not require distributional assumptions concerning the inefficiency term as in the maximum likelihood equivalent. This benefit does come at a cost though, as it requires the assumption that inefficiency does not vary over time, which is restrictive.

For long time periods, the assumption of time invariant inefficiency is clearly problematic, and a number of approaches which allow for inefficiency to vary, whilst retaining some structure to the variation, have been developed. Time varying models have been developed for both the traditional panel data methods (e.g. Cornwell et al., 1990) and the maximum likelihood approach (e.g. Battese and Coelli, 1992; Cuesta, 2000). Kumbhakar and Lovell (2000) describe these approaches in detail. A key distinction in the literature is between those models which make the assumption of independence in inefficiency over time (e.g. pooled SFA; Battese and Coelli, 1995) and those which permit firms' inefficiency to change in a structured and not random way over time (Cuesta, 2000). The latter seem to have advantages from a regulatory and economic perspective.

An important and relatively recent development in the literature has revolved around the problem of disentangling inefficiency from unobserved heterogeneity. In the standard panel literature, fixed and random effects are assumed to represent unobserved, time invariant factors that vary between firms. As noted, in the efficiency literature these models have been applied as efficiency estimation approaches, with the firm effects reinterpreted as inefficiency. This approach risks badging unobserved factors – genuine heterogeneity between railways – as inefficiency. Methods have therefore been developed in the literature to address this (Greene, 2005; Farsi et al., 2005; Kumbhakar et al., 2014; Colombi et al., 2014). One version of Greene's approach includes a firm-specific dummy, to capture unobserved heterogeneity between firms, which is assumed to be time invariant (e.g. environmental factors, such as topography or climate) as well as the one-side inefficiency term (which varies over time). The decomposition therefore relies on the assumption that inefficiency varies randomly over time whereas unobserved heterogeneity is time invariant (as well as on the distributional assumptions of the model). The model is then estimated via maximum likelihood. This is one of the so-called "true" models, and there is also a random effects version of this approach.

The Farsi et al. (2005) approach separates inefficiency from unobserved heterogeneity by making the assumption that the former is assumed not to be correlated with the regressors whilst the latter may be (inefficiency being a function of the ability of management to control costs given the exogenous set of output requirements and input prices that it faces – hence this would not be expected to be correlated with the regressors). Finally, the approaches set out by Kumbhakar et al. (2014) and Colombi et al. (2014) seek to go further and separate the model residual into four components: random noise, time varying inefficiency, time invariant inefficiency and time invariant unobserved heterogeneity. This model relies entirely on distributional assumptions to make this separation, which is a limitation. It further assumes that unobserved heterogeneity is uncorrelated with the regressors, which may not be valid. It is worth noting that these are relatively new approaches with relatively few applications in transport.

2.5.5 A Note on Production and Distance Functions

As noted above, we focus on cost function estimation in this section, since ultimately it is cost that regulators care about. Production functions – or their multi-input, multi-output counterparts – may be used in circumstances where cost data or input prices are not available. These can provide useful insights, though they do not permit the analysis of allocative efficiency. That said, in railways and network industries it may not be possible for firms to adjust all inputs optimally, so technical efficiency analysis may be pertinent. Kennedy and Smith (2004) use a distance function approach that also aims to include bad outputs (see section 2.3 above). This paper is important from a regulatory perspective as it comprises an internal (within-country) comparison on rail infrastructure regions within the United Kingdom – such an approach is often the most pragmatic in transport applications where there is only one infrastructure provider within a given country, and international comparisons are hard to achieve.

2.6   CONCLUDING REMARKS

There exists a range of methods used in the academic literature to assess efficiency and productivity performance both between firms and over time. These include productivity indices, the simplest of which is labour productivity; with more advanced indices covering all inputs (total factor productivity). Non-parametric methods such as data envelopment analysis (DEA) permit the analysis of efficiency as well as productivity analysis, and parametric methods likewise permit such a rich analysis.

Perhaps a key advantage of the parametric method is that it readily yields information on the relationship between costs and the regressors (which can be checked and challenged), which data envelopment analysis does not (in terms of its usual application, although with further steps measures of scale elasticities can be obtained).[4] Whilst parametric methods do require the choice of a functional form – which can be challenging – DEA is not necessarily an antidote to that problem, because it can be seen as a "black box" that "hides" the underlying shape of the frontier. In regulatory applications, our experience is that parametric methods are more used than DEA. In any case, where there are many cost drivers, DEA often requires a parametric second stage, thus reducing the difference between the methods to some extent.

Particularly important aspects of any benchmarking method are that it controls for heterogeneity between firms and over time, and that it deals with the possibility of economies of scale and density that are so widespread in transport applications particularly, and in network industries more widely. It needs to be credible; and potentially it also needs to be transparent, which may mean that simplicity could be preferred by regulators in some cases.

There exists a wide range of methods for estimating cost inefficiency in the literature, some of them relatively simple and widely used, particularly by regulators, and others more complex. However, some of the more complex methods are now entering the economic regulation sphere. In the UK, for example, the British rail (and road) regulator, i.e. the Office of Rail and Road (ORR), has adopted a range of advanced methods, and others, such as Ofwat, have considered these approaches at least, though to date have fallen back on simpler methods, given the data and results obtained.

In the regulatory context in the UK, the Competition and Markets Authority (CMA) which, inter alia, acts as a referee in disputes between regulators and regulated firms, has also tended to prefer simpler methods, partly from a transparency perspective. Panel methods offer much more scope for a rich analysis of the cost structure (economies of scale and density) and inefficiency and these are the most widely used in railways. The question of dealing with random noise and heterogeneity (observed and unobserved) remains a key issue for all regulators, in all sectors. Here there can be a choice between simpler approaches such as COLS, augmented via an upper quartile adjustment, versus SFA techniques to distinguish between random noise and inefficiency. DEA in general does not deal with the problem of decomposition of cost gaps into random noise and inefficiency (though this could be dealt with via an upper-quartile-type adjustment as in COLS).[5]

Ultimately, the choice of technique will depend on a number of factors, including the number of data points, availability of cost driver data, model performance, economic theory and practical considerations. Usually, it is appropriate to run a range of approaches and compare the results and in some cases it will not be possible to choose between them easily. Economic regulators in that case tend to average the efficiency results across a range of models.

NOTES

1. The material in this section draws partly on Smith and Nash (2014).
2. The material in this section draws partly on Fraquelli and Vannoni (1996).
3. The material in this section draws partly on Erbetta and Fraquelli (2012).

4. Though it should be noted that the piecewise shape of the DEA frontier would produce extreme values for elasticities at certain points.
5. However, there are other approaches in the literature, which seek to give a statistical dimension to DEA. These are rather complex for a regulatory environment and start to blur the distinction between DEA and statistical methods.

REFERENCES

Agrell, P.J. and P. Bogetoft (2017), "Regulatory benchmarking: models, analyses and applications", *Data Envelopment Analysis Journal*, 3(1–2). Version retrieved from www.researchgate.net/publication/305490664_Regulatory_Benchmarking_Models _Analyses_and_Applications.

Arrow, K.J., H.B. Chenery, B.S. Minhas and R.M. Solow (1961), "Capital–labor substitution and economic efficiency", *Review of Economics and Statistics*, August, 225–250.

Banker, R.D., A. Charnes and W.W. Cooper (1984), "Some models for estimating technical and scale inefficiencies in data envelopment analysis", *Management Science*, 30(9), 1078–1092.

Battese, G.E. and T.J. Coelli (1992), "Frontier production functions and the efficiencies of Indian farms using panel data from ICRISAT's village level studies", *Journal of Quantitative Economics*, 5, 327–348.

Battese, G.E. and T.J. Coelli (1995), "A model for technical inefficiency effects in a stochastic frontier production function for panel data", *Empirical Economics*, 20, 325–332.

Beattie, B.R. and C.R. Taylor (1985), *The Economics of Production*, Wiley, New York.

Bitzan, J.D. and W.W. Wilson (2007), "A hedonic cost function approach to estimating railroad costs", *Research in Transportation Economics*, 20(1), 69–95.

Blades, D. (1998), *Measuring Depreciation*, OECD, Paris.

Bogetoft, P. and L. Otto (2010), *Benchmarking with DEA, SFA, and R*, Springer-Verlag, New York.

Caves, D.W., L.R. Christensen and W.E. Diewert (1982), "The economic theory of index numbers and the measurement of input, output and productivity", *Econometrica*, 50(6), 1393–1414.

Caves, D.W., L.R. Christensen and M.W. Tretheway (1984), "Economies of density versus economies of scale: why trunk and local service airline costs differ", *Rand Journal of Economics*, 15, 471–489.

Charnes, A., W.W. Cooper and E. Rhodes (1978), "Measuring the efficiency of decision making units", *European Journal of Operational Research*, 2(6), 429–444.

Christensen, L., D. Jorgenson, and L. Lau (1971), "Conjugate duality and the transcendental logarithmic production function", *Econometrica*, 39, 255–256.

Chung, Y. and R. Färe (1995), "Productivity and undesirable outputs: a directional distance function approach", Discussion Paper 95-24, Southern Illinois University at Carbondale.

Coelli, T., D.S. Prasada Rao, C.J. O'Donnell and G.E. Battese (2005), *An Introduction to Efficiency and Productivity Analysis*, Springer, New York.

Colombi, R., S.C. Kumbhakar, G. Martini and G. Vittadini (2014), "Closed-skew normality in stochastic frontiers with individual effects and long/short-run efficiency", *Journal of Productivity Analysis*, 42, 123–136.

Cook, W.D. and J. Zhu (2013), "Data envelopment analysis: balanced benchmarking", *Create Space Independent Publishing Platform*.

Cook, W.D. and J. Zhu (2014), *Data Envelopment Analysis: A Handbook on Modelling of Internal Structures and Networks*, Springer Science, New York.

Cornwell, C., P. Schmidt and R.C. Sickles (1990), "Production frontiers with cross-sectional and time-series variation in efficiency levels", *Journal of Econometrics*, 46, 185–200.

Cuesta, R.A. (2000), "A production model with firm-specific temporal variation in technical inefficiency: with application to Spanish dairy farms", *Journal of Productivity Analysis*, 13(2), 139–152.

Debreu, G. (1951), "The coefficient of resource utilization", *Econometrica*, 19(3), 273–292.

Diewert, W. (1971), "An application of Shephard duality theorem: a generalised Leontief production function", *Journal of Political Economy*, 79, 481–507.

Diewert, W.E. (1976), "Exact and superlative index numbers", *Journal of Econometrics*, 115–145.

Diewert, W.E. (1981), "The theory of total factor productivity measurement in regulated industries", in T.G. Cowing and R.E. Stevenson (eds), *Productivity Measurement and Regulated Industries*, Academic Press Inc., New York.

Diewert, W.E. and D. Lawrence (1999), "Measuring New Zealand's productivity", Treasury Working Paper 99/5, www.treasury.govt.nz/workingpapers/99-5.htm.

Efron, B. (1979), "Bootstrap methods: another look at the jackknife", *The Annals of Statistics*, 7(1), 1–26.

Erbetta, F. and G. Fraquelli (2012), "Managerial efficiency and size: an assessment of strategic potential of Italian manufacturing firms", *European Review of Industrial Economics and Policy*, *ERIEP*, 4.

Färe, R., S. Grosskopf, M. Norris and Z. Zhang (1994), "Productivity growth, technical progress, and efficiency change in industrialized countries", *The American Economic Review*, 84(1), 66–83.

Farrell, M.J. (1957), "The measurement of productive efficiency", *Journal of the Royal Statistical Society*, 120(3), 253–281.

Farsi, M., M. Filippini and M. Kuenzle (2005), "Unobserved heterogeneity in stochastic cost frontier models: an application to Swiss nursing homes", *Applied Economics*, 37(18), 2127–2141.

Fraquelli, G. and D. Vannoni (1996), "Regulation and total productivity in electricity: a comparison between Italy, Germany and France", *Vierteljahrshefte zur Wirtschaftsforschung*, 65(4), 512–524.

Greene, W. (2005), "Reconsidering heterogeneity in panel data estimators of the stochastic frontier model", *Journal of Econometrics*, 126, 269–303.

Kennedy, J. and A.S.J. Smith (2004), "Assessing the efficient cost of sustaining Britain's rail network: perspectives based on zonal comparisons", *Journal of Transport Economics and Policy*, 38, 157–190.

Kumbhakar, S.C. and C.A.K. Lovell (2000), *Stochastic Frontier Analysis*, Cambridge University Press, Cambridge.

Kumbhakar, S.C., G. Lien and J.B. Hardaker (2014), "Technical efficiency in competing panel data models: a study of Norwegian grain farming", *Journal of Productivity Analysis*, 41, 321–337.

Lintner, J. (1965), "The valuation of risk assets and the selection of risky investments in stock portfolios and capital budgets", *The Review of Economics and Statistics*, 13–37.

Martini, G., A. Manello and D. Scotti (2013), "The influence of fleet mix, owner-ship and LCCs on airports' technical/environmental efficiency", *Transportation Research Part E: Logistics and Transportation Review*, 50, 37–52.

Meinen, G., P. Verbiest and P.P. de Wolf (1998), *Perpetual Inventory Method. Service Lives, Discard Patterns and Depreciation Methods*, OECD, Paris.

Mossin, J. (1966), "Equilibrium in a capital asset market", *Econometrica*, 768–783.

Organisation for Economic Co-operation and Development (OECD) (2001), *Measuring Productivity, Measurement of Aggregate and Industry-Level Productivity Growth*, OECD, Paris.

Pitt, M.M. and L.-F. Lee (1981), "The measurement and sources of technical ineffi-ciency in the Indonesian weaving industry", *Journal of Development Economics*, 9, 43–64.

Schmidt, P. and R.C. Sickles (1984), "Production frontiers and panel data", *Journal of Business & Economic Statistics*, 2(4), 367–374.

Sharpe, W.F. (1964), "Capital asset prices: a theory of market equilibrium under condi-tions of risk", *The Journal of Finance*, 19(3), 425–442.

Shephard, R.W. (1953), *Cost and Production Functions*, Princeton University Press, Princeton, NJ.

Simar L. and P.W. Wilson (1998), "Sensitivity analysis of efficiency scores: how to bootstrap in nonparametric frontier models", *Management Science*, 44(1), 49–61.

Simar, L. and P.W. Wilson (2000a), "Statistical inference in nonparametric frontier models: the state of the art", *Journal of Productivity Analysis*, 13, 49–78.

Simar, L. and P.W. Wilson (2000b), "A general methodology for bootstrapping in nonparametric frontier models", *Journal of Applied Statistics*, 27(6), 779–802.

Smith, A.S.J. and C.A. Nash (2014), "Rail efficiency: cost research and its implications for policy", International Transport Forum Discussion Paper 22, OECD.

Smith, A.S.J., P. Wheat and G. Smith (2010), "The role of international benchmarking in developing rail infrastructure efficiency estimates", *Utilities Policy*, 18, 86–93.

Solow, R. (1957), "Technical change and the aggregate production function", *Review of Economics and Statistics*, 39, 312–320.

Spady, R.H. and A.F. Friedlaender (1978), "Hedonic cost functions for the regulated trucking industry", *The Bell Journal of Economics*, 9(1), 159–179.

Star, S. and R.E. Hall (1976), "An approximate Divisia index of total factor productiv-ity", *Econometrica*, 44(2), 257–263.

Syverson, C. (2011), "What determines productivity?", *Journal of Economic Literature*, 49(2), 326–365.

Wheat, P.E. and A.S.J. Smith (2015), "Do the usual results of railway returns to scale and density hold in the case of heterogeneity in outputs? A hedonic cost function approach", *Journal of Transport Economics and Policy*, 49(1), 35–47.

Zellner, A. (1962), "An efficient method of estimating seemingly unrelated regressions and tests for aggregation bias", *Journal of American Statistical Association*, 57, 348–368.

3. The issue of data

Ginevra Bruzzone and Chris Nash

3.1 INTRODUCTION

Benchmarking requires the use of data, in particular data on costs, inputs and outputs (including quality indicators) of comparable undertakings. Information on control variables is also needed to take into account the different situations in which companies operate.

The availability of proper data, in terms of quantity and quality, is a crucial issue for any benchmarking technique, from the simplest to the most sophisticated. Meaningful econometric assessments can only be carried out if the quantity of data is sufficiently high. If data is based on self-declarations by companies, it must be checked and, whenever necessary, cleaned.

3.2 SOURCES OF DATA

Transport companies publish annual reports and accounts, but these are rarely sufficient for benchmarking purposes. Firstly, data is generally published at the company-wide level only, and many companies are responsible for a variety of types of services (local, regional and long distance), sometimes different modes and sometimes in different countries. Secondly, even if the financial data is usable, the accompanying physical data and data on control variables are often missing. British train operating company data is unusually useful in this respect, as most passenger services are franchised and whoever wins the franchise takes control of an existing company for the duration of the franchise. Thus the data in its accounts refers to a single British franchise. Often the franchise offers a single type of service, and relevant physical data and data on control variables are published by the regulator.

A second source of data may be national or international associations such as UIC (rail – Union internationale des chemins de fer), UITP (local public transport – Union internationale des transports publics) and CEDR (highways – Conference of European Directors of Roads). Many such organisations publish yearbooks with relevant annual data. However, they do not necessarily provide everything needed, and data may not be totally consistent between companies, unless the organisation concerned is strict in its quality control.

Thirdly, some of the companies concerned (or even all of them) may voluntarily produce data specifically for benchmarking, because they recognise the value of such benchmarking exercises for themselves in understanding how they could improve efficiency. Datasets for benchmarking based on voluntary cooperation are usually collected and managed by a private organisation or a research centre. For instance, UIC undertook the Lasting project, whilst Imperial College runs the COMET and NOVA metro benchmarking clubs. But in this case neither the data nor the results may be published, or if they are, they may be anonymised, greatly reducing their value to researchers. Moreover, any voluntary cooperation between undertakings aimed at collecting economic data on the performance of individual companies requires special care to ensure compliance with competition law. The reason is that the exchange among undertakings, either direct or by means of an intermediary, of information on competitive variables such as prices or costs, may facilitate collusion and thus, according to the case law, may constitute an anticompetitive agreement.[1]

However, in its 2011 Guidelines on horizontal cooperation agreements (point 95), the European Commission acknowledges that information exchange for benchmarking can lead to efficiency gains ("Information about competitors' costs can enable companies to become more efficient if they benchmark their performance against the best practices in the industry and design internal incentive schemes accordingly").

Therefore the exchange of such information among competitors can still be considered compatible with EU competition rules provided that all the conditions indicated in Article 101(3) of the Treaty on the Functioning of the European Union (TFEU) are met. In particular, the exchange of information should not go beyond what is necessary to achieve the efficiency gains, a fair share of the benefits should be passed on to consumers and competition should not be eliminated in respect of a substantial part of the products concerned.

Fourthly, relevant data may be collected and published routinely by national or international statistical offices, such as Eurostat. These publications will seldom be adequate for benchmarking by themselves, but may be a good source of some types of data, for example control variables.

Fifthly, provision of data for benchmarking may be required by a public authority for regulatory purposes. In this case the authority must have adequate powers to do so (see below), and again the data may be confidential or anonymised and, therefore, not available to external researchers. The British rail regulator utilises such powers to require data on Network Rail in Britain, not just at national level but also at regional level and the level of individual routes, facilitating internal benchmarking within the organisation.

The European Commission undertakes a two yearly Rail Market Monitoring Study, which collects data from all Member States. This started on a voluntary basis, but participation is now required under Regulation (EU) 2015/1100 on the reporting obligations of the Member States in the framework of rail market monitoring.

Data for benchmarking exercises may be collected not only from the companies concerned, but also from third parties, for example, by means of surveys.

Given that most of the relevant data cannot be drawn from companies' financial statements and is typically not publicly available, it is crucial that regulatory arrangements and contracts for management of infrastructure or provision of public transport services make provision for the supply of adequate data for benchmarking in all areas indicated in Chapter 1 of this volume where benchmarking can be used to support public policy (efficiency-enhancing regulation; design of public contracts for the management of infrastructure or the provision of public transport services; enforcement of competition rules).

In most jurisdictions, this issue is addressed by granting public authorities the power to collect the relevant information from companies. The task differs depending on whether data is needed by public authorities for an ad hoc purpose (such as conducting a general fact-finding market investigation or assessing under competition law whether a dominant company is applying excessive prices) or, instead, to carry out permanent regulatory duties.

Whereas for ad hoc exercises it may be sufficient to collect the data on a case-by-case basis, for regulated activities it is usually more efficient to organise a structured system of data collection. In particular, companies may be asked to prepare the relevant information by means of regulatory accounting at pre-established time intervals.

The more systematic and structured is the collection of the relevant data, the easier it is to compare the information on individual companies. A further advantage of regularly collecting data from companies, on the basis of stable criteria, is that the resulting databases allow the carrying out of time series analysis.

Whatever the source of the data, some cleaning may be necessary. This may comprise simply scanning the data for outliers, or comparing alternative sources of data where these are available. Data considered unreliable may either simply be dropped, or may be estimated, for instance by interpolation of numbers from adjacent years, or may be checked by going back to the organisation concerned.

3.3 INTERNAL BENCHMARKING AND INTERNATIONAL BENCHMARKING

In those markets where at the national level there is only one company, or a very small number of comparable companies, sometimes regulators carry out intra-group benchmarking, in order to assess whether there are different efficiency levels between the divisions of the same company. The British rail regulator, for instance, utilises its powers to require data on Network Rail in Britain not just at national level but also at regional level and the level of individual routes, facilitating internal benchmarking within the organisation. In this way, the quantity of data is increased. The more autonomy is granted by the company to local managers, the more useful will be this intra-group benchmarking; however, it cannot be ignored that local divisions/subsidiaries are not fully independent, since they are controlled by the same entity.

Therefore, in such situations, benchmarking with companies in other Member States should also be considered. Provided that it is possible to take the different settings into account, international benchmarking offers the opportunity to compare fully independent corporate experiences. This is typically the situation for rail, where the UIC (Union internationale des chemins de fer) has already promoted some international benchmarking on the basis of a panel of data covering 13 European countries over 11 years (for more details, see Chapter 5).

The development of international datasets for benchmarking efficiency in the transport sector would strongly benefit from the setting of common standards for the collection of information.

3.4 THE LEGAL FRAMEWORK

Both EU legislation and national legislation provide public authorities with powers to collect information from companies for the fulfilment of their institutional tasks, both for regulation and for competition law enforcement, although the legal framework is different.

As to the EU framework for the application of competition rules (Arts 101–109 of the TFEU), both the European Commission and national competition authorities are empowered to collect information for the application of the Treaty provisions prohibiting anticompetitive agreements and the abuse of a dominant position (Regulation (EC) 1/2003; Directive (EU) 2019/1, the so-called "ECN+ Directive"). Recently, the European Commission has also been empowered to collect information from companies for the application of the rules on State aid, whereas previously it could request such information only through the public administration of the Member State (Regulation (EU) 2015/1589).

For national regulatory authorities, there are no equivalent EU rules aimed at ensuring a minimum common level of investigative powers across European countries. However, looking at the general principles of EU and national law, it is possible to point out some shared features.

First of all, the power to collect information from companies should not go beyond what is necessary and proportionate for the performance by public authorities of their institutional tasks.

A second general principle of EU and national law attains to protection of confidential information, which can be considered a corollary of the freedom of enterprise and the protection of private life contemplated by the EU Charter of Fundamental Rights.[2] Pursuant to this principle, a balance must be ensured between, on the one hand, the need to allow regulatory authorities to collect information in the public interest and, on the other hand, the protection of business secrets and other confidential information.

Therefore, when collecting and using data for benchmarking, with special reference to the disclosure of such data, public authorities must be aware of whether the relevant data may be considered confidential information.[3]

Usually the types of information collected by regulatory authorities for benchmarking do not represent trade secrets, which by definition are to be considered confidential information.[4] For types of information that are different from trade secrets, the assessment of whether they should be considered confidential should be done on a case-by-case basis, depending on the features of the information involved. Pursuant to the case law of the European Court of Justice, evidence can be considered confidential information when all the following requirements are met:

a. The information is known only to a limited number of persons.
b. Its disclosure is liable to cause serious harm to the person who provided it or to third parties (which is usually the case when the information has commercial, financial or strategic value).
c. The interests liable to be harmed by disclosure are objectively worthy of protection.

In the case of data concerning costs, inputs and outputs of individual companies, for instance, the confidentiality may be justified by the need to protect the competitive process as well as the freedom of enterprise.

Looking at the guidelines of the European Commission which, in different areas, deal with confidential information, it emerges that usually information which dates from five years or more ago is considered historical and lacking commercial value, whereas current internal business plans and forward-looking commercial information which are not disclosed by the company are usually considered confidential information.[5]

In order to ensure a proper balancing between access by regulatory authorities to company data and the protection of confidential information, the legal framework contemplates different tools and procedural safeguards.

Beyond being granted the power to collect information only when necessary and proportionate for the fulfilment of their institutional tasks, usually public authorities are allowed to use such information only for the purpose for which it is collected (the "purpose limitation" principle), unless express consent is given by the company involved. Moreover, public officials are bound by a confidentiality constraint.

Specific rules ensure the right of access to the file held by public authorities by the parties that are individually affected by the decisions taken on the basis of this information, which typically includes the regulated company (see for instance Regulation (EC) 1049/2001 on access to data held by European institutions). When the balancing of the different rights results in the decision to grant access to the file, public authorities may use specific arrangements in order to ensure to the maximum extent the protection of confidential information. Such arrangements include, for instance, ensuring access to documents only when sensitive data has been redacted, or restricting the persons allowed to see the data (confidentiality rings), or producing summaries of the information in an aggregated or otherwise non-confidential form (European Commission, 2020).

3.5   INTERNATIONAL COOPERATION BETWEEN REGULATORS

International cooperation between regulators, including establishing a shared database for benchmarking, typically requires some institutional arrangements in order to make it consistent with the limited purpose constraint and the protection of confidential information. For competition law enforcement and consumer protection, for instance, the scope of exchange of information between the competent authorities of the Member States is strictly regulated by EU rules; in particular, national officials are bound to professional secrecy also for data received from other authorities.[6]

The same kind of rules for the exchange of information between national regulators would facilitate international benchmarking in the transport sector. This approach would be of the utmost importance to support the development of shared and interoperable international databases in the transport sector, which might be accessible to national regulators for the fulfilment of their respective tasks.

Shared high quality international databases accompanied by strict procedural safeguards might be beneficial also from the point of view of companies, since they would reduce duplications of requests of information, consistently with the "once only" principle whereby public administrations should avoid requesting information from companies that is already held by another public administration.

3.6   CONCLUSIONS

There are a number of sources of data available for benchmarking exercises, including published annual reports and accounts, data published by international organisations and voluntary benchmarking clubs. But this data is rarely adequate, so regulators will often need to gather data specifically for the task. European legislation makes provision for this, subject to requirements that the data is proportionate and that confidentiality is respected.

NOTES

1.   On the EU case law, see Court of Justice, case C-194/14 P, *AC Treuhand v. Commission*, and case C-286/13 P, *Dole Food and Dole Fresh Fruit Europe v. Commission*. See also the Guidelines on horizontal cooperation agreements by the European Commission, 2011.

2.   See Court of Justice, case C-450/06, *Varec SA v. Belgian State*, paragraph 48:

> It follows from the case-law of the European Court of Human Rights that the notion of "private life" cannot be taken to mean that the professional or commercial activities of either natural or legal persons are excluded (see *Niemietz v Germany*, judgment of 16 December 1992, Series A no 251-B, §29; *Société Colas Est and Others v France*, no 37971/97, §41, ECHR 2002-III; and also *Peck v The United Kingdom* no 44647/98, §57, ECHR 2003-I).

3.   Article 339 of the Treaty on the Functioning of the European Union (on professional secrecy for members of EU institutions) includes, among the information covered by the obligation of professional secrecy, information about undertakings, their business relations or their cost components.

4.   Trade secrets are defined by Directive (EU) 2016/943 as information which meets three cumulative requirements:

    a.   It is secret, i.e. it is not generally known among or readily accessible to persons within the circles that normally deal with the kind of information in question.

    b.   It has commercial value because it is secret.

    c.   It has been subject to reasonable steps in the relevant circumstances by the person lawfully in control of the information to keep it secret.

5.   See, for instance, European Commission, 2020.

6.   On professional secrecy in the application of EU competition rules, see Art. 28 of Regulation (EC) 1/2003; on exchange of information between authorities in charge of consumer protection, see Art. 33 of Regulation (EU) 2017/2394. For cooperation among regulators in the communications sector, similar provisions are contained in Arts 38–40 of Regulation (EU) 2018/1971 ("BEREC regulation").

REFERENCES

European Commission (2011), Guidelines on the applicability of Article 101 of the Treaty on the Functioning of the European Union to horizontal cooperation agreements, 2011/C 11/1.
European Commission (2020), Communication on the protection of confidential information for the private enforcement of EU competition law by national courts, 2020/C 242/01.

PART II

Benchmarking and regulation in the different transport modes

4. Benchmarking in roads and tolled highways

Carlo Cambini and Chris Nash

4.1 INTRODUCTION

Roads and highways in Europe are for the most part provided by public authorities (although both construction and maintenance may be contracted out) and free at the point of use. A small number of cities now have road pricing schemes, and several countries have toll roads, bridges or tunnels. In some cases, these are provided as concessions, either let by a process of competitive tendering or directly awarded.[1] In principle, competitive tendering should give a strong incentive for efficiency provided that there is a genuine transfer of cost risk to the contractor. Even where roads are built under a concession contract, however, renegotiation or the extension of concession periods without competitive tendering is common. In short, the provision of roads is an area where competition is relatively weak, and where the use of benchmarking and yardstick competition may therefore be seen as important.

There is a long history of benchmarking highways, but most of this literature simply compares key performance indicators with no formal way of allowing for differences in environment, highway quality, user satisfaction or input prices (Wheat, 2017). There is a second strain of analysis of highway costs, but this is from the point of view of assessing marginal costs for use in pricing decisions, with no allowance for inefficiency. Much of this work formed part of EC projects in infrastructure costs and charges. Since it usually utilizes data on short sections of road which do not form decision-making units, it is not able to shed light on issues of economies of scale in road maintenance and renewal. It does, however, suggest strong economies of density, with elasticities for renewal cost between 0.5 and 0.8 and for maintenance cost between 0.4 and 0.7, while the elasticity for operations cost appears to be more or less zero (Link et al., 2016). Thus, comparing costs per unit of traffic between road systems without allowing for traffic density would be very misleading, but since the elasticities for maintenance and renewals are far from zero, comparing systems on the basis of costs per road or lane kilometre without allowing for the costs related to traffic levels would also be misleading.

Neither of these strands of the literature will be further reviewed here; instead, we shall concentrate on benchmarking studies using formal statistical and econometric methods, of which there appear to be relatively few. In section 4.2, we look at studies on the efficiency of the provision of roads by national or local authorities worldwide; we then look specifically at studies of tolls roads (section 4.3), and finally we consider the Italian experience, in which benchmarking has played an important part in regulation of toll roads in recent years (section 4.4).

4.2   BENCHMARKING ROADS USING FORMAL STATISTICAL TECHNIQUES

Use of formal benchmarking methods requires a sample of different decision-making units whose efficiency may be compared. Where major highways are run by a single national body, with no allocation of responsibility to lower levels of disaggregation, then such studies can only be done with a cross section of countries, involving all the problems of international comparability such studies encounter. Where there are separate bodies responsible for highways for different regions, or where there is significant delegation of authority to regions within a single national body, such studies may use regional data. In most countries local roads are the responsibility of states or local authorities, hence benchmarking studies may use within-country data. Finally, as noted above, some countries award concessions for construction and maintenance of roads within an area, usually toll roads. This again permits within-country benchmarking.

In England, the Office of Rail and Road (ORR), which is responsible for assessing the efficiency of the national provider of main roads (Highways England), has commissioned a review of experience and possibilities for road benchmarking (KPMG, 2016). They conclude that the scope and detail of the publicly available information is high relative to that found in most other regulated sectors. Information can be sourced from international datasets, including those produced by the OECD, World Bank, International Road Federation, European Road Federation and World Economic Forum, but there is uncertainty about comparability.

Several international benchmarking studies have been undertaken for roads, but most, such as Conference of European Directors of Roads (2010), do not use formal analytical methods. An exception is Braconier et al. (2013), which uses data envelopment analysis (DEA), but considers inputs and outputs of the road system as a whole, including number of vehicles, accidents and carbon emissions, and does not consider infrastructure cost, noting that this is a small part of the cost of the road system as a whole. Quality of service is very important given its impact on vehicle operating costs, which constitute the majority of the costs of the system.

ORR is now developing methods for benchmarking costs of Highways England regions using a stochastic cost frontier approach; an initial presentation on this work was given at the European Transport Conference in 2017 (Spencer-Bickle, 2017).

There is debate in the literature on how the outputs of highways agencies should be measured (e.g. Massiani and Ragazzi, 2008). It is generally agreed that costs depend both on the capacity provided (usually measured as lane kilometres, although the costs of 100 km of two-lane roads may differ from those of 50 km of four-lane roads) and traffic volumes. Vehicle km may be relevant for toll collection costs, but in terms of damage done to road surfaces, standard axle km would be a more appropriate measure. However, this data is rarely available; the best that can be done usually is to consider whether the proportion of traffic made up by heavy goods vehicles (the main determinant of standard axle km) varies across the sample. Most studies examine operating, maintenance and renewals costs rather than capital costs. Costs may also vary significantly with the characteristics of the network, such as the presence of bridges and tunnels, and the charging mechanism used. Quality of service, including the smoothness of the road surface and waiting times at manual toll booths, may also be relevant variables, although ones on which data is scarce.

In practice, the main source of econometric studies of road infrastructure costs is within-country comparisons. The earliest study we have found is Sikow-Magny and Talvitie (1996). This used a Translog cost function to examine economies of scale and scope for road construction, rehabilitation and maintenance for 20 districts and 100 construction projects in Finland. Outputs consisted of kilometres of each of three types of roads, in terms of traffic density, and other explanatory variables included traffic volumes, numbers of bridges and interchanges and kilometres of cycleway and walkway. This was not really a benchmarking study, but did produce important conclusions for the efficient design of contracts in the industry. It found economies of scale in both construction and maintenance at existing organization size in Finland; the most efficient size of maintenance district was found to cover 800–1,000 km. There were no economies of scope, but, surprisingly, contracting out was found to raise costs. It was speculated that this was because, in the short run, in-house organizations were unable to reduce their staff in line with reductions in workload.

More recent studies have used data envelopment analysis. For instance, Ozbek et al. (2012) use a variable returns to scale DEA model to examine the relative efficiency of road maintenance in eight counties in Virginia, USA. Their input is expenditure and outputs are road condition and area of road maintained (i.e. the sum of length times width of the roads in the system). They start with a long list of uncontrollable variables representing traffic levels, climate, terrain, subsurface conditions and type of road, but use earlier research to group regional factors into a categorization of low, medium and severe in terms of their impact on maintenance costs. The variation in efficiency scores is very large, indeed implausibly so. The same authors have applied a similar model to examine the efficiency of bridge maintenance in Virginia (Ozbek et al., 2010). A similar study with some of the same authors (Fallah-Fini et al., 2012) examined the efficiency of maintenance of the Interstate Highway system in Virginia. A bootstrapping method was used to correct for bias, and this reduced the variability of efficiency scores. The main interest in the results is that Virginia at the time used a mix of traditional contracts that specified the work to be done and performance-based contracts that specified the target road condition sought but left the method to the contractor. Surprisingly, the traditional contracts were found to be the more efficient approach, although the authors suggest that this may be partly because performance-based contracts were still in their infancy, and a hybrid of the two might prove to be best.

Wheat (2017) estimates a stochastic cost frontier model using maintenance costs for 51 British local authorities for five years with road length, traffic levels, mix of road types, quality (number of defects) and user satisfaction as explanatory variables. He finds there are strong economies of scale for small authorities, but that these are exhausted by road network sizes of 4,000–8,000 km, after which diseconomies of scale set in. He finds that poor road quality raises costs. At low and high levels of public satisfaction, there is a strong positive relationship between satisfaction and cost, but this relationship is weak in the middle range.

In a follow-up to this, Wheat et al. (2019) studied highway maintenance costs in England. To estimate cost functions, they use data on 70 English unitary authorities and county councils in 2015–16. They use road length and traffic variables as output variables while separating total network length into urban and rural road lengths and including a set of variables relating to road classification. To control for network quality, they include three road condition indicators available from the Department for Transport (where maintenance is required) and weight these by the corresponding share of road classifications in total network length. Their input price variables are: the median hourly wage in civil engineering and a national index of materials prices in road construction. They also include a time trend control variable. They use a modified Cobb–Douglas functional form to estimate a total cost function. Comparing the results obtained from the two models they show that, while both models result in generally similar parameter estimates, the student's t-half normal model has a considerably narrower distribution of efficiency predictions comparing to the normal–half normal model. Their results also show that, in the t-half normal model, the minimum efficiency estimate is considerably higher (0.527 compared to 0.225) and the maximum is significantly lower (0.855 compared to 0.918). Therefore, the range of efficiency scores is remarkably smaller in the t-half normal model. As for the mean efficiency score, the value is higher in the t-half normal model, equal to 0.721, compared to 0.660 in the normal–half normal model.

4.3 BENCHMARKING TOLLED HIGHWAYS USING FORMAL STATISTICAL TECHNIQUES

A number of econometric benchmarking studies relate to toll road concessions in Italy, Norway and England. The main elements of these studies are summed up in Table 4.1.

Among the Italian toll concession studies, Massiani and Ragazzi (2008) estimate a set of cost functions using standard regression as well as stochastic frontier analysis (SFA) models to measure the cost efficiency of different Italian concessionaires. They use a cross section of 18 concessions for the year 2006. The dependant variable in the cost function in both models is the operating costs, which is considered to be the sum of the costs of raw materials and intermediate goods, services, rental, leasing and personnel. The two outputs are capacity and traffic. Capacity is measured as weighted road km (where the weights are the number of lanes) and traffic is measured as vehicle km (it is argued that the proportion of heavy goods vehicles varies little in the sample). It should be noted that since this is a simple cross-section analysis within a single country, amortization and financial costs are not considered to be a part of operating costs due to their time-based characteristic. In addition, input prices are not introduced in the cost function as they are assumed to be constant across the sample. With respect to the marginal costs of traffic and capacity, results using a Translog cost function are found to be very sensitive to the exact specification of the error term of the model. Therefore, the authors prefer to use a simple linear model with these marginal costs falling within the minimum and maximum range of the Translog models. For this reason, no clear results on economies of scale are obtained. However, the authors do find evidence of considerable inefficiency and suggest that yardstick competition could help drive this out. The authors try to explore whether these diverse efficiency scores might be affected by the cost of toll collection. They specifically run a rough estimate of the efficiency in toll collection by comparing the personnel employed in collection with traffic volumes. They conclude that while diversity in the number of collectors per billion vehicle km is significant, such differences cannot be attributed to different degrees of efficiency. They correctly argue that this is due to the fact that efficiency scores also depend on factors such as the length of the network, the number of gates and the average travelling distance of vehicles on each concessionaire's network.

In a second study, Benfratello et al. (2009) estimate a Translog cost model for 20 Italian motorway concessionaires over the period 1992–2004. This is not a frontier model as the aim was to examine economies of scale and density and technical change rather than efficiency. So, strictly speaking, it is outside the scope of this review, but it is included because of the interest of its results regarding Italian highway concessions. They use length of the road network and volume of traffic as output measures and input prices for labour, maintenance cost per vehicle km and other cost per road km. They also use the number of viaducts or tunnels and the percentage of the system that is three lane to control for other characteristics of the road network and a time trend for technical progress.

The authors find considerable technical progress, strong economies of density (with an elasticity of around 0.5) and economies of scale at least up to networks of 300 km. Beyond this length, it is estimated that economies of scale are exhausted by 600 km, but the authors warn that the estimates of economies of scale are dependent on inclusion of a single large operator, so no clear conclusion can be reached. Privatization reduces costs by 3 per cent, whilst the introduction of a price cap rather than cost plus regulation appears to have had no discernible effect.

It is noticeable that, for what it is worth, the results of Benfratello et al. (2009) suggest that economies of scale are exhausted at a very much lower level of road kilometres than the one found by Wheat (2017) for Britain. Of course, his results are for local roads, where spending levels are much lower, so it may be expected that economies of scale persist at much higher levels of road kilometres than for inter-urban roads. Nevertheless, the difference is pronounced.

The Norwegian studies are also interesting, even though highway construction and maintenance in Norway are the responsibility of the Norwegian Public Roads Administration, and thus studies of toll road company costs only include the cost of tolling and administrative costs, and not road maintenance and renewals.

Among the studies, Amdal et al. (2007) estimate average cost functions with the aim of restructuring the toll collection systems. They utilize an unbalanced panel dataset of 26 concessions for the years 1998–2004. They estimate a Translog cost function to assess whether or not toll companies are characterized by economies of scale. To this aim, they use average operating costs per paying vehicle as the dependent variable and traffic, and not network length, as an output variable. As control variables, they introduce a set of economic, technological and institutional variables including the number of lanes in the toll station(s), total debt by the end of each year, share of vehicles using on-board units, a dummy variable for toll cordon, a dummy variable for passenger charging and a dummy variable for competitive tendering, as well as a full set of time dummies included to control for any effects of aggregate factors common to all companies. The reason for including financial debt as a variable is that toll companies report that a considerable part of their operating cost is related to financial management, whilst number of lanes, use of on-board units, presence of a cordon and passenger charging all affect the cost of toll collection.

Results show that the average operating costs decrease with traffic volume. Unexploited economies of scale are found up to a traffic volume of approximately 190 million paying vehicles per year, but as network length is not included nothing can be deduced about the appropriate size of a concession. The results also show that for a given traffic volume, while the average operating costs increase as the number of lanes increase, they will reduce as the number of paying vehicles using on-board units increases. Competitive tendering is found to reduce costs by 24 per cent. The authors also run a sensitivity analysis and estimate several modified specifications for robustness checks and conclude that the estimation of traffic and the share of paying vehicles using on-board units are always statistically significant and very robust with respect to the specification.

Welde and Odeck (2011) apply both DEA and stochastic frontier analysis to analyse efficiency of a sample of 20 toll companies, representing 45 per cent of total toll companies in Norway, over the period 2003–2008. As output they use the number of vehicles handled per lane, and as inputs, operational and administrative costs. To control for the impact of exogenous variables on performance of the companies, they include a set of inefficiency determinants, including dummy variables for how long the toll company has been in operation (age), percentage of vehicles using on-board units and the collection system determined by the Norwegian Public Roads Administration (NPRA). They also use several variables related to the form the tolls take, including the extent to which the system for collecting tolls is based on electronic toll collection, whether there is a charge per passenger as well as the charge per vehicle, and whether the company being assessed is a cordon toll company.

For the DEA model, to capture the impact of exogenous variables, they use a truncated regression to regress these variables on inefficiency scores. For the SFA model they estimate a standard production function with a Translog functional form in which the dependent variable is the output. Their results confirm the importance of operating costs in the production of toll companies compared to administrative costs. For the inefficiency determinants, they find that in both models the tolling technologies significantly increase efficiency in contrast to the pure manual tolling. Interestingly, while the age of the toll company is significant in the SFA model, it is not the same in the DEA model.

As for the efficiency scores, while the mean efficiency varies in both models between 0.5 and 0.6, they find considerable variation in efficiency measures (standard deviation is large at about 17–30 per cent). Both methods demonstrate large inefficiencies in the performance of the toll companies, although this result varies between the DEA and cost frontier methods. Their results also show that larger companies have higher efficiency scores in both models, which is considered to be a sign of unexploited economies of scale in the sector.

4.4   REGULATORY BENCHMARKING IN TOLLED HIGHWAYS: AN IMPLEMENTATION IN ITALY

An interesting example of practical implementation of benchmarking in tolled highways by a regulatory authority is given by the Italian Transport Authority, which used the econometric frontier cost analysis to intervene in the Italian highway sector. In what follows, we first briefly provide a snapshot of the Italian market and institutional framework and then present this first interesting benchmarking experience.

4.4.1   The Italian Institutional Background and Market Data

The road and highway network in Italy is around 257,000 kilometres, much less than in France (more than 1 million km), Poland and the UK (more than 400,000 km) but larger than in other European countries.[2]

The management of national roads is entrusted to Anas, a State-owned company currently within the FSI group. For other roads the competence is of regional or local administrations, at the provincial and municipal level. Pursuant to a decree of 2018,[3] approximately 6,250 km of the latter are being brought within the competence of Anas.

The construction and maintenance of roads are usually contracted out, following the rules on public procurement.

As to tolled highways, in 2018 the total length of the network was around 6,960 km, almost the double that in the United Kingdom (3,768) and slightly over half those in France (11,599) and Germany (12,993) (Eurostat).[4] The entire network is managed by means of concessions. The toll component is dominant, with about 6,023 km; the remaining 938 kilometres are managed by Anas.

Three-quarters of the network was built during the 1960s and 1970s, following law no. 463/1955 ("Legge Romita") and law no. 729/1961 ("Piano Zaccagnini"). The largest part of the network was built by Società Autostrade, which at that time was a State-owned enterprise, controlled by the IRI holding.

Table 4.1   Empirical analysis for cost estimation of tolled highway concessionaires

Author	Data	Dependent variable	Output	Input	Environmental or context variables	Functional form
Amdal, Bardsen, Johansen and Welde (2007)	26 road operators 1998–2004	Operating costs	# Total paying vehicles	– Price of inputs (assumed as constant and therefore not included) – # Lines at toll stations	– Financial debts of the operator – Type of payment system (electronic, manual …) – Vehicles equipped with electronic toll systems – Dummy for award with competitive procedures	Cobb–Douglas
Massiani and Ragazzi (2008)	18 concessionaires 2006	Operating costs	Vehicles per km	Network average capacity indicator		Cobb–Douglas and Translog

Author	Data	Dependent variable	Output	Input	Environmental or context variables	Functional form
Benfratello, Iozzi and Valbonesi (2009)	20 concessionaires 1992–2004	Operating costs (long term)	Traffic volumes	– Price of labour: labour cost/annual average number of employees – Maintenance price: maintenance costs/traffic volumes – Price of other costs (total operating costs – labour costs – maintenance costs) / network km	– Network length (km) – # Major works (bridges, viaducts …) – % of network with three or more lanes – Public/private ownership dummy – Regulatory regime dummy (price cap/rate of return)	Translog (with hedonic variables)
Welde and Odeck (2011)	20 road operators 2003–2008	Operating costs + administrative costs	Total # of paying vehicles / # of sections	– Price of inputs (assumed as constant and therefore not included)	– Years of activity of the operator – Type of payment system (electronic, manual …) – Vehicles equipped with electronic toll systems – Dummy for award with competitive procedures	Translog

The traffic on the toll highway network has grown almost fivefold from 1970 to 2010, going from 15 to 83 billion vehicles-km; the trend was reversed from 2010 to 2013, with a reduction of almost 10 per cent of the traffic; since 2013 traffic has started growing again, reaching 82.7 billion vehicles-km in 2017. The heavy vehicle component of the traffic is 23 per cent of the total figure.

The toll highway network is divided among 28 concessionaires (Table 4.2), although the number is much lower (approximately reduced to half) if one considers control shareholdings. Autostrade per l'Italia Spa (ASPI) is the largest operator, with slightly less than 2,900 km (3,020 km taking into account controlled companies). The second largest operator is SIAS Spa (Gavio group), which accounts for around one-fifth of the entire network (1,423 km), mainly in the north-western regions of Italy.

In terms of ownership, slightly less than 66 per cent of the network is operated by entirely private companies, about 13 per cent is totally public, and the remaining 23 per cent is operated by public–private companies, mainly under control of the public partners.

The sector is highly concentrated also in some other European Member States: in France, the three largest concessionaires have a market share of more than 90 per cent, and in Spain, the largest concessionaire has a market share of more than 60 per cent. Interestingly, concentration as measured by the Herfindahl–Hirschman Index is higher in terms of traffic than in terms of toll revenues or network length.

From the institutional point of view, for several years in Italy concessions have been awarded to both public and private operators without any competitive process, on the basis of undisclosed financial plans and for a long duration, recently extended for some important concessionaires.

Although reference to a price cap methodology has been required since 1996, the approaches followed in practice are heterogeneous and often do not include reference to an efficiency-enhancing X factor attaining the expected productivity. Several methods entail an *ex ante* reimbursement of investment plan, with no penalties if the investments are not carried out. Moreover, there is heavy compensation to be paid in the case of termination of the contracts. In total, concessionaires are facing six different methods for setting tolls in existing contracts.[5] The most frequent approach is "footing the bill", i.e. a "cost-plus" approach with no efficiency-enhancing factors. Under this approach, concessionaires are in principle incentivized to maximize investments, maintenance and the related unit costs, since all costs are reimbursed, but at the same time there is no incentive to improve efficiency and productivity.

A different approach is followed in the case of the largest concession. ASPI has been privatized with a form of regulation that can be defined as "lump sum sale" to the concessionaire, i.e., given the investment plan authorized by the

Benchmarking and regulation in transport

Table 4.2   Concessionaires (2018)

Concessionaires	Km	% of total	Traffic (million v-km)	%	Toll revenue (thousands/€)	% of total
Autostrade per l'Italia S.p.A.	2857.5	47.4	47.218	56.1	3,809.336	55.1
Autostrada del Brennero S.p.A.	314	5.2	5.046	6.0	324.984	4.7
CAS – Consorzio per le Autostrade Siciliane	298.4	5.0	n.d.		n.d.	
Strada dei Parchi S.p.A.	281.4	4.7	1.901	2.3	176.813	2.6
Autostrada Brescia Verona Vicenza Padova S.p.A.	235.6	3.9	5.624	6.7	338.983	4.9
Autovie Venete S.p.A.	210.2	3.5	2.641	3.1	188.911	2.7
Milano Serravalle – Milano Tangenziali S.p.A.	179.1	3.0	3.111	3.7	234.552	3.4
SATAP S.p.A. Tronco A21	164.9	2.7	2.021	2.4	177.783	2.6
ATIVA S.p.A.	155.8	2.6	1.852	2.2	129.259	1.9
SALT S.p.A. – Tronco Ligure Toscano	154.9	2.6	1.893	2.3	188.936	2.7
Autostrada dei Fiori S.p.A. – Tronco A6 Torino – Savona	130.9	2.2	930	1.1	69.973	1.0
SATAP S.p.A. Tronco A4	127.0	2.1	2.291	2.7	270.542	3.9
Autostrada dei Fiori S.p.A. – Tronco A10 Savona – Ventimiglia	113.3	1.9	1.230	1.5	156.622	2.3
Autovia Padana S.p.A.	105.5	1.8	855	1.0	51.175	0.7
SALT S.p.A. – Tronco Autocisa	101.0	1.7	847	1.0	100.138	1.4
SITAF – Società Traforo Autostradale del Frejus S.p.A.	82.5	1.4	340	0.4	141.562	2.0
CAV – Concessioni Autostradali Venete S.p.A.	74.1	1.2	1.818	2.2	139.909	2.0
SAV – Società Autostrade Valdostane S.p.A.	67.4	1.1	351	0.4	68.630	1.0
BRE.BE.MI. Brescia – Bergamo – Milano	62.1	1.0	455	0.5	80.398	1.2

Concessionaires	Km	% of total	Traffic (million v-km)	%	Toll revenue (thousands/€)	% of total
Autostrada Asti – Cuneo S.p.A.	55.7	0.9	156	0.2	19.497	0.3
SAT – Società Autostrada Tirrenica S.p.A.	54.6	0.9	293	0.3	35.738	0.5
SAM – Società Autostrade Meridionali S.p.A.	51.6	0.9	1.690	2.0	90.389	1.3
Pedemontana Lombarda	41.5	0.7	265	0.3	35.259	0.5
TEEM – Tangenziale Est Esterna di Milano	33.0	0.5	308	0.4	61.081	0.9
RAV – Raccordo Autostradale Valle d'Aosta S.p.A.	32.4	0.5	113	0.1	27.861	0.4
Tangenziale di Napoli S.p.A.	20.2	0.3	847	1.0	64.511	0.9
SITRASB – Società Italiana Traforo Gran San Bernardo S.p.A.	12.8	0.2	9	0.0	9.857	0.1
SITMB – Società Italiana per Azioni per il Traforo del Monte Bianco	5.8	0.1	11	0.0	61.552	0.9
TOTAL	6023.2		84.116		6,918.331	–

Note: The totals for columns five and seven do not total 100 due to rounding.
Source: SIVCA – Ministry of Transport (2018).

grantor, the level of profits is set free, in exchange for an up-front payment to the State of about €7 billion. As the economic literature on regulation shows (Armstrong and Sappington, 2006), this approach incentivizes efficiency (the concessionaire has direct advantages in minimizing costs), but information asymmetries are left untouched.[6]

A distinct overall regulatory issue concerns the quota of works that are allowed to be assigned "in house" in relation to what has to be tendered out. A sharp debate is still going on about this issue, including the impact in terms of increased transaction costs. The main objective of monitoring this aspect is collecting evidence on efficient benchmarks, since the financial plans of concessionaires apparently are quite differentiated.

In a broader perspective, a revision of public policy in respect of roads and highways should also reconsider the separation of the sector into toll and free motorways, especially since the larger part of the traffic is served by under-financed and under-planned local roads in the metropolitan areas.

4.4.2   Regulatory Issues and the Implementation of Benchmarking

Currently in Italy the issue of how to ensure a proper public policy for toll highways is being hotly debated (see the report by the Corte dei Conti, 2019), and it is widely acknowledged that in this sector both competition in the market and benchmarking can play a role in ensuring efficiency and effectiveness in construction, maintenance and management activities.

The regulatory powers originally assigned by the law (decree law no. 201 of 6 December 2011) to the Italian Authority pertained mainly to the design of new awards of concessions. In particular, a uniform tariff-setting methodology based on the price cap method, with determination of a five-year "X productivity factor" for each concession, has to be developed in order to replace the six methods applied before. The goal of the law is thus to make the market more easily understandable and its operating conditions more transparent. In addition, the Authority has to define the optimal management area; the length of a highway concession above and below which there are no significant economies of scale and scope.

The first application of benchmarking by the Italian Authority was carried out to "define optimal management areas of toll motorway sections so as to promote plural management and foster competition by comparison", pursuant to the law establishing the Authority.[7] For this purpose, since the beginning of 2014, the Authority started an analysis of production costs of all highway concessionaires so as to determine the so-called "efficient cost frontier" by taking into account the output level (e.g. traffic volumes), the prices of production factors, the length of the section under concession and other qualitative and quantitative characteristics of existing technology. In more detail, drawing on the before-mentioned studies, and in particular on the analysis by Benfratello et al. (2009), the Authority defined a method to study the costs of Italian motorway concessionaires by introducing some innovations in the existing studies. The analysis performed by the Authority examined a total cost function (including labour, maintenance and other operating costs as well as an estimation of capital costs given by the sum of amortization and financial expenses). Further, a number of control variables have been introduced in order to better capture the concessionaire heterogeneity, such as different depreciation policies with respect to remaining life of the concession, quality of service (in relation to the road surface) and the capital structure of the concessionaire. The Authority applied both the Cobb–Douglas and Translog functions. Technically, the total cost function is

$$C = f(V, LKm, P_i, H),$$

where:

- V is the total number of km travelled (output),
- LKm is the length in km of the concession,
- Pi are the input prices defined as follows:

  (a) *labour price*, given by labour costs/average number of employees;
  (b) *maintenance price*, given by maintenance costs/number of km travelled;
  (c) *other service price*, given by (cost for third party services + other operating costs)/network length;
  (d) *capital price*, given by (amortization + financial expenses)/network length;

- H are additional firm-level and structural control variables including:

  (a) *stoneworks/km*, given by length of viaducts, bridges, tunnels in km/ network length;
  (b) *high lanes/km*, given by (3-lanes and 4-lanes km)/network length;
  (c) *quality measure*, given by the IPAV index, i.e. a pavement quality indicator;
  (d) *residual period of concession*, given by the years at the end of the concession/length of the concession in year;
  (e) *debt/equity* = debt to equity ratio.

The analysis applies a stochastic frontier analysis (with time invariant and time varying decay) to a dataset made by data from 23 concessionaires tracked from 2005 to 2016.

By applying the approach by Caves et al. (1984) in assessing the degree of economies of scale, the results transposed into Decision no. 70/2016 show that the value of 180 km (corresponding to the 75th percentile of distribution in the sample examined) is the minimum threshold value for the optimal length (km) of the motorway infrastructure subject to a concession, i.e. the length at which the average cost of a concession reaches its minimum level. The maximum threshold was estimated at approximately 315 km, whereas for lengths exceeding 315 km no additional efficiency gains related to industrial and structural aspects of motorway concessions seem to be generated and thus the economy of scale seems to expire.

Benchmarks resulting from the estimation of efficient cost frontiers may also play a role in the definition of efficiency enhancing incentives in service contracts with concessionaires. On the basis of these estimates the Authority has to set the X productivity parameter for the price cap formula.

In Decision no. 119/2017, the Authority has defined, upon request of the adjudicating body, schemes for the award of new concessions to be included in specific tender offers as well as toll schemes, based on a price cap methodology and an X productivity factor, to be revised every five years. The tariff scheme identifies the admissible costs and investments, and contains both a component concerning the operation of the infrastructure (including ordinary maintenance costs) and a component to cover construction costs (for the recovery of new investment costs, including costs possibly incurred in case of takeover by a new concessionaire). Subsequently, the same approach has been followed to outline tariff schemes, in the absence of a tender, for the direct award of a toll highway concession (Decision no. 73/2018).

More recently, Decree law 28 September 2018, no. 109 ("decreto Genova") has made a step into completely reforming the regulation of the Italian tolled highway sector. The task of establishing toll schemes based on price cap regulation, with the determination of the X productivity index every five years, has been extended to the updating or revision of existing contracts. Following this new law, the Authority defined the pricing schemes for 16 concessionaires using the same price cap formula adopted in the previous case (Decision no. 16/2019 and Decisions 64–79/2019). In so doing, the Authority pursued the goal of introducing a unique price cap mechanism with efficiency-enhancing targets. In performing its benchmarking analysis using the same econometric approach previously described, the Authority finds that the efficiency gap in the sector is considerable, ranging from 1.95 per cent to 27.6 per cent.

4.5   CONCLUDING REMARKS

In conclusion, it seems that although there are many sources of data on roads, data availability is still a significant problem. Ideally, benchmarking of road costs would use both measures of traffic, including vehicle and standard axle kilometres, and of capacity, such as lane km, as outputs, and also network characteristics, the form of tolling and quality of service as control variables. Often these are not available and proxies have to be used.

There is strong evidence of economies of density in roads, but the situation regarding economies of scale is less clear. For local roads, Wheat (2017) finds economies of scale persist up to road lengths of 4,000–8,000 km, whilst according to the limited evidence available, economies of scale for Italian toll highways are exhausted at a much lower network size (around 320 km).

Finally, all studies have found considerable levels of inefficiency, suggesting a role for benchmarking and yardstick competition where other forms of competition are not feasible, as well as competitive tendering for any new concessions.

From a policy perspective, this implies that benchmarking methodologies are expected to play an increasing role for highways, both for the design of tenders and the design of contracts, in the case also of in-house awards. The implementation by the Italian Transport Authority of the tasks established by the law shows how benchmarking can be used to promote more uniform efficiency-enhancing regulatory methods. Monitoring the maintenance and investment costs of non-toll highways and roads would also be useful to broaden the information basis for the entire sector and perform robust benchmarking across firms.

NOTES

1. The British example is interesting in this respect. Despite not, in most cases, having road tolls, Britain has a public–private partnership (PPP) scheme under which certain roads are essentially contracted out long term, including construction or upgrading and maintenance, following a competitive tendering process. Initially, the British approach remunerated the private contractor by a system of shadow tolls, but it was realized that it was not sensible to give an incentive to generate more car traffic, so the shadow tolls for cars have been replaced by availability payments, but with incentive payments for reliability of journey times and safety.
2. Eurostat, which, however, suggests using these data with caution, due to problems of comparability.
3. Decree of the President of the Council of Ministers of 20 February 2018.
4. AISCAT, data at 31 December 2017.
5. A description of these methods can be found in the illustrative Report of the ART Decision no. 3/2018: www.autorita-trasporti.it/wp-content/uploads/2018/09/Relazione-illustrativa-delibera-n.-88_2018.pdf, in particular pp. 13–23. See also Beria et al. (2015) and P. Sestito (2015), Hearing before the 8th Commission of the Chamber of Deputies within a Sectoral Inquiry on highway concessions, www.bancaditalia.it/pubblicazioni/interventi-vari/int-var-2015/sestito-audizione-110615.pdf.

6. The price cap in this case depends on the real inflation rate (i.e. price increases by 70 per cent of the inflation rate), the remuneration of investments approved in the additional Convention of 1997 and the remuneration of new investments.
7. Article 37(2)(a) of Decree law no. 201 of 6 December 2011, converted with amendments into law no. 214 of 22 December 2011.

REFERENCES

Amdal, E., G. Bardsen, K. Johansen and M. Welde (2007), "Operating costs in Norwegian toll companies: a panel data analysis of 26 concessions for the years 1998–2004", *Transportation*, 34(6), 681–695.
Armstrong, M. and D. Sappington (2006), "Regulation, competition and liberalization", *Journal of Economic Literature*, 44, 325–366.
Benfratello, L., A. Iozzi and P. Valbonesi (2009), "Technology and incentive regulation in the Italian motorways industry", *Journal of Regulatory Economics*, 35, 201–221.
Beria, P. F. Ramella and A. Laurino (2015), "Motorways economic regulation: a worldwide survey", *Transport Policy* 41(C), 23–32.
Braconier, H., M. Pisu and D. Bloch (2013), "The Performance of Road Transport Infrastructure and its Links to Policies", OECD Economics Department Working Papers, No. 1016, OECD Publishing, Paris.
Caves, D.W., L. Christensen and M. Tretheway (1984), "Economies of density versus economies of scale: why trunk and local service airline costs differ", *The RAND Journal of Economics*, 15(4), 471–489.
Conference of European Directors of Roads (CEDR) (2010) *Report on BEXPRAC*, CEDR, Brussels.
Corte dei Conti (2019), Le concessioni Autostradali, Deliberazione del 18 Dicembre 2019, n. 18/2019/G, Rome.
Fallah-Fini, S., K. Triantis, M. Jesus and W.L. Seaver (2012), "Measuring the efficiency of highway maintenance contracting strategies: a bootstrapped non-parametric meta-frontier approach", *European Journal of Operational Research*, 219(1), 134–145.
KPMG (2016), *Benchmarking Highways England: A Report to the Office of Rail and Road*, KPMG, London.
Link H., C.A. Nash, A. Ricci and J.D. Shires (2016), "A generalised approach for measuring the marginal social costs of road transport in Europe", *International Journal of Sustainable Transport*, 10(2), 105–119.
Massiani, J. and G. Ragazzi (2008), "Costs and efficiency of highway concessionaires: a survey of Italian operators", *European Transport*, 38, 85–106.
Ozbek, M.E., J.M. de la Garza and K. Triantis (2010), "Efficiency measurement of bridge maintenance using data envelopment analysis", *ASCE Journal of Infrastructure Systems*, 16(1), 31–9.
Ozbek, M.E., J.M. de la Garza and K. Triantis (2012), "Efficiency measurement of the maintenance of paved lanes using data envelopment analysis", *Construction Management and Economics*, 30, 995–1009.
Sikow-Magny, C. and A.P. Talvitie (1996), "Efficient organization of highway construction, rehabilitation, and maintenance", *Transportation Research Record*, 1558(1), 117–121, doi:10.1177/0361198196155800116.
Spencer-Bickle, A. (2017), "Initial benchmarking of Highways England's regional maintenance spending", European Transport Conference, Barcelona.

Welde, M. and J. Odeck (2011), "The efficiency of Norwegian road toll companies", *Utilities Policy*, 19(3), 162–171.

Wheat, P. (2017), "Scale, quality and efficiency in road maintenance: evidence for English local authorities", *Transport Policy*, 59, 46–53.

Wheat, P., A.D. Stead and W.H. Greene (2019), "Robust stochastic frontier analysis: a student's t-half normal model with application to highway maintenance costs in England", *Journal of Productivity Analysis*, 51, 21–38.

5.   Rail benchmarking

Andrew Smith and Chris Nash

5.1   INTRODUCTION

Traditionally European rail systems have been structured as government-owned, vertically integrated monopolists. In that situation, one would have expected governments to be very interested in benchmarking as a way of determining the efficiency of their own rail systems. Some benchmarking studies did take place (for instance British Rail/University of Leeds (1979), which, however, made no use of formal statistical techniques), but perhaps it is surprising that governments did not make more use of this technique, although of course most of the methodology in use today had not then been developed.

Starting with Directive 91/440, the European Commission encouraged the division of rail companies into what it saw as the natural monopoly element (the infrastructure) and the potentially competitive element (train operations). Subsequent legislation has required the establishment of an independent regulator and provision of incentives for efficiency, either as part of the regulatory process or as part of a multiannual contract between the infrastructure manager and the transport ministry. Track access charges may be based on the costs of an efficient infrastructure manager. That left an obvious need for benchmarking of the costs of infrastructure managers, although again surprisingly little use has been made to date of benchmarking techniques. The British regulator has, however, used these in its determinations, as described in Chapter 8.

For train operations, under the European rail packages, new entry has been permitted into all freight and international passenger sectors. As from December 2020, new entry is permitted into commercial passenger operations and from 2023 competition for public service contracts will be required (in both cases with some possible exceptions); although these measures to liberalise the domestic rail passenger market have already been implemented in some countries. Thus it may reasonably be argued that actual competition in or for the market may render yardstick competition redundant in train operations. However, the stage when competition plays this role has not yet been reached. Even in the freight market, the incumbent still has more than half of the market in most EU markets, whilst in the passenger sector there is often little or no competition in or for the market (with Britain, Sweden and Germany being notable exceptions because of the extensive use of benchmarking; a few countries, such as Italy, have some competition in the commercial passenger market, but only on one or two profitable routes). Even where there is competitive tendering for the market, benchmarking may play an important role in providing a comparator model to ensure the bidding process is providing value for money; this is obviously particularly important in the case of a direct award or if there is only one bid. Thus we would see benchmarking as having an important role in train operations as well, at least for some years to come. Experience of benchmarking in the two sectors will be considered in turn, followed by an examination of the evidence relating to rail systems as a whole.

5.2   BENCHMARKING INFRASTRUCTURE MANAGERS

The only case where we are aware of a rail regulator making formal use of benchmarking techniques is in Britain. After use of internal benchmarking in 2003, two approaches were adopted during the 2008 review. The first used a panel of 13 European infrastructure managers over an 11-year period. The data was provided from the Lasting Infrastructure Cost Benchmarking (LICB) project undertaken by the UIC (Union internationale des chemins de fer). This data had been used by the UIC to carry out (normalised) unit cost comparisons across countries, but had not previously been subject to analysis using econometric methods. The dataset included data on costs (adjusted based on PPP (purchasing power parity) exchange rates), traffic volumes (by type), measured in both train-km and tonne-km, network length, and a range of other variables characterising differences between the companies (for example, extent of electrification, network density). Ideally, both train-km (as determinants of capacity requirements) and gross tonne-km (as determinants of maintenance and renewals costs) would be included.

A time varying inefficiency model (Cuesta, 2000), which permits inefficiency to vary by firm over time, was used, but in a structured way that recognises the panel nature of the dataset. The results are shown for Network Rail in Figure 5.1 (data on other companies cannot be revealed for confidentiality reasons); see Smith (2012). Results are shown for maintenance and renewals costs, with the additional model variant to allow for Network Rail's renewals costs to be reduced downwards prior to modelling to allow for the fact that the company was renewing at above steady-state levels in terms of renewal volumes (the lines in Figure 5.1 are thus labelled 'with and without steady-state adjustment'). The overall message of Figure 5.1 is that Network Rail's efficiency deteriorated sharply after 2000, compared to its European comparators, leaving the company with an efficiency gap of around 40 per

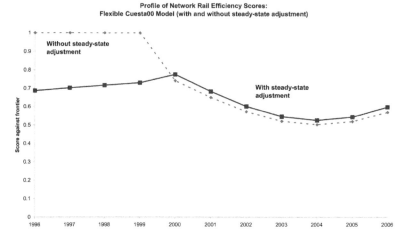

Source: Reproduced from Smith (2008); see also Smith (2012).

Figure 5.1   Profile of Network Rail efficiency scores: preferred model

cent by the end of the period. The analysis was carried out by the University of Leeds, with the Office of Rail and Road (ORR) and in conjunction with Network Rail and the UIC.

In a separate, supporting study, the ORR and the University of Leeds collected a new dataset comprising five other rail infrastructure managers in Europe and North America. This included data on costs, outputs, and network characteristics at the regional level within each country. Thus, although the number of companies included was smaller than in the LICB dataset, the sample size was expanded via the use of regional data within companies (sub-company data structure). The dataset also allowed the ORR to study within-country variations in inefficiency. The results broadly confirmed the results of the main study using LICB data (see Smith et al., 2010; Smith and Wheat, 2012b).

It is further worth noting that the ORR carried out a range of other studies, principally based on bottom-up evidence. These confirmed the existence of a substantive gap, supported by examples of best practice in other countries (see Table 5.1).

Although the ORR carried out/commissioned a wide range of studies – all of which pointed in the direction of a large efficiency gap – it was the output of the LICB-based econometric model which was used to set Network Rail's efficiency targets. The ORR chose to compare Network Rail against the upper quartile of the peer group, rather than the frontier, thus meaning that the starting efficiency gap for its analysis – based on the preferred econometric model from the analysis of the LICB data – was 37 per cent rather than 40 per cent. The ORR also gave the company ten years to close the gap, with only two-thirds of the gap targeted to be closed during the immediate control period (control period 4 (CP4); 2009–2014).

In the next periodic review (PR13), the ORR shifted the emphasis of its approach to bottom-up methods. This was driven by a number of factors, but in part reflected increased doubts after 2008 about the quality of the LICB data and the commitment of the different companies to providing accurate information. A rerun of the sub-company approach was also attempted, but again it was considered that there was insufficient time to get enough certainty about the quality and comparability of the data received. Therefore, although Network Rail acknowledged the size of the efficiency gap resulting from the PR08 econometric modelling, emphasis switched in the PR13 review to bottom-up analysis. Whilst new econometric modelling with an updated LICB dataset was carried out and reported, in the process also applying more advanced techniques, the econometric modelling played a supporting role to the bottom-up analysis (thus reversing the approach taken in PR08; see ORR, 2013).

Perhaps one of the lessons that may be learned here is that international benchmarking is problematic because it takes considerable time and commitment from a group of countries to make the analysis credible and usable. In PR08 the ORR had the advantage of a ready-to-go dataset, produced by the UIC, and this enabled top-down, econometric international benchmarking to play a more significant role than it has in other regulated sectors. If international benchmarking is to work, then it may require concerted efforts by regulators/governments across Europe, working together to establish a common benchmarking framework against which all companies can be compared, thus also implying that data can be requested and audited by regulators and policymakers. Finally, a further opportunity for benchmarking remains the notion of internal benchmarking. Whilst not without its problems, it remains a useful part of a regulator's toolkit as it establishes the savings that could be achieved if best practice (within-country) were consistently applied. The existence of disaggregation into units that have managerial autonomy (at least to some degree), as with Network Rail's routes, is of course a prerequisite for such an approach, but these groupings/disaggregations do also exist in other railways.

5.3   TRAIN OPERATIONS

Again the evidence on train operating costs comes mainly from Britain and from the passenger sector. The reason is that Britain has 20–25 passenger franchises (the number has changed a little over time), each of which is constituted

Table 5.1   *Examples of European best practice which may be relevant*
                 for Network Rail

Asset inspection and asset management.	In general best practice European railways undertake fewer track inspections but inspections are generally of higher quality. It is estimated that similar techniques applied in Britain could reduce foot patrolling inspection costs by around 75% and tamping expenditure by 20%.
Recycling components	This is common European practice. In Switzerland, for example, rail, point motors, sleepers and signal heads are regularly refurbished then cascaded from higher to lower category routes. Cascaded rail on lines re-laid with steel sleepers could lead to savings. Additionally ballast cleaning (partial renewal) as opposed to traxcavation (complete renewal) could reduce ballast renewal cost in Britain by 40%.
High output rail stressing	Stressing continuously welded rail by heating it rather than physically stretching it is a process discontinued in Britain in the 1960s and 1970s. Some European networks (using modern equipment) have re-introduced this method which doubles on-site productivity and, if applied to the renewals re-railing workbank in CP4, could lead to significant annual savings for Network Rail.
Formation rehabilitation trains	Modern high output European plant is regularly used to undertake formation and also ballast renewals. If applied to Network Rail's CP4 category 7 and 12 track renewals RailKonsult estimate that it could reduce unit costs for both activities by around 40%.
Lightweight station platforms	The use of modular construction polystyrene station platforms in the Netherlands could provide opportunities in Britain, given the substantial CP4 platform extension workbank. Analysis suggests a unit cost saving of around 25% in Britain.
Efficient European re-railing techniques.	This particular study brought together many themes from the previous RailKonsult work by focussing upon the Swiss re-railing method. Bespoke plant, high output welding techniques and dedicated teams are applied routinely. Put together for basic re-railing work alone this method is around 40% more efficient than current Network Rail practice.
Use of dedicated teams	Contractors are widely used by most continental railways, as they are in Britain. However, there is generally a greater degree of specialisation by activity in continental Europe (such as S&C renewal or tamping). This ensures a highly skilled and productive workforce dedicated to particular tasks in contrast to the situation in Britain where contractors are often not even dedicated to rail.

Source: Taken from Smith et al., 2010.

as a separate company publishing its own accounts. In most countries such data for a number of individual train operators is not available.

Both DEA and cost function (including stochastic frontier) methods have been used. However, the purpose of the studies has typically been to examine issues such as franchising policy or economies of scale and density rather than benchmarking per se.

Whatever approach is taken to the measurement of efficiency, there is an immediate need to determine what are the outputs and inputs of a train operator and that issue will be considered first, before we look at actual studies.

For outputs, there is typically a choice of considering passenger-km, train-km or vehicle-km. Passenger-km may be considered the ultimate output of passenger train operators, although their costs may vary sharply with the type and quality of service (a passenger-km seated in a luxury coach of a long-distance train is both more expensive and more valuable than a passenger-km standing in a crowded commuter train). However, neither commercial nor social considerations would suggest that train operators minimise costs per passenger-km by operating long, infrequent and overcrowded trains. Frequency of service is an important quality of service characteristic and is often stipulated in public service contracts. This suggests train-km may be a better output measure, although obviously costs vary with the characteristics of the train, including its speed and number of stops. Since both staff and rolling stock are paid for per unit of time rather than distance, costs per train-km tend to be reduced by increases in speed, although at high speeds this may be partly offset by increased energy and maintenance costs. Obviously costs also increase with length of train, although not proportionately, as longer trains still only require one locomotive (for locomotive-hauled stock) and one driver.

This suggests that passenger-km, train-km, vehicle-km and average speeds may all be relevant measures, although only the study by Wheat and Smith (2015) was able to use all these measures or derivatives of them; usually not all are available. Ideally some measure of the peakedness of traffic would also be valuable, as it is peak demand that determines the size of the vehicle fleet required.

On the input side, providing a rail service requires locomotives, passenger coaches or freight wagons (or self-powered vehicles), track, signalling, terminals and a variety of types of staff (for train crew, signalling, track and rolling stock maintenance, terminals and administration). While ultimately all may be regarded as forms of labour and capital, the length of life of the assets and government intervention over employment and investment will often mean that at a particular point in time an undertaking will not have an optimal configuration of assets and staff. This renders attempts to measure inputs simply as labour and capital difficult, as measures of the value of capital stock will need to allow for excess capacity and inappropriate investment. An alternative is to simply look at physical measures of assets (e.g. kilometres of track, numbers of locomotives, carriages and wagons for railways), but this obviously makes no allowance for the quality of the assets. Further, and importantly, physical measures such as staff numbers can be greatly affected by contracting out and, unless a balancing item such as other costs is included as an input, substantially distort measures of productivity and efficiency.

A key problem in measuring technical efficiency is that of joint costs and economies of scale and density. For instance, a single-track railway may carry both passenger and freight traffic, a passenger train, first- and second-class passengers, and a freight train, a variety of commodities. In this situation, only some of the costs can be specifically attributed to one of the forms of traffic; the remaining costs are joint. The result is that railways are typically character-ised by economies of scope; i.e., the costs of a single railway handling a variety of types of traffic are less than if each distinct product were to be handled by a different railway. Moreover, most evidence suggests that railways are subject to economies of traffic density. Putting more traffic on the same route gener-ally reduces unit costs and raises measures of total factor productivity, unless the route is already heavily congested.

The result is that apparent rises in productivity may be caused by diversi-fication into new products or by increased traffic density rather than being relevant to the measurement of performance. Of course, under conditions of economies of density, running more services (and possibly different types of service) on the network does lead to a genuine improvement in productivity. The argument here, however, is that the improvement in productivity arises naturally as a result of the shape of the cost function, and not because of any improvement in working practices. Of course, to the extent that the method used contains relevant measures of outputs and output characteristics such that it can capture some of these features of the technology (e.g. scale and density effects; quality; network complexity), then it should be possible to obtain measures of technical efficiency after having taken account of these effects.

As noted above, a variety of methods have been used in studies of British passenger train operating costs, including non-parametric DEA (Affuso et al., 2003; Cowie, 2009; Merkert et al., 2009) and index number approaches (Cowie, 2002a; Smith et al., 2009), as well as parametric estimation of cost functions (Cowie, 2002b; Smith and Wheat, 2012a; Wheat and Smith, 2015), production functions (Cowie, 2005) and distance functions (Affuso et al., 2003). Clearly the former methods (DEA and index number approaches) can only consider cost or technical efficiency and produce no estimates regarding the actual cost structure.

An important issue is whether to include an infrastructure input in any analysis of train operating costs. Clearly the infrastructure input may be an important part of the transformation function and so should be considered for inclusion in any analysis. The four papers by Cowie all include some measure of infrastructure input in the analysis which is some combination of route-km and access charges paid by operators to the infrastructure manager (to form a price if applicable).

This in turn raises two important and related problems: (1) the infrastructure input is hard to measure (this is particularly the case in Britain where access charges change significantly from year to year depending on the degree of subsidy); and (2) the inclusion of this input turns the analysis into an assessment of rail industry costs/production, rather than being targeted on the train operating companies (TOCs). In their study, Affuso et al. (2003) produce two models: one including the infrastructure input, and one not. The results differ as a consequence, although this problem is less severe during the early period after privatisation (which the study covers), since access charges and infrastructure costs were fairly stable during that period. Whilst there are good reasons for capturing the infrastructure input in a study of TOC performance to capture the possibility that this input affects the TOC transformation function, Smith and Wheat (2012a) and Wheat and Smith (2015) argue that, given the measurement problems noted above, infrastructure inputs are best left out of the analysis. The dependent variable in their paper is thus defined as TOC costs, excluding fixed access charges. Route-km is also included as an explanatory variable in their model, not as a measure of the infrastructure input, but to distinguish between scale and density effects.

The focus of Smith and Wheat (2012a) was on the impact on cost efficiency of contract regimes after several renegotiations and temporary contracts were introduced following franchise failure. It used a panel data stochastic frontier framework that allowed efficiency to evolve over time (based on Cuesta, 2000). They also included dummy variables in the cost function to allow the extent of cost effects of different contract types to be directly estimated.

The focus of the Wheat and Smith (2015) work, in contrast, was how best to model the cost structure of the industry. This work utilised a hedonic cost function, and the description of the data used is given in Table 5.2. In particular, they defined three generic outputs (route-km, train-hours and number of stations operated) and defined nine characteristics of train services which go into the train-hours output function. These characteristics control for the heterogeneity in train service provision. They also define two inputs and associated prices.

Finally, Wheat et al. (2018) and Stead et al. (2019) studied the cost structure of open-access operators in Britain. Whilst there has been extensive study of open-access operations, these papers offer rare insights into costs and, in particular, the comparison of costs against the 'incumbent' franchised operator, since such data is seldom available.

Findings on the cost structure of passenger train operations

In this subsection we present some results of the work undertaken to date to illustrate the richness and usefulness of the methods employed. Returns to

Table 5.2   *Data used in Wheat and Smith (2015)*

Symbol	Name	Description	Data Source
y_1	Route-km	Length of the line-km operated by the TOC. A measure of the geographical coverage of the TOC	National Rail Trends
y_2	Train hours	Primary driver of train operating cost	National Modelling Framework Timetabling Module
q_{12}	Average vehicle length of trains	Vehicle-km /Train-km	Network Rail
q_{22}	Average speed	Train-km/Train hours	National Modelling Framework Timetabling Module
q_{32}	Passenger load factor	Passenger-km/Train-km	Passenger-km data from National Rail Trends. Train-km data from Network Rail.
q_{42}	Intercity TOC	Proportion of train services intercity in nature	National Rail Trends for the categorisation of TOCs into intercity, LSE and regional. Where TOCs have merged across sectors a proportion allocation is made on an approximate basis with reference to the relative size of train-km by each pre-merged TOC.
q_{52}	London South Eastern indicator	Proportion of train services into and around London (in general commuting services)	
q_{62}	$q_{42}q_{52}$	Interaction between Intercity and LSE proportions	
q_{72}	$q_{42}(1 - q_{42} - q_{52})$	Interaction between intercity and regional (non-intercity and non-LSE services) proportions	
q_{82}	$q_{52}(1 - q_{42} - q_{52})$	Interaction between LSE and regional proportions	
q_{92}	Number of rolling stock types operated	Number of 'generic' rolling stock types operated	National Modelling Framework Rolling Stock Classifications
y_3	Stations operated	Number of stations that the TOC operates	National Rail Trends
Prices			
P_1	Non-payroll cost per unit rolling stock		TOC accounts for cost, Platform 5 and TAS Rail Industry Monitor for rolling stock numbers
P_2	Staff costs (on payroll)		TOC accounts (both costs and staff numbers)

Source: Reproduced from Table 1 in Wheat and Smith (2015).

scale (RtS) and returns to density (RtD) can be defined specifically for operations (as distinct from infrastructure). RtS measure how costs change when a firm grows in terms of geographical size. RtD measures how costs change when a firm grows by running more services on a fixed network.

The DEA analysis yields few results in relation to economies of scale or density. Indeed the paper by Cowie (2009) imposes constant returns to scale. Merkert et al. (2009) did estimate a variable returns to scale model and found that British and Swedish TOCs were below minimum efficient scale, while the largest German operators were above. Of the parametric papers, Cowie (2002b) estimates a cost model which provides evidence on economies of scale. Cowie finds evidence for increasing returns to scale and that these are increasing with scale. There is no attempt to differentiate between scale and density economies in the analysis.

Smith and Wheat (2012a) put forward a model which yields estimates of the extent of both economies of scale and economies of density, where the primary usage output is train-km. They found constant returns to scale and increasing returns to train density. The policy conclusion of this finding is that whilst there would not be scale benefits from merging franchises, such mergers may reduce costs by allowing greater exploitation of economies of density, i.e. a single operator running trains more intensively down a given route (though see further discussion on economies of density and heterogeneity below). One limitation of the Smith and Wheat (2012a) work was the inability to estimate a plausible Translog function. Instead, a restricted variant was estimated, selected on the basis of general to specific testing and on whether key elasticities were of the expected sign. This implicitly restricts the variation in economies of scale and economies of density.

Further work by Wheat and Smith (2015) estimated a Translog simultaneously with the cost share equations and adopted a hedonic representation of the train operations output in order to include characteristics of output in a parsimonious manner. This work provides new insights into the scale and density properties of train operations, since it allows RtS and RtD to vary with the heterogeneity characteristics of output. Figures 5.2 and 5.3 summarise the findings on RtD and RtS.

Figure 5.2 shows that all TOC types exhibit increasing RtD and that this does fall with density, although RtD are never exhausted within the middle 80 per cent of the sample. At any given train-hours per route-km level, intercity TOCs exhibit the lowest RtD, while LSE (commuter services into London) exhibit the strongest (and indeed even at the 90th percentile density in sample the RtD estimate is in excess of 1.2). Intuitively, the curve for mixed TOCs is somewhere in between the curves for intercity and regional. The policy conclusion from the analysis of RtD is that most TOCs should be able to reduce unit costs if there is further growth in train hours (on a fixed network) in response to future increases in passenger demand.

Figure 5.3 provides a similar plot for RtS. This shows that for all of the central 80 per cent of the train-hours distribution, intercity (and mixed) TOCs exhibit decreasing RtS. LSE TOCs exhibit increasing returns to scale only for the very smallest in sample, whilst regional TOCs are the only TOC type to have an appreciable range exhibiting increasing returns to scale. The results are consistent with a U-shaped average cost curve, although it would appear that most TOCs are operating at or beyond the minimum unit cost point. This finding has important implications for examining the optimal size of TOCs and was relevant to franchise policy changes in Britain in recent years that resulted in substantial franchise re-mapping, and in turn larger franchises. The evidence that some of the British TOCs may be too large also concords with evidence from Germany, where evidence of decreasing returns for the larger franchises has been reported (see Link, 2016).

The overall conclusion from this section is that modelling returns to scale and density in passenger train operations potentially requires a rich model to fully capture the effects. The initial work published in Smith and Wheat (2012a) based on a restricted Translog model suggested broadly constant returns to scale combined with fairly strong economies of density. This may

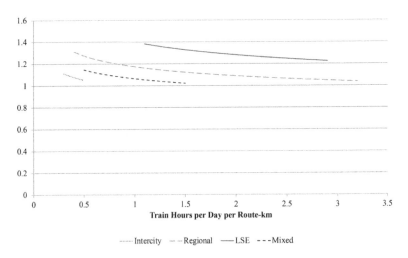

Source: Reproduced from Wheat and Smith (2015).

Figure 5.2   *Returns to density for different TOC types holding other variables constant*

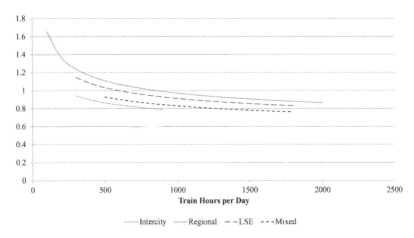

Source: Reproduced from Wheat and Smith (2015).

Figure 5.3   Returns to scale for different TOC types holding other variables constant

suggest that there could be a case for making franchises smaller, which could additionally help in reducing the risk of franchise failure, which has been a key problem in Britain. Britain's franchises are already considerably larger, in general, than those elsewhere in Europe. However, if reducing the size of franchises also increases the degree of franchise overlap, then important economies of density may be lost in the process, so it is not a clear policy conclusion. Turning the argument the other way round, larger franchises that result in reductions in franchise overlap and the exploitation of economies of density may reduce costs.

That said, Wheat and Smith (2015) develop a richer model, which takes account of service heterogeneity (in particular, in terms of train speed and TOC type) in relation to returns to scale and density. In that later paper it is found that the ability to exploit economies of density may be constrained by service heterogeneity. Likewise, the losses of economies of density from reducing franchise size might be smaller than indicated above. It is further found that some franchises in Britain are operating at decreasing returns to scale, and may therefore be too large (as noted above, a similar finding has been reported for Germany).

What the above research suggests is that it is possible to shed new light on the structure of costs of passenger train operations, and draw broad conclusions about the economies of scale and density of those operations. The most recent work suggests that there could be cost savings from reducing franchise size (because of scale diseconomies) and that losses in economies of density might be reduced by service heterogeneity. Some new work in the area of open-access operations (Wheat et al., 2018 and Stead et al., 2019) has also suggested that open-access operators in Britain, though much smaller than their franchised comparators, have similar unit costs. This finding is surprising as these companies are unable to benefit from economies of density as they run far fewer services than the franchised operators, although being subsidiaries of larger companies they do share some resources with other companies in the group. Potentially this analysis suggests that open-access operators may be able to reach lower costs than franchisees, perhaps because they are free to determine their own salaries and working conditions, whereas in Britain franchisees take over an existing company. Further, the work suggests that open-access operators perform worse in respect of punctuality than franchised operators and thus may be offering low-quality, low-cost services.

5.4   EUROPEAN RAIL SYSTEM BENCHMARKING

Whereas separate studies of infrastructure and operations are largely confined to Britain, there are many studies of European rail systems (infrastructure and operations) as a whole. These studies add together infrastructure and train operating costs. However, there remain serious data problems and these are getting worse. Most past studies concentrate on the impact of reforms at the European level and have applied data envelopment analysis to physical data; the problems with that approach have been outlined above. Moreover, they have usually used the data published by the UIC,[1] data which has been shown to contain inconsistencies (van de Velde et al., 2012). Moreover, this source only contains data on UIC members, generally the incumbent, but not new entrants, and in some cases covers their activities in a number of countries rather than just their home country. A rare example of the estimation of cost functions to study the impact of European reforms is Asmild et al. (2009); they also went to considerable efforts to clean up and supplement the UIC data. They found that competitive tendering for passenger services, open access for freight services and accounting separation of infrastructure from operations all improved efficiency, but could find no further effect of complete separation of infrastructure from operations. However, their data series ended in 2001, before many reforms took place.

A number of studies have been undertaken using DEA. In one of the more recent studies, Cantos et al. (2010) use data envelopment analysis on physical data for 16 railways for the period 1985–2005. In a first stage they use two outputs (passenger-km and freight tonne-km) and four inputs – employment, number of passenger-carrying vehicles, number of freight wagons and route-km – to compile measures of efficiency. They then regress these measures on variables reflecting the operating conditions of the railway concerned (percentage of train-km that are passenger, traffic density in terms of train-km per route-km, mean passenger train load and mean freight train load) and on variables reflecting vertical separation and introduction of competition.

They find separate beneficial effects of vertical separation and introduction of competition in the freight market, whereas passenger franchising has no such effect. However, of the four countries in their sample in which passenger franchising has been introduced, only in Sweden and Germany has it covered a significant proportion of regional services and in none has it covered commercial services. That vertical separation has improved efficiency over and above the impact of competition is surprising; a key concern is that this may be because vertically separated systems undertake more subcontracting and that this has not been picked up in the physical data, but there is no clear evidence on this issue.

Cantos et al. (2012) use a larger sample of 23 countries and a more up-to-date period of 2001–2008. It repeats the data envelopment analysis approach of the earlier paper, but also applies a stochastic frontier approach, showing that this leads to much lower efficiency scores, although the ranking of countries in terms of efficiency is similar. The results of the second stage analysis are rather different, however. Vertical separation has no significant effect on efficiency, whilst the strongest positive effect on efficiency comes from passenger tendering. Freight open access has a positive effect on efficiency that is significant in one of the models. Unfortunately, they seem to have a less adequate set of variables as controls in the second stage analysis in this paper. They only include population density and rail route length. The results could be considerably biased by the lack of data on passenger and freight train loads, which tend to be heavily influenced by the geography of the country and government policy, but which are major determinants of efficiency.

A recent example of the use of a Translog cost function with panel data from a large number of countries is Mizutani and Uranishi (2013). They used data for 30 railway companies from 23 OECD countries for the years 1994 to 2007, giving 420 observations. Whilst most of the observations were from Europe, they included the vertically integrated passenger railways of Japan, and also South Korea and Turkey. Where vertical separation had been implemented, they added together the infrastructure manager and the train operating company to form a single observation. The basic source of data was the UIC, but this was supplemented as necessary by data from company annual reports.

Two separate models were estimated, one using passenger-kilometres and freight tonne-kilometres as outputs and the other, total train-kilometres, with the share of passenger revenue to total revenue, passenger load factors and length of haul and freight number of cars per train to reflect differences in the characteristics and therefore costs of the train-kilometres. Factor prices for labour, track, rolling stock and other materials were estimated. Finally route-kilometres, train-kilometres per route-kilometre and the percentage of line electrified were included as descriptors of the network.

The rail reform variables were dummies reflecting complete vertical separation (the holding company model being regarded as integrated) and horizontal separation of passenger and freight operations. It was found that whilst horizontal separation unequivocally reduces costs, vertical integration only reduced costs for densely trafficked railways; for most European railways it increased them. Given that there are no separate variables representing the degree to which competition is permitted or actually takes place, it must be assumed that these impacts are the net effect of any additional costs directly caused by vertical separation and of the impact of any increase in competition. The explanation given for the impact on costs varying with density is that given above, that the transactions costs caused by vertical separation will be much greater in densely trafficked networks than in less densely trafficked ones.

Van de Velde et al. (2012) take this work further by updating and improving the dataset and introducing separate dummy variables for holding companies and complete vertical separation (this work was also later published in the academic literature, see Nash et al. (2014) and Mizutani et al. (2015)). They also add data for Britain, the country in which the most radical reforms had taken place, but which had been excluded from most previous studies due to lack of data. Finally, they introduce dummy variables representing passenger and freight market competition.

They confirm the previous finding that, compared with complete vertical integration, vertical separation reduces costs at low levels of density but increases them at high; at mean European density levels, costs are not affected by the change. This effect is not likely to be one of pure transactions costs (negotiating and enforcing contracts), which have been shown to be a relatively small proportion of total system costs (Merkert et al., 2012) but is more likely a problem of misalignment of incentives leading to poor integration of infrastructure and operations, in circumstances (dense traffic) when this is particularly important. They find weak evidence (significant at 10 per cent only) that the holding company model reduces costs compared with vertical integration, but this does not vary with density, so the holding company would be preferred to vertical separation at high levels of density but not at low.

Within the range of the data, the introduction of competition seems to have had no effect on costs. Horizontal separation of freight and passenger undertakings seems to have sharply reduced costs (perhaps because this has typically been associated with preparation of the freight undertaking for privatisation), whilst a high proportion of revenue coming from freight rather than passengers tends to increase the costs of vertical separation (perhaps because planning freight services efficiently requires closer day-to-day working than for passenger services, since freight services vary from day to day whereas passenger services are generally fixed for the duration of the timetable). The paper also provides qualitative evidence on the issue of how misalignment of incentives may raise costs and shows how, whilst efficiently set track access charges and performance regimes are important, they do not provide incentives for railway undertakings to assist infrastructure managers in seeking the minimum cost solution to infrastructure provision. A mechanism for sharing of changes in costs and revenues would be required to achieve that. Such a mechanism was a feature of the one 'deep' alliance negotiated in Britain between a train operator and the infrastructure manager, but it is not clear how successful this was and it has not been possible to negotiate such an alliance again.

Finally, using similar data, but focusing only on Europe, Smith et al. (2018) find evidence that strong economic regulation has led to lower costs; though that economic regulation seems to work best when combined with vertical separation. To an extent then, strong regulation could overcome some of the misalignment issues noted above, even for separated railways – though further research is needed, with more up-to-date data.

The conclusion of the studies in this section is that there is no one-size-fits-all policy for European railways. Based on a mixture of qualitative and quantitative research, the evidence suggests that vertical separation may perform less well than the holding company model for intensely used networks, whilst being the structure of choice for less dense networks. Whilst this is in part intuitive, it is not totally clear why separation reduces costs for lightly used networks, particularly if there is little competition. It is also disconcerting that it has not been possible to find clear competition effects in the data; though potentially there is evidence that strong regulation can have an impact on costs. A final note must be that although we consider the cost function approach to be the best approach, and with the van de Velde et al. (2012) study incorporating data from the Community of European Railway and Infrastructure Companies (CER) members to supplement published data, there nevertheless remains work to be done on the data side to improve its comparability.

5.5   CONCLUDING REMARKS

The literature contains a rich set of studies focused on analysis of rail costs for efficiency (and other) purposes, covering infrastructure, train operations and the vexed question as to what extent infrastructure and operations should be separated or combined. Key issues in all cases are to develop a technology that reflects the possibility of economies of scale and density, and to deal with heterogeneity through specifying a rich set of explanatory variables. This often then leads to a parametric approach as the most readily able to deal with these issues in a transparent way. Where data does not exist on key variables, it is accepted that the residual contains both unobserved factors, and inefficiency; and decomposition of the residual has been dealt with through either advanced econometric techniques or through regulatory judgement (e.g. through the application of upper quartile techniques). In addition to questions of model specification and efficiency decomposition, the general question of whether the data is of good quality and comparable across firms (and particularly across countries) is a key challenge (perhaps the greatest challenge) for economic regulators doing benchmarking. Measurement of capital can be a particular challenge – e.g. lumpy renewal volumes and costs – and a number of methods have been applied to deal with this problem.

Past studies have also made good use of internal benchmarking to overcome the issues associated with international studies and sometimes combined these two approaches, joining together regional data within countries from several different countries. This latter point enables the study of what might be the optimal size of an infrastructure region. In the train operations literature this leads to a similar question – what is the optimal size of a rail franchise? Indeed these questions of scale (and density), though not formally captured as inefficiency, could lead to large cost savings if answered correctly. Broadening the discussion, it can be difficult to view rail infrastructure in isolation from train operations, and much study has been done to look at whether it is cheaper to integrate the two. A key finding in a literature with somewhat mixed results is that the answer may depend on the density of usage; with more intensely used networks more amenable perhaps to full vertical integration or to the holding company model. Finally, is important to link benchmarking analysis with underlying business and engineering understanding. The latter can come in two forms. First, in helping to interpret the elasticities on cost drivers in a cost function – do they make sense? If so this implies that the model has greater credibility. Second, bottom-up analysis can help understand why there is an efficiency gap. This approach was used most notably by the ORR in 2008 (and since), when the econometric model indicated a gap between Network Rail and the best infrastructure managers in Europe of up to 40 per cent. Bottom-up analysis of best practice provided supporting evidence to explain that gap. More recent policy in Great Britain has focused on bottom-up studies – it is accepted that a gap exists, and the focus has been on identifying ways of getting costs down (see Chapter 8).

ACKNOWLEDGEMENT

This chapter draws heavily on work undertaken jointly with our colleague Dr Phill Wheat, and we are very grateful to him for his contribution.

NOTE

1. Note this is published data as distinct from the confidential data from the LICB project described earlier.

REFERENCES

Affuso, L., A. Angeriz, and M.G. Pollitt (2003), 'Measuring the Efficiency of Britain's Privatised Train Operating Companies', mimeo (unpublished version provided by the authors).

Asmild, M., T. Holvad, J.L. Hougaard and D. Kronborg (2009), 'Railway reforms: do they influence operating efficiency?', *Transportation*, 36(5), 617–638.

British Rail/University of Leeds (1979), *A Comparative Study of European Rail Performance*, British Rail, London.

Cantos P., J.M. Pastor and L. Serrano (2010), 'Vertical and horizontal separation in the European railway sector and its effects on productivity', *Journal of Transport Economics and Policy*, 44(2), 139–160.

Cantos, P., J.M. Pastor and L. Serrano (2012), 'Evaluating European railway deregulation using different approaches', paper given at the workshop on Competition and Regulation in Railways, *Transport Policy*, 24, November, 67–72.

Cowie, J. (2002a), 'Subsidy and productivity in the privatised British passenger railway', *Economic Issues*, 7(1), 25–38.

Cowie, J. (2002b), 'The production economics of a vertically separated railway – the case of the British train operating companies', *Trasporti Europei*, August, 96–103.

Cowie, J. (2005), 'Technical efficiency versus technical change – the British passenger train operators', in D.A. Hensher (ed.), *Competition and Ownership in Land Passenger Transport: Selected Refereed Papers from the 8th International Conference (Thredbo 8) Rio de Janeiro, September 2003*, Emerald Group Publishing, Bingley, UK.

Cowie, J. (2009), 'The British passenger rail privatisation: conclusions on subsidy and efficiency from the first round of franchises', *Journal of Transport Economics and Policy*, 43(1), 85–104.

Cuesta, R.A. (2000), 'A production model with firm-specific temporal variation in technical inefficiency: with application to Spanish dairy farms', *Journal of Productivity Analysis*, 13(2), 139–152.

Link, H. (2016), Liberalisation of passenger rail services: case study – Germany, report for the Centre on Regulation in Europe (CERRE).

Merkert, R., A.S.J. Smith and C.A. Nash (2009), 'Benchmarking of train operating firms – a transaction cost efficiency analysis', *Journal of Transportation Planning and Technology*, 33(1), 35–53.

Merkert, R., A.S.J. Smith and C.A. Nash (2012), 'The measurement of transaction costs: evidence from European railways', *Journal of Transport Economics and Policy*, 46(3), 349–365.

Mizutani, F. and S. Uranishi (2013), 'Does vertical separation reduce cost? An empirical analysis of the rail industry in OECD countries', *Journal of Regulatory Economics*, 43(1), 31–59.

Mizutani, F., A.S.J. Smith, C.A. Nash and S. Uranishi (2015), 'Comparing the costs of vertical separation, integration, and intermediate organisational structures in

European and East Asian railways', *Journal of Transport Economics and Policy*, 49(3), 496–515.

Nash, C.A., A.S.J. Smith, D. van de Velde, F. Mizutani and S. Uranishi (2014), 'Structural reforms in the railways: incentive misalignment and cost implications', *Research in Transportation Economics*, 48, 16–23.

Office of Rail and Road (ORR) (2013), Periodic Review 2013 Final Determination of Network Rail's outputs and funding for 2014–19, ORR, London.

Smith, A.S.J. (2008), International Benchmarking of Network Rail's Maintenance and Renewal Costs: An Econometric Study Based on the LICB Dataset (1996–2006), Report for the Office of Rail Regulation, October 2008. Available at: www.rail-reg .gov.uk/server/show/nav.2001.

Smith, A.S.J. (2012), 'The application of stochastic frontier panel models in economic regulation: experience from the European rail sector', *Transportation Research Part E*, 48, 503–515.

Smith, A.S.J. and P.E. Wheat (2012a), 'Evaluating alternative policy responses to franchise failure: evidence from the passenger rail sector in Britain', *Journal of Transport Economics and Policy*, 46(1), 25–49.

Smith, A.S.J. and P.E. Wheat (2012b), 'Estimation of cost inefficiency in panel data models with firm specific and sub-company specific effects', *Journal of Productivity Analysis*, 37, 27–40.

Smith, A.S.J, C. Nash and P. Wheat (2009), 'Passenger rail franchising in Britain – has it been a success?', *International Journal of Transport Economics*, 36(1), 33–62.

Smith, A.S.J., P.E. Wheat and G. Smith (2010), 'The role of international benchmarking in developing rail infrastructure efficiency estimates', *Utilities Policy*, 18, 86–93.

Smith, A.S.J., V. Benedetto and C.A. Nash (2018), 'The impact of economic regulation on the efficiency of European railway systems', *Journal of Transport Economics and Policy*, 52(2), 113–136.

Stead, A.D., P.E. Wheat, A.S.J. Smith and M. Ojeda Cabral (2019), 'Competition for and in the passenger rail market: comparing open access versus franchised train operators' costs and reliability in Britain', *Journal of Rail Transport Planning & Management*, 12.

Van de Velde, D., C. Nash, A. Smith, F. Mizutani, S. Uranishi, M. Lijesen and F. Zschoche (2012), 'EVES-Rail – Economic effects of vertical separation in the railway sector', Report for CER – Community of European Railway and Infrastructure Companies, by inno-V (Amsterdam) in cooperation with University of Leeds – ITS, Kobe University, VU Amsterdam University and Civity management consultants, Amsterdam/Brussels.

Wheat, P.E. and A.S.J. Smith (2015), 'Do the usual results of railway returns to scale and density hold in the case of heterogeneity in outputs: a hedonic cost function approach', Journal of Transport Economics and Policy, 49(1), 35–47.

Wheat P.E., A.S.J. Smith and T. Rasmussen (2018), 'Can competition for and in the market co-exist in terms of delivering cost efficient services? Evidence from open access train operators and their franchised counterparts in Britain', Transportation Research Part A: Policy and Practice, 113, 114–124.

6. Local public transport

Giovanni Fraquelli

6.1 BENCHMARKING THE COST STRUCTURE AND THE QUALITY OF THE BUS INDUSTRY

The operation of public transport services has a significant impact on the budget of territorial bodies, since in most cases the revenues from end users' tickets and subscriptions are not sufficient to recover the costs of providing the service. Cost-based compensation instead of incentive-based mechanisms predominated in the last decades. In recent years, in order to induce more efficiency, enhance productivity and reduce huge deficits, many countries have put in place reforms in which the institutional reorganisation of the industry is combined with the design of new regulatory measures that foresee specific incentives to increase efficiency.

At the same time, the focus on quality is becoming increasingly important. Improvements that increase the load factors of public transport, attracting new passengers, can provide significant benefits. Having a large public transport system is not enough. Most benefits are related to its use, the satisfaction of the passengers, the capability to stimulate a reduction in automobile travel and the relative vehicle ownership and operating costs. Modal substitution is a strategic aspect of addressing demand towards sustainable transport, and this process can be favoured by modal options that provide high-quality services.

6.2 BENCHMARKING EFFICIENCY

The study of the comparative efficiency of public transport companies contributes to decreasing the information asymmetry between policymakers and public transport firms and represents a good input to the debate on public transport regulation. Results of empirical analyses on efficiency and productivity of single operators are sensitive to the context of the study, to the methodological approaches adopted to measure efficiency and to the nature of inputs and outputs. Within the wide range of available literature, we shall refer to two reviews that adopt different visions and summarise the most significant results.

The first one has a mainly economic perspective (section 6.2.1), while the second one combines economic and engineering approaches (section 6.2.2).

6.2.1   Benchmarking Efficiency: An Economic Perspective

The review by Jarboui et al. (2012) considers 24 works relating to the period 2001–2011 and therefore represents a useful benchmarking tool for the first decade of the 2000s. The works are classified by paying attention to whether the analysis is theoretical or empirical, to the countries covered by the study, to the methodological approach and to the nature of outputs and inputs.

In Table 6.1 we summarise the results. We can see that Norway (five studies) and the USA (four studies) are the countries analysed most frequently. However, another 11 countries (Canada, France, Germany, Great Britain, Greece, India, Italy, Portugal, Spain, Switzerland, Taiwan) are also involved in the reviewed works. Only the studies concerning Brazil versus seven European countries (Sampaio et al., 2008) and Norway and France (De Borger et al., 2008) adopt an international comparative perspective. As to the methodological approaches, the majority of the works have adopted the DEA technique (21 studies); other studies adopt the stochastic frontier analysis approach (SFA, four studies), free disposal hull (FDH, one study) and three of them combine the different methods, i.e. DEA–SFA, DEA–SFA–FHD and DEA–MEA (multidirectional efficiency analysis).

With regard to datasets, in the first years of the decade we find some cross sections or time series, but starting from the year 2007 studies usually use panel data in their applications. The output variables, in most of the works, consist of supply-oriented measures such as vehicle-km and seat-km, or demand-oriented measures such as passenger-km, bus utilisation and ridership; moreover, revenues and sales are used in several studies. The output specification represents a very important issue and the debate in literature is broad:

> The main arguments have been summarised by Berechman (1993). First, inputs do not vary systematically with demand-oriented output measures so that they do not allow an adequate description of transport technology. Second, supply-oriented output indicators are to a larger extent more under the control of transport companies than demand-oriented outputs … Third, independently of the achievement of frontier aims defined in terms of passenger transport services really consumed, supplying the transport services in the least costly way may be considered a best requirement for transport operators. Therefore, the focus should be on pure supply indices when measuring productivity and efficiency. (Jarboui et al., 2012, p. 122).

As inputs, most studies refer to labour, capital and energy, although measured by different variables. For example, labour can be expressed by the number of staff employed, by the driving hours, or in terms of driver costs. Capital

Table 6.1   Main results of the review

Years and countries of the studies covered by the review	Methodological approach (number of uses)	Outputs	Inputs	Efficiency scores
2001 Spain, Norway	DEA (18)	*Supply side*	*Physical measure*	Non-parametric and parametric approaches generate different efficiency scores.
2002 Great Britain	SFA (2)	Vehicle-km	No. of employees	
2002 Theoretical	DEA-SFA (1)	Seat-km	No. of staff employed	Technical inefficiency occurs in many countries (USA, Canada, Italy, India) and the average value is about 20–25%.
2003 USA, Norway	DEA-SFA-FDH (1)	Frequency	Driving hours	Comparative studies in different countries (Brazil versus 7
2004 USA, Norway, Canada	DEA-MEA (1)	Bus-km/inhabit	Vehicles operated	European countries and Norway–France) indicate a great
		Average t. time	Vehicle capacity	variability, both between and among countries.
			Fleet size	
2006 Switzerland		Accessibility	Network length	As to economies of scale: decreasing returns to scale (R.S.)
2007 USA, Greece, Italy		Comfort, safety	No. of intersections	in USA 2004; in Brazil vs 7 European countries (2008), 56%
2008 Norway, Brazil vs		Accident rate pop.	Service duration	transport systems have increasing R.S., 29% decreasing R.S.,
7 European countries,			Priority lines	India (2011) increasing R.S. are dominant.
Norway–France			Fuel consumption	

Years and countries of the studies covered by the review	Methodological approach (number of uses)	Outputs	Inputs	Efficiency scores
2009 Spain, Taiwan 2010 Portugal 2011 India (3 studies), USA		*Demand side* Passenger-km No. of passengers Annual ridership Bus utilisation Load factor Passenger / distance t. Sales, revenue	*Operating expenses* Driver costs Energy cost Fuel cost Total operating expenses Capital measure Liquid assets	Small operators – increasing R.S.; average-sized firms: constant or increasing R.S.; large systems: decreasing R.S. Several factors can affect efficiency but there is agreement about the relevance of working and operations practices, the quality of the management and the presence of low financial constraints (2002). Technical investment seems to be an important source to recover efficiency. Regulation (or deregulation) and privatisation may improve efficiency, but their relevance is strongly debated.

Source: Our synthesis from Jarboui et al. (2012).

includes prevalently vehicles operated, fleet size and vehicle capacity. Among the energy variables, we find the fuel used, the fuel cost and the lubricant cost. In some cases, the quantities of inputs are missing and are replaced by the total operating expenses. Many studies include environmental variables to better account for the configuration and the quality of the network.

As for the empirical outcomes, technical inefficiency is reported with respect to many countries (USA, Canada, Italy, India) and the average value is about 20–25 per cent. We know that deterministic-non-parametric and stochastic-parametric approaches studies (Brazil versus seven European countries and Norway–France) indicate great variability of the technical inefficiency, both within and among countries. De Borger et al. (2008) attribute such variability to the heterogeneity of the service management in the different countries and in particular to the differences in the regulatory framework, population density, quality management and operating environment. The works cited are not specifically oriented to the evaluation of the economies of scale but provide useful information on this subject. In general, small firms are characterised by increasing returns to scale, while average-sized operators evidence increasing or constant returns to scale, and we find decreasing returns to scale for large companies.

A great number of variables can affect efficiency, but many authors agree about the working and operations practices, the quality of the management and the presence of low financial constraints. Technical investments seem to be an important source of efficiency recovery. Sometimes regulation (or deregulation) and privatisation are good solutions to improve efficiency, although this topic is strongly debated. Studies of the different operating contexts based on different approaches and representative indicators are lacking.

6.2.2   Benchmarking Efficiency: An Engineering Approach

The review by Daraio et al. (2016) provides a classification of the existing literature on economic efficiency in the urban public transport sector. The analysis concerns 124 papers starting from 1970. The authors identify five areas of research dealing with efficiency. The study aims to address different issues:

- technical efficiency (efficiency/productivity literature, focusing on cost minimisation and/or profit maximisation);
- the factors affecting technical efficiency, by means of non-parametric frontier analysis (NFA) and parametric frontier analysis (PFA);
- the effect of alternative regulatory regimes on the efficiency of the operation;
- the relative advantages of public versus private ownership and/or operation;

- the economies of density, scope and scale (space and time dimension of service provision and features of transportation technology).

The authors propose a general evaluation framework, summarising the different approaches of research with respect to six dimensions (economic goals; service performance; role in relieving road congestion; impact on environmental sustainability; social inclusion issues; territorial accessibility), reported in Table 6.2. "The first one summarises the economic perspective, the second one the key interest of the travellers, while the last four represent the main benefits that are typically expected by the community when implementing public transports systems" (Daraio et al., 2016, p. 3).

In all the reviewed works, profit and cost aspects related to the operation of the service are considered. Service performance is examined mainly in terms of travel and waiting times, equally addressing the viewpoint of the operator and the customer. In contrast to the economic literature, the engineering literature gives less attention to the other four evaluation perspectives (the last four rows) listed in Table 6.2. However, congestion issues have an important role in the analysis of competing transport means, while sustainability issues, related to external environmental costs, represent an essential component in every process of design of public transport.

As to the choice of input and output variables the situation is similar to the one already discussed in section 6.2.1.

> Input variables, these normally fall in two main categories: "physical" production factors with their own measurement units (number of employees, hours of work etc.) on one side, and costs in monetary units on the other, that are further split into capital expenses and operating expenses …. The number of employees (or hours of work), fuel consumption, number of vehicles in the fleet are largely the most considered variables since they represent the main inputs in the production process. … As regards the other clusters of input variables we analogously find that the prices of labour, capital and fuel are the far more utilised while only a limited number of papers … consider a broader set of cost oriented input variables such as maintenance and overhead costs … (Daraio et al., 2016, p. 6).

On the output side, the authors categorise three main groups: variables that measure the efficiency of the service from the supply point of view (vehicles or seats by travelled km are the ones most frequently used); variables related to the effectiveness of the production process with respect to the demand (number of passengers and passengers by travelled km); and monetary variables related to the service revenues.

An additional set of variables that can be considered as inputs or outputs refers to quality and characteristics of the service, such as service performance (commercial speed, punctuality), and accessibility (length of network, number of stops). Some works consider the average age of the fleet (this variable refers

Table 6.2   *Matching evaluation aspects with producer viewpoint and with literature on efficiency*

Evaluation aspect	Relevance for the producer viewpoint (efficiency)	Relevance for the evaluation of efficiency and productivity	Relevance for the evaluation of determinants of technical efficiency
Profit/cost analysis	***	***	***
Service performance	**	***	***
Road congestion	**	*	**
Sustainability	*	**	**
Social inclusion	*	*	*
Accessibility	*	*	*

Notes: * = little relevant; ** = relevant to some extent; *** = strongly relevant.
Source: Our synthesis of Table 1, Daraio et al., 2016, p. 3.

contemporarily to efficiency and effectiveness). Variables describing the socio-economic characteristics of the service and the management approach are also typically considered. In synthesis, the input–output variables emerging from the engineering literature are related to the following aspects: operational efficiency, intensity of use of the service by passengers, service use related to input (expenses/passenger-km), relative service dimension (fleet dimension/ population of the service area), service coverage (route lengths/population of the service area), dimension of the potential market (passengers/population of the service area), revenues generation, externalities (number of accidents/ (vehicles*kilometres)).

As for the methodological approach, the review identifies two groups of methods that are prevailing in local public transport (LPT) studies. On the one hand, it points out the dominance of the parametric methods (Cobb–Douglas cost functions and Translog cost functions). These studies use stochastic frontier analysis (SFA) and multistage analyses of cost functions in relation to total cost estimates. To investigate costs, however, a smaller group of studies adopt DEA and total factor productivity indexes (Malmquist indexes). On the other hand, non-parametric methods based on DEA and indexes dominate the empirical analysis of factor productivity. They "are more flexible and are char-acterised by a wider range of used variables" (Daraio et al., 2016, p. 9). The effects of external environmental variables on efficiency are widely studied in the field of non-parametric efficiency analysis: the efficiency scores, estimated in a first stage, are regressed on environmental variables using a "two-stage approach".

6.2.3   Benchmarking Economies of Scale and Scope

In a public policy perspective, evidence about the optimal dimension of the local transport network plays an important role for planning and designing the provision of the service, especially the extension of the service area, the frequencies of buses and the number of bus routes. On the other hand, the knowledge of the underlying production technology gives the possibility to set pricing policies. "A finding of diseconomies of scale can imply that, for example, a city can have different parts of its system operated by separated companies at a lower unit cost of output" (Karlaftis and McCarthy, 2002, pp. 1–2).

Moreover, the operators are often multi-service firms. They operate in regulated markets such as urban and intercity transport and in non-regulated markets, such as long-distance express coach and long-distance chartered coach services. Coach services can represent an important complement of the regular transit system (Talley 2007). They can be easily interconnected with other modes of transport. Chartered coach travel is typically characterised by non-scheduled times and non-fixed routes. For this reason this service is mainly addressed to occasional users, such as the tourist sector. Conversely, after the process of transport liberalisation (2009), long-distance coach transport is growing exponentially so as to compete directly with railways and airline services. If multi-service firms are exploiting scope economies, it is desirable to let them run integrated production in regulated and unregulated services.

Early studies on the analysis of costs in transportation were mainly focused on the effects of diversification among different transit modes within the same urban area.

Colburn and Talley (1992), by analysing different modes of transport in urban systems, find evidence of limited cost complementarities. Viton (1993), by investigating the processes of aggregation between different suppliers, shows that cost savings resulting from mergers depend on the transport modes of the companies as well as on the number of firms involved in the merger. Farsi et al. (2007), exploring a Swiss multimodal transport system, show the presence of economies of scale and scope and support integrated multimode operations as opposed to unbundling. As these authors argue,

> ... when transport modes are legally unbundled, bidding can be opened to both single-mode operators and multi-mode companies. Whereas in the present situation the competition is difficult for companies specialised in a single transit service because of the comparative advantage of the incumbent multi-mode companies. In this case, due to fewer potential bidders, the benefits from competition for the market would be lower ... Therefore, it is relevant for the local authorities to know

if and how much a multi-mode supplier could use the scope and scale economies to reduce their costs in comparison to a group of single-mode operators. (p. 2)

In order to estimate scale and scope economies, the most popular method is to use a multi-output specification of the cost function.

As for scale economies, Gagnepain et al. (2011) report that a significant number of empirical studies are in line with a U-shaped average cost curve, exhibiting increasing returns to scale for smaller operators and decreasing returns beyond a certain output level. As an example, Cowie and Asenova (1999) estimate that small companies (with a bus fleet of fewer than 200 vehicles) experience some economies of scale.

6.2.4   Efficiency and Economies of Scale and Scope: Some Findings about Italy

Fraquelli et al. (2004) investigate the cost behaviour and the existence of scope economies by relying, for the estimation, on a set of dummy variables to distinguish between specialised operators (in urban or intercity services) and integrated companies, and find evidence of lower costs for integrated bus transport firms.

Cambini et al. (2007), focusing on a set of medium and large Italian municipalities, find evidence of economies of scale in most cases, suggesting that companies should operate across the entire system of the urban network, without fragmentation of the service. They also argue that mergers between operators of neighbouring cities or between suppliers of urban and intercity transit services would be desirable in order to reduce operating costs.

Di Giacomo and Ottoz (2010) estimate a total cost function for multi-service LPT companies. They highlight very mild scope economies (around 2 per cent) between urban and intercity services. The extent of scope economies tends to decrease as the firm size increases, and modest scale economies are observed for the median firm. Ottoz and Di Giacomo (2012), analysing the LPT system of a specific Italian region (Piedmont), provide empirical evidence of the impact on costs of different diversification strategies. The results show the presence of scope economies for the median firm, ranging between 16 per cent and 30 per cent depending on the cost function specification as well as on the number of outputs. Lower global scope economies are found for publicly owned firms and, more generally, for large operators.

A recent analysis including coach operators (Abrate et al., 2016) investigates the presence and the magnitude of scale and scope economies in the provision of passenger transport services, using a sample of Italian bus and coach operators. They estimate a multi-product cost function including chartered coach, urban and intercity passenger services as three separate outputs.

The research uses an unbalanced panel of 47 firms observed during the years 2008–2012, for a total of 147 observations. Of these, 30 observations refer to specialised firms, while nine observations refer to fully integrated firms. Most, however, are firms performing a couple of services (in particular intercity and charter services, or intercity and urban). Data related to costs, output quantities and input prices were obtained by integrating the information available in the annual reports of each company with additional information drawn from questionnaires sent directly to managers. The long-run total cost includes the expenditure for fuel and other raw materials and services, labour and capital costs of each firm. The monetary values are expressed in 2010 constant prices. The three output categories (urban transit, intercity transit and charter transit), are measured by vehicle-kilometres. As to the methodology, a composite cost function econometric model (Pulley and Braunstein, 1992) was used. It allows the disentangling of potential synergies that emerge when firms provide different combinations of the three types of transit services.

The research finds evidence that the average firm exhibits constant aggregate returns to scale and is characterised by the absence of global scope economies. Small multi-service firms, however, may benefit from cost reductions with respect to specialised operators. As the size of the firm increases, the cost savings survive only for the intercity bus service. For firms larger than the average, the presence of decreasing returns to scale counterbalances the effect of scope economies. When the core business is urban transport, the service can benefit from diversifying into intercity services, while firms specialising in intercity services can exploit scope economies by diversifying into coach hire services. A diversification strategy involving all three activities is not beneficial (except for very small operators).

6.3   BENCHMARKING QUALITY OF LOCAL TRANSIT SERVICES

6.3.1   Quality Performance Measures: Aims and Nature

In order to ensure a continuous improvement of the service provided by public transport, appropriate performance measures must be identified. These are a fundamental tool for outlining the objectives of companies, verifying their achievement and allocating public resources in a selective way.

Performance measures can be qualitative or quantitative, but when they are intended to document progress towards a particular objective, or to make comparisons between operators, quantitative indicators that lead to objective evaluations are necessary. In the literature, we find various classifications of the transit performance measures, and the options proposed by the researchers can be grouped with reference to four fundamental aspects (Carter and Lomax,

1992; Dalton et al., 2001; Meyer, 2000; Vuchic, 2007; Litman, 2009; Guirao et al., 2016):

- efficiency measures (cost efficiency, vehicle utilisation, vehicle-kilometres/vehicle/year, passengers/vehicle-kilometres, labour productivity, energy efficiency);
- effectiveness measures (cost effectiveness – outcome value compared to the cost of input, cost per passenger trip, intensity of network service, passenger trips per capita, passenger trips per hour);
- service quality measures (route length per square kilometre, vehicle-kilometre, vehicle-hour, average speed, average headway, number of incidents, users' satisfaction, quality desired);
- transportation quantity or volume (number of vehicles, fleet size, fleet capacity, number of lines and network length, annual number of passengers, service area population, passenger trips).

6.3.2 Quality Determinants of Bus Services

Research on the quality of local public transport services has been carried by many authors in recent years and is characterised by the use of different methodologies and indicators. The main quality-related attributes concern bus routes in terms of direction and coverage, bus stops (number, distance, location), service frequency, span of service, travel time, need for transfers. Taking into account the different components contributing to the quality of the service, the variables that have turned out to be of greatest interest from the various studies concern: service availability, service reliability, comfort, cleanliness, safety and security, fares, information, customer care and environmental impacts. Eboli and Mazzulla (2012), Redman et al. (2013) and Litman (2019) present a comprehensive review of the literature. Below we report a brief summary of the nature of the main attributes that qualify the bus service.

- **Service reliability**: this concerns the capacity of the transport system to respect departure times and journey times. Obviously, the greater or lesser reliability affects positively or negatively the number of passengers. The proposal illustrated in the document TCRP Synthesis 10 (Transportation Research Board, 1995) considers journeys to be on time if running up to one minute early and up to five minutes late and the same criteria are adopted by the Italian regulations (DPCM 30.12.1998).
- **Comfort**: this concerns both the physical condition of the vehicles and the amenities on the vehicles or at waiting points. Attention goes to seating quality, temperature, crowding, noise and convenience of access to vehicles. Regarding crowding, Eboli and Mazzulla (2011), hypothesise

a quadratic relationship between the proposed indicator and the ratio of the number of passengers to the number of offered seats, with value close to ten for the case of small number of passengers, and to zero when the number of passengers is equal to or higher than the number of available seats.

–   **Cleanliness**: the degree of cleanliness concerns the vehicle, both internally and externally and the related facilities. The cleaning of public transport has a profound influence on the image of the service and the consequent use.

–   **Safety and security**: these terms indicate the possibility that passengers will be involved in a road accident (safety) or become the victim of a crime (security). Various aspects of safety of bus drivers are included. The European Commission attributes great importance to these variables in defining the hierarchy of quality determinants in public transportation in Europe (Transportation Research Board, 2003a, 2003b). The security category consists of three aspects: safety from crime (staff/police presence, lighting, visible monitoring, layout, identified help points), safety from accidents (presence/visibility of supports, avoidance/visibility of hazards, active safeguarding by staff), and perceptions of security (congruity of safety measures, ability to control the network, media relations image).

–   **Fares**: this concerns the level of the monetary cost of the journey by bus. Although many studies give evidence that transit demand is inelastic to the fare level (Dargay and Hanly, 1999, 2002; Deb and Filippini, 2010), the average fare paid per passenger is important to manage the trade-off between efficiency, subsidies and affordable fares.

–   **Information**: without correct information, potential passengers will not be able to use the transit service. "Passengers need to know how to use the transit service, where the access is located, where to get off in the proximity of their destination, whether any transfers are required, and when transit services are scheduled to depart and arrive" (Eboli and Mazzulla, 2012, p. 14). The passenger should have information at every stage of his journey and today's technology offers great help through "customer information systems" provided through visual, voice or other media. These automated systems, available both at bus stops and on board, can significantly improve the quality of services from both the operational and users' point of view. Good information before the trip can optimise the route and its time of travel, while during the journey it reduces the perceived waiting time.

The case studies of Madrid and Bremerhaven, reported by Monzon et al. (2013), highlight the benefits of the introduction of "Real Time Passenger Information (RTPI) systems". Both cities present improvements in the area of "information to passengers". In Madrid, multimodal services were available via the web, SMS, displays and Bluetooth. In Bremerhaven, the information devices introduced on the bus and at the bus stops produced an increase in the quantity and quality of the real-time information. In addition, passengers perceived a higher quality of service in respect of punctuality, reliability, information while travelling and frequency.

- **Customer care**: this variable relates to the attitude of the personnel towards the users and the reliability of the ticket offices. It includes the courtesy and preparation of drivers and controllers, access to ticket offices and automatic ticket machines and the reliability of online information and sales platforms.
- **Environmental impacts**: the technological improvement of recent years in the performance of engines and in batteries has enormously improved the options available to local transport companies to reduce pollution. The management of the bus fleet needs to find the right balance between acquisition, operation and disposal costs and the level-of-service requirements and environmental impact (Durango-Cohen and McKenzie, 2018).

Table 6.3 provides a summary of the connections between the attributes and their indicators.

6.3.3 Passenger Satisfaction

Previously we examined the attributes that characterise the quality of the service, mainly from the supply side point of view. The attributes are consequences of the investments in buses, bus stops and information technology and in the operation management of the service (staff, maintenance, cleaning, attention to reliability and safety). The approach essentially responds to the control systems implemented by the operators to measure the ability to offer services that meet customer expectations. This is an important point, but it is necessary to understand if and to what extent the various initiatives undertaken by the carriers meet the needs of actual and potential users.

Customer satisfaction is a useful tool to explain the relationship between the offer of products and services of the company and the appreciation of the consumer. In the management of the LPT, the attention to this relationship is fundamental because it allows the carrier to understand what the traveller considers important as an effective or potential user and, from another point of view, the degree of fulfilment of the suppliers to the "performance-based contracts".

Different perspectives
We mentioned the "effective or potential user" because the customer evaluation can be carried out according to two perspectives. We can measure the expected quality (a pre-consumption attitude and evaluation) for the various components of the service or consider the perceived quality (the degree of

Table 6.3   Quality determinants of bus services

Nature of performance	Attributes	Indicators
Service availability	Bus line in terms of direction and coverage, bus stops (number, distance, location), service frequency, span of service, travel time, need for transfers	Route coverage as spacing distance between bus routes, route miles per square miles, proportion of population served by transit, bus stop spacing, walking distance, number of runs for each hour of the day, vehicle-km per inhabitant, number of hours per day of transit service
Service reliability	On-time performance, regularity in the amount of time between vehicles in the transit system (headway regularity) and running time	Percentage of vehicles departing from or arriving at a location on time, ratio of the average difference between the actual and the scheduled headway to the scheduled headway, average difference between the actual and the scheduled running times compared to the scheduled running time
Comfort	Quality of seats and level of crowding, temperature, noise and vibrations, access to vehicle	Seat-back slope, seat width and available leg room, number of passengers on board divided by the capacity of the vehicles, passengers per seat, standing passengers, ratio of the number of buses with a functioning air conditioning system to the total number of buses used on the route
Cleanliness	The physical condition of vehicles and facilities, and specifically the cleanliness of the bus interior and exterior	Frequency of interior cleaning and exterior washing

Nature of performance	Attributes	Indicators
Safety and security	Possibility that passengers will be involved in a road accident (safety) or become the victim of a crime on board or at a stop (security). Various aspects of the safety of bus drivers are included	Number of passenger fatalities, number of road accidents during the year compared with the average number of road accidents in the last three years, number of complaints during year compared with the average number in the last three years
Fares	Characteristics of the monetary cost of the journey by bus. Affordability of bus fares	The average one-way ticket cost, the cost of a monthly passes, percentage of monthly wage for a monthly average of journeys
Information	Availability of information concerning the planning and execution of a journey, availability of schedule/maps on bus, passenger information during the trip, announcements, availability of schedule/maps at bus stops	Ratio of the number of vehicles with functioning information device on board to the total number of vehicles sampled in a certain time period, score assigned to the availability of schedule/maps to each stop
Customer care	Courtesy and knowledge of drivers, courtesy and helpfulness of ticket agents, personnel appearance, effectiveness of the ticket issuing and selling network	Ratio of the number of uniformed staff to the total staff number, scores assigned to staff helpfulness and courtesy, scores regarding availability of tickets, position and visibility of signs
Environmental impacts	Emissions, noise, visual pollution, effect of vibrations on road, consumption of energy or space	Ratio of the number of low-emissions vehicles to the total number of vehicles needed for the line, degree of vehicle noise emissions

Source: Our synthesis from Eboli and Mazzulla (2011, 2012) and Litman (2019).

satisfaction) from the traveller, or refer to both perspectives. The evaluations in terms of expectations "represent what customers expect of the service", and in terms of perceptions "represent what customers receive from the service" (Eboli and Mazzulla, 2012, p. 5). Levinger and McGehee (2008) stress this side of the evaluation (demand side), suggesting some attributes useful to attract new riders: the service must be easy to use (in relation to the timetable), effective (operating on time and with predictable schedules), comfortable (traveller must be safe, secure and relaxed) and appealing.

Table 6.4   Calculation of the Customer Satisfaction Index (CSI)

Parameter P	Average weighting (1–10) A	Average score (1–10) B	Average unit weighting C	Weighted average score D = B * C
P1	8	6	1.33	7.98
P2	6	8	1	8
P3	2	8	0.33	2.64
P4	4	4	0.67	2.68
P5	9	5	1.5	7.5
P6	7	6	1.17	7
	Average of the average weighting P1– P6 = 6			CSI 5.97

6.3.3.1 Methodological approach: statistical analysis

Customer satisfaction can be measured relying on two methodological approaches. The first approach includes methods of *statistical analysis*, such as factor analysis, scatter grams, bivariate correlation and cluster analysis. In this way, we can have an evaluation of the single attributes or of the relationship between attributes and overall satisfaction expressed in terms of indexes. In the literature, some indexes were proposed by Kano et al. (1984), Berger et al. (1993), Hill (2003), Cuomo (2000) and Bhave (2002). The SERVQUAL index (Parasuraman et al., 1988) is probably the most frequently applied by academics and industry operators. It has been developed by marketing researchers to measure the gap between consumer expectations and perceptions along five dimensions of service quality (reliability, assurance, tangibles, empathy and responsiveness). Despite its merits, the length of the questionnaire and the difficulty of capturing true pre-consumption expectations make the use of this model complex.

The Customer Satisfaction Index (CSI)

Bhave (2002) proposes a simpler index, frequently used in the field of transport services: the Customer Satisfaction Index (CSI), which summarises as a percentage the overall satisfaction obtained by the weighted average of the attributes that contribute to customer satisfaction. To understand the calculations, in Table 6.4 we provide an example following the approach of Bhave (2002).

The index can be determined in the following manner:

1. Parameter P: attribute definition: attributes are selected, e.g. service availability, cleanliness, fares, safety and security, information, customer care.

2. Defining a weight: for each attribute the respondents assign a weight ranging from 1 to 10.
3. Column A, average weight: the average of the weights, attributed by all the customers to each attribute, is computed. Average P1–P6 = (8 + 6 + 2 + 4 + 9 + 7)/6 = 6.
4. Assigning score: respondents assign a score to each parameter ranging from 1 to 10.
5. Column B, average score: the average of the scores attributed by all the customers to each attribute is computed.
6. Column C, average unit weightings: dividing the average weight of every attribute (in column A), by the average of the average weighting, for all the attributes, the unit weight of each attribute (the relative weigh) is determined (C). Attributes with higher priority will have an average unit weight higher than ones which are less important or with lower priority. E.g., Attribute P1 with a unit weight of 1.3 has much higher relevance if compared to attribute P3 with a unit weight of 0.33.
7. Column D: finally, the CIS is obtained as a weighted average, multiplying the average score of each attribute by the respective unit weight (B * C). CSI = (7.98 + 8 + 2.64 + 2.68 + 7.5 + 7)/6 = 5.97.

The case of a bus service serving a campus of the University of Calabria
Mazzulla and Eboli (2006) conducted an investigation concerning the bus service provided to a campus of the University of Calabria sited in the urban area of Cosenza (attended by approximately 32,000 students and 2,000 members of staff). In interviews based on a standard questionnaire, students were asked to give information about their transport mode and about some service quality attributes. Three different groups of travellers were interviewed: public transport non-users (non-user reasons), public transport users (user reasons), and both users and non-users (ranking service quality attributes). A total of 382 students living outside the urban area of Cosenza were interviewed. A statistical-descriptive analysis of the stated preferences proves that:

– The main public transport non-use reasons are: low service frequency (first reason for 40 per cent respondents), vehicle overcrowding (first reason for 16 per cent of respondents), slowness of the vehicles (12.5 per cent).
– The most important public transport use reasons are: car non-availability (36.8 per cent), no driving licence (15.5 per cent), difficulty of car parking (3.6 per cent). "The percentages of stated preferences on the headings excluded from the analysis indicate that public transport is primarily used for reasons not related to service quality, but only to a difficulty in the use of the private car" (p. 47). Service quality factors in favour of the user

reasons are service inexpensiveness (45.4 per cent), less tiring trip (36.1 per cent), and a considerable percentage is represented by lower risk of road accidents (10.3 per cent).
–   The most chosen quality attributes are: frequency (51.3 per cent), availability of seats on bus (17.9 per cent) and number of bus stops (6.2 per cent).

The user's preference analysed within the survey (p. 49) made it possible to calculate the weighted average for each service quality attribute. Service quality attributes with a major weight were service frequency (38.3) and seats on bus (21.9).

The case of nine European cities
Fellesson and Friman (2008) conducted a review of the works related to the measure of customer satisfaction and present the results of a statistical analysis, with data coming from public transport users, concerning nine important European cities. They justified their approach by stating that:

> Even within the same industry, there might be considerable differences in how the service is perceived by the customers, due to various ways of producing the actual service and due to customer differences. Such differences do not reduce the value of satisfaction measurement, however. They could indicate fundamental aspects of the service industry under study that should especially be attended to. (p. 95)

The data for the nine cities (Stockholm, Barcelona, Copenhagen, Geneva, Helsinki, Vienna, Berlin, Manchester and Oslo) were collected through a telephone survey. The interviewers reached 1,000 respondents in each city. The questionnaire took into account 17 attributes rated on five levels of service appreciation (from (1) – don't agree at all – to (5) – fully agree). The 17 items of the survey were subjected to principal component analysis (PCA).

> The overall pattern of factors shows clear signs of an industry generic structure consisting of four basic quality dimensions, i.e. safety/security system (with supply and reliability items), comfort, and staff behaviour. This clearly indicates that there is, in fact, a uniform way of perceiving public transport in major European cities … [p. 99], but there are differences in how these dimensions are cognitively structured. (p. 100)

6.3.3.2   Methodological approach: regression models

The second category of techniques consists of estimation of the coefficients, related to the importance attached to each attribute, by modelling the relationship between quality (dependent variable) and the explanatory attributes (independent variables) (Louviere et al., 2000; Hensher et al., 2003; dell'Olio et al., 2010). We can employ linear models, like multiple regression models, and non-linear models, like the structural equation model (SEM) and logit models.

The Service Quality Index (SQI)

Hensher et al. (2003) deepen the ways of measuring the service quality by using stated choice methods and estimating multinomial logit models (MNL). They "assume that the overall level of passenger satisfaction is best measured by how an individual evaluates the total package of services offered. Appropriate weights attached to each service dimension will reveal the strength of positive and negative sources of overall satisfaction" (p. 500).

In 2000, two important operators in Sydney (one public and one private operator) were involved in the research. The study concerned nine geographical segments and 13 attributes describing the dimension of service quality from a passenger's perspective. In the stated preference approach (SP) the attributes were ranged on three levels, referring to the trip in progress during the on-board survey (for example: bus travel time: L1 25 per cent less, L2 same, L3 25 per cent more). The combinations of the three levels of the 13 attributes (3^{13}) were restricted to 81 choice sets using a fractional design (Louviere et al., 2000). In this way, respondents had the chance to evaluate three sets resulting in 27 different survey forms. The bus operators distributed about 4,500 surveys, relating to peak and off-peak runs in each segment, with an average response rate of more than 25–30 per cent. "Each passenger was given a choice set of three alternatives to evaluate (the current and two SP designed packages selected from the 81 available sets. They evaluated them and chose one. This was repeated a total of three times" (p. 506). The importance of weight relative to each attribute in the sample in each segment was estimated by a multinomial logit model (Louviere et al., 2000). Multiplying each attribute level associated with the current trip by the parameters estimated, measuring the relevant weight, and summing the values of all attributes, the SQI for each passenger was determined. The average across the values of SQI of the passengers using a specific segment provided the SQI of the segment.

The evaluation of the contribution of each attribute to the overall level of SQI by segment reveals that travel time and fare are the greatest sources of negative satisfaction. On the other hand, service frequency and getting a seat are the greatest sources of positive satisfaction. As the fare level gives the most important contribution to the passenger disaffection for all segments (except one segment) it is clear that reducing fares (and travel time) will give a great contribution to improving the SQI.

6.3.4   The "Desired" Quality

So far, we have addressed the issue of the quality perceived by the traveller, but if we want to retain the users or increase their number, we have to examine the desired quality. Dell'Olio et al. (2011) underline that:

> The desired quality is different from the perceived quality because it does not represent the daily experiences of the users, but rather what they desire, hope for or expect from their public transport system ... knowledge of which gives local authorities the background information for personalised marketing policies based on the user's requirements rather than their daily perceptions. (p. 217)

The study by Dell'Olio et al. (2011) is important both methodologically and in terms of results. The study was carried out in Santander, capital of Cantabria, with a population of about 250,000 inhabitants, taking peripheral boroughs into account. The municipal service is provided by 19 daily bus routes and three night routes (20 million journeys in 2008). To choose the variables that can be improved and the importance (weight) that the travellers place on them, the authors use the focus groups approach. The design methodology for the stated preferences surveys can be summarised as follows: design a preliminary survey; test the preliminary version by focus group (checking the variables); SWOT analysis ("strengths – weaknesses – opportunities – threats") as a support to design and administer a pilot survey; efficient design of the definitive survey (using a measure known as D-error); distribution of the definitive surveys; modelling bus user and potential user behaviour for their desired qualities; modelling the sample's behaviour to find more efficient policies.

Through a pilot survey, the authors collected the data of the revealed preference, which was useful to define the design of the definitive stated preferences surveys. A utility function was estimated by a multinomial discrete choice model, measuring the relative relevance of each variable of the desired service quality.

> Certain variables contribute greater weight to the utility function for all the defined categories of current bus users, independently of socio-economic characteristics. These variables are waiting time (with a negative sign), comfort on board and cleanliness in the bus (both with positive signs). However, the contribution of comfort and cleanliness to the utility functions can be seen to have no weight for potential bus users. These variables have not been considered when defining what they expect from a high-quality public transport service ... (p. 226)

In respect of policies aimed at increasing the number of users of public transport in Santander, the authors suggest: reducing waiting time; improving comfort during the journey; introducing information campaigns aimed at potential bus users; strengthening the busiest routes at rush hour by providing more services.

6.3.5   The Management of Quality

EQUIP (Extending the Quality of Public Transport, 2000 – a project funded by the EC), developed a handbook for self-assessment of the internal performance of local public transport operators. "The major, and most tangible, output of EQUIP is the Handbook for the self-assessment of internal quality performance by land-based public transport operators" (p. 3).

EQUIP has focused on local surface-based public transport (bus, trolley bus, tram/light rail, metro and local heavy rail). The work relates to the management of the efficiency and quality of the public transport operators, paying attention to the capability to achieve planned outputs by the optimal use of resources. The methodology is based upon the continuous improvement process, a cyclical model that proceeds from self-assessment by direct benchmarking with other operators.

> Continuous Improvement is an ongoing process within an organisation, and can be considered as a corporate frame of mind. The organisation recognises that it must evolve to meet the changing environment and market, and its customers (external and internal) have ever increasing expectations. The organisation identifies its weak points, and implements actions to adapt or restructure itself for better performance. This assures customer satisfaction, and minimises opportunities for competitors. Overall, the process aims to add value throughout, by optimising both efficiency and effectiveness ... (p. 4)

The continuous improvement process is all-inclusive and, in a cyclical contest, involves operation management, administration and staff levels. The process, reported in Table 6.5, is composed of nine stages characterised by the identification of the critical factors of success and related indicators (1–3), the comparison of the operator's performances (4–6) and finally learning and implementing best practices (7–9).

Benchmarking is suggested as a fundamental tool. EQUIP (2000) defines three progressive levels where benchmarking is viewed as an instrument of measurement and comparison. The performance of an organisation can be compared with that of its peers using standardised indicators at the following levels (summary, Table 0.1, p. 6):

1. Self-assessment (measure your own performance).
2. Comparison (compare your performance with a database of values; identify improvement areas and best "standards").

Table 6.5   The nine stages of the continuous improvement process

1	Define and agree on critical success factors of business.
2	Develop indicators to measure performance.
3	Measure indicators for an individual operator.
4	Compare performance with that of others.
5	Identify areas to be improved.
6	Review relevant business processes.
7	Learn best practice from benchmark partners.
8	Plan and implement improvements.
9	Monitor performance.

Source: EQUIP (2000), p. 5.

3. Partnering (work with relevant partners, perhaps with some outside your direct business sector; exchange confidential information; learn best practice and the means of implementing the change; ideally, this should be a two-way process.

This approach gives three "primary" results, i.e. the identification of:

–   the strengths of the organisation;
–   the weaknesses and potential improvements;
–   the size of potential improvements.

"After the benchmarking phase whether at Level I, II or III, the organisation has gained an in depth knowledge of itself. There is a common understanding by all of the participants, and it removes doubts and wrong perceptions ..." (p. 6). It is emphasised that this process "does not lead to improvement in itself, but is the catalyst for change. The true value is only added through achieving real improvements ..." (p. 6).

The handbook is composed of two parts: Part I, Method, describes the rationale for benchmarking and the data handling methodology used in EQUIP; Part II is composed of a list of indicators in a format ready for self-completion, together with an accompanying guide, including a checklist for completing the process.

6.4   CONCLUSIONS

In the first paragraphs of this chapter, we focused on the issue of efficiency in local public transport. Strong inefficiencies emerged in almost all the analysed countries, with an average technical inefficiency value of about 20–25 per cent. Although different works and different methodological approaches indicate great variability of the technical inefficiency, both within and among countries, the problem cannot be underestimated and definitely deserves significant attention. However, it should be noted that often the main issue is not the reduction of the operational and environmental costs, but the increase of the number of passengers. This aspect suggests the need for further insights with respect to the variables related to modal transfer, such as the switch from private car to bus or to other public transport options. This approach shifts the focus to the quality of the service.

The analyses of service quality, from the supply side point of view, list service availability and reliability, comfort, cleanliness, safety and security, fares, information, customer care and environmental impact as the quality attributes of bus services. Investments in these attributes and other operations undertaken by carriers are important, but it is essential to understand whether they are appreciated by consumers. Customer satisfaction can be measured with different instruments and from different perspectives, but the cases reported by the literature, although conditioned by the local context, show consistent results in relation to the importance of the service frequency (or waiting time) and the comfort on board (in particular, getting a seat). As far as an optimisation process is concerned, the desired service quality can be incentivised through subsidy mechanisms, but concrete results can only be achieved through the direct commitment of companies. Self-assessment of internal quality and constant comparison with other operators can prove crucial to meeting the challenge.

REFERENCES

Abrate, G., F. Erbetta, G. Fraquelli and D. Vannoni (2016), "Bet big on doubles, bet smaller on triples. Exploring scope economies in multi-service passenger transport companies", *Transport Policy*, 52, 81–88.
Berechman, J. (1993), *Public Transit Economics and Deregulation Policy*, North-Holland, Amsterdam.
Berger, C., R. Blauth, D. Boger, C. Bolster, G. Burchill, W. DuMouchel, F. Pouliot, R. Richter, A. Rubinoff, D. Shen, M. Timko and D. Walden (1993), "Kano's methods for understanding customer-defined quality", *The Center for Quality Management Journal*, 2(4), 1–36.
Bhave, A. (2002), "Customer satisfaction measurement", *Quality & Productivity Journal*, February.
Cambini, C., M. Piacenza and D.Vannoni (2007), "Restructuring public transit systems: evidence on cost properties and optimal network configuration from medium and large-sized companies", *Review of Industrial Organisation*, 3, 183–203.
Carter, D.N. and T.J. Lomax (1992), "Development and application of performance measures for rural public transportation operators", *Transportation Research Record*, 1338, 28–36.

Colburn, C.B. and W.K. Talley (1992), "A firm specific analysis of economies of size in the U.S. urban multiservice transit industry", *Transportation Research Part B*, 3, 195–206.

Cowie, J. and D. Asenova (1999), "Organisation form, scale effects and efficiency in the British bus industry", *Transportation*, 26, 231–248.

Cuomo, M.T. (2000), *La customer satisfaction. Vantaggio competitivo e creazione di valore*, CEDAM, Padova.

Dalton, D., J. Nestler, J. Nordbo, B. St. Clair, E. Wittwer and M. Wolfgram (2001), "Transportation data and performance measurement", *Transportation Research Board Conference Proceedings*, 26, 75–87.

Daraio, C., M. Diana, F. DiCosta, C. Leporelli, G. Matteucci and A. Nastasi (2016), "Efficiency and effectiveness in the urban public transport sector: a critical review with directions for future research", *European Journal of Operational Research*, 248, 1–20.

Dargay, J. and M. Hanly (1999), *Bus Fare Elasticities. Report to the UK Department of the Environment, Transport and the Regions*, ESRC Transport Studies Unit, University College London.

Dargay, J.M. and M. Hanly (2002), "The demand for local bus services in England", *Journal of Transport Economics and Policy*, 36(1), 73–91.

De Borger, B., K. Kerstens and M. Staat (2008), "Transit costs and cost efficiency: bootstrapping non-parametric frontiers", *Research in Transportation Economics*, 23(1), 53–64.

Deb, K. and M. Filippini (2010), "Public bus transport demand elasticities in India", *Journal of Transport Economics and Policy*, 47(3), 419–436.

Dell'Olio, L., A. Ibeas and P. Cecın (2010), "Modelling user perception of bus transit quality", *Transport Policy*, 17, 388–397.

Dell'Olio, L., A. Ibeas and P. Cecın (2011), "The quality of service desired by public transport users", *Transport Policy*, 18, 217–227.

Di Giacomo, M. and E. Ottoz (2010), "The relevance of scale and scope economies in the provision of urban and intercity bus transport", *Journal of Transport, Economics and Policy*, 44(2), 161–187.

Durango-Cohen, P.L. and E.C. McKenzie (2018), "Trading off costs, environmental impact, and levels of service in the optimal design of transit bus fleets", *Transportation Research Part A: Policy and Practice*, 114, 354–363.

Eboli, L. and G. Mazzulla (2011), "A methodology for evaluating transit service quality based on subjective and objective measures from the passenger's point of view", *Transport Policy*, 18(1), 172–181.

Eboli, L. and G. Mazzulla (2012), "Performance indicators for an objective measure of public transport quality service", *European Transport / Trasporti Europei*, 51, Paper no 3.

EQUIP (Extending the Quality of Public Transport) (2000), *Final Report*, UR-98-RS.3076.

Farsi, M., A. Fetz and M. Filippini (2007), "Economies of scale and scope in local public transportation", *Journal of Transport, Economics and Policy*, 41(3), 345–361.

Fellesson, M. and M. Friman (2008), "Perceived satisfaction with public transport service in nine European cities", *Journal of the Transportation Research Forum*, 47(3), 93–103.

Fraquelli, G., M. Piacenza and G. Abrate (2004), "Regulating public transit networks: how do urban-intercity diversification and speed-up measures affect firms' cost performance?", *Annals of Public and Cooperative Economy*, 75(2), 193–225.

Gagnepain, P., M. Ivaldi and C. Muller (2011), "The industrial organization of competition in local bus services", in A. de Palma, R. Lindsey, E. Quinet and R. Vickerman (eds), *A Handbook of Transport Economics*, Edward Elgar Publishing, Cheltenham.

Guirao, B., A. García-Pastor and M.E. Lopez-Lambas (2016), "The importance of service quality attributes in public transportation: narrowing the gap between scientific research and practitioners' needs", *Transport Policy*, 49, 68–77.

Hensher, D.A., P. Stopher and P. Bullock (2003), "Service quality – developing a service quality index in the provision of commercial bus contracts", *Transportation Research Part A*, 37, 499–517.

Hill, N. (2003), *How to Measure Customer Satisfaction*, Gower Publishing Ltd, Aldershot.

Jarboui, S., P. Forget and Y. Boujelbene (2012), "Public road transport efficiency: a literature review via the classification scheme", *Public Transport*, 4(2), 101–128.

Kano, N., N. Seraku, F. Takahashi and S. Tsjui (1984), "Attractive quality and must-be quality", *Hinshitsu*, 14(2), 147–156.

Karlaftis, M.G. and P. McCarthy (2002), "Cost structures of public transit systems: a panel data analysis", *Transportation Research Part E*, 38, 1–18.

Levinger, D. and M. McGehee (2008), "Connectivity: responding to new trends through a usability approach", *Community Transportation*, 33–37.

Litman, T. (2009), Sustainable Transportation Indicators. A Recommended Research Program for Developing Sustainable Transportation Indicators Data, Transportation Research Board Annual Meeting, Paper 09-3403.

Litman, T. (2019), *Evaluating Public Transit Benefits and Costs, Best Practices Guidebook*, www.vtpi.org/tranben.pdf.

Louviere, J.J., D.A. Hensher and J. Swait (2000), *Stated Choice Methods: Analysis and Applications in Marketing, Transportation and Environmental Valuation*, Cambridge University Press, Cambridge.

Mazzulla, G. and L. Eboli (2006), "A service quality experimental measure for public transport", *European Transport / Trasporti Europei*, 34, 42–53.

Meyer, M. (2000) "Measuring that which cannot be measured at least according to conventional wisdom", Transportation Research Board – Proceedings from the 26th Annual Meeting on Performance Measures to Improve Transportation Systems and Agency Operations, Irvine, 29 October–1 November.

Monzon, A., S. Hernandez and R. Cascajo (2013), "Quality of bus services performance: benefits of real time passenger information systems", *Transport and Telecommunication* 14(2), 155–166.

Ottoz, E. and M. Di Giacomo (2012), "Diversification strategies and scope economies: evidence from a sample of Italian regional bus transport providers", *Applied Economics*, 44(22), 2867–2880.

Parasuraman, A., V.A. Zeithaml and L.L. Berry (1988), "SERVQUAL: a multiple-item scale for measuring consumer perceptions of service quality", *Journal of Retailing*, 64(1), 12–40.

Pulley, L.B. and Y.M. Braunstein (1992), "A composite cost function for multiproduct firms with an application to economies of scope in banking", *Review of Economics and Statistics*, 74, 221–230.

Redman, L., M. Friman, T. Gärling and T. Hartig (2013), "Quality attributes of public transport that attract car users: a research review", *Transport Policy*, 25, 119–127.

Sampaio, B.R., O.L. Neto and Y. Sampaio (2008), "Efficiency analysis of public transport systems: lessons for institutional planning", *Transportation Research Part A, Policy and Practice*, 42(3), 445–454.

Talley, W.K. (2007), "Classifying urban passenger transportation services", in V. Coto-Millán and V. Inglada (eds), *Essays on Transport Economics*, Springer, New York.

Transportation Research Board (1995), *A TCRP Synthesis 10, Bus Route Evaluation Standards*, Transit Cooperative Research Program, Washington DC.

Transportation Research Board (2003a), *A Guidebook for Developing a Transit Performance-Measurement System*, Transit Cooperative Research Program, Report 88, Washington DC.

Transportation Research Board (2003b), *Transit Capacity and Quality of Service*, Transit Cooperative Research Program, Report 100, 2nd edn, Washington DC.

Viton, P. (1993), "How big should transit be? Evidence from San Francisco Bay Area", *Transportation*, 20, 35–57.

Vuchic, V.R. (2007), *Urban Transit: Systems and Technology*, Wiley, New York.

7. Seaports and airports

Eddy Van de Voorde and Chris Nash

7.1   INTRODUCTION

Ports and airports are important parts of the transport system. This is due to the large volume of goods and passengers they handle, but also to derived effects in terms of employment and investment. Both ports and airports are crucial nodes in complex logistics chains and as such a welfare-generating actor for a region and/or country.

Competition between and within ports and airports is therefore fierce. Many actors are involved in that competition. Consequently, port and airport competition is influenced by a multitude of related and sometimes even conflicting interests. For a port, three types of competition may be discerned, i.e. intra-port competition at operator level (competition between port undertakings within a single port), external port competition at operator level (competition between port undertakings from different ports), and inter-port competition at port authority level (Van de Voorde and Winkelmans, 2002). The same types of competition apply to airports. A daily fight for throughput and passengers!

But the question arises whether all ports and airports do face strong competition. There may be a case in which one or more forms of market failure lead to allocative inefficiency. Possible causes of market failure include market power, asymmetric information, externalities and public goods. At that moment one starts thinking about regulation. A major argument in favor of regulation is based on the natural monopoly character of some industries. Production at the minimum possible long-run average cost will happen only if one firm controls the industry's total production, i.e. the minimum efficient scale (MES) is more or less equivalent to, or larger than the total market size. Whilst some market areas may be able to support several ports and airports of minimum efficient scale, in smaller geographical markets this may not be possible. Even where it is possible, planning constraints and environmental considerations may prevent the development of competing facilities, giving existing ports and airports monopoly power.

So in the case of seaports and airports, first of all, one should raise the question of whether or not they always work in a competitive environment.

In the latter case, there might be a need for regulation. If so, should regulation be applied to all ports and/or airports? If we regulate, do we opt for structural regulation focusing on market structure, or conduct regulation seeking to influence the behavior of firms?

In what follows we start from the heterogeneous character of seaports and airports, stressing the relationship between a high number of different actors. No two seaports or airports are physically and economically the same. We refer to already existing forms of regulation, the market evolution towards fewer and bigger market players and/or alliances and the consequences in terms of regulatory requirements.

7.2   THE SEAPORT: A HETEROGENEOUS MIX OF ACTORS

7.2.1   Introduction

Major port activities deal with the physical throughput of goods and passengers. In the course of time, this throughput function has become separated with the emergence of new, specialized functions such as, among others, forwarding and agency, and a distribution function. Each port in itself became a chain of consecutive links, while the port as a whole also constitutes a link within a global logistics chain. Over time, the relative importance of the various links has clearly changed, due to significant efficiency-increasing technological developments (Meersman, Van de Voorde and Vanelslander, 2009).

The port that contributes to the cheapest logistics chain is, in theory at least, most likely to be called at. The ultimate decision process of the port user is whether the port considered does offer advantages compared to other ports serving the same hinterland. Or does the port offer sufficient advantages in order to be considered as an additional port of call for an existing or yet-to-be-established liner or feeder service.

Port operations involve a great many players, both at management level and at operational level. These actors may be united in a single company, as is the case in some privately owned ports in the UK, or they may constitute a mixture of firms and authorities within the port. A typical European port consists of more than a port authority and a terminal operating company. Many different players and decision makers are active within ports, including shipping companies, port authorities, goods handlers, agents, industrial and production companies, etc. Moreover, activities of actors are changing, as are the mutual relationships between their companies.

The question arises of which player in the chain takes which decisions. Earlier studies have shown very clearly that certain players are particularly influential, namely the owner and/or shipper of the goods, the forwarder and the shipping companies (see e.g. Coppens et al., 2007). Terminal operating companies (TOCs), on the other hand, are highly dependent upon the decisions taken by these three other parties, even though TOCs themselves are also required to make long-term commitments: investment in superstructure (e.g. storage capacity) and terminal infrastructure (e.g. cranes, straddle carriers, and so on).

Figure 7.1 gives the structure of a typical maritime supply chain, including the potential relationships between actors. The possibility of monopoly power, and of the need for regulation, may arise at any point in the chain. Cost minimization, for example, is important for every actor in that chain, but clearly a shipping company has greater scope than some other actors for restricting costs while being able to maintain a price level that guarantees a large profit margin. Ultimately, the (new) owner of the goods will have to pay the bill.

Within that maritime logistics chain, we concentrate as a next step on the pricing and payment of port bills (see Figure 7.2). By quantifying these relationships between actors one gets an idea about the relative power of the actors (Meersman, Van de Voorde and Vanelslander, 2009). This has been done for the port of Antwerp. Drawing on empirical data, a quantified understanding has been reached of the mutual relationships between the port actors, and their mutual dependency. The influence of a port actor (Antwerp in this case) on its customer (in this case another port actor) is measured by means of forward linkages. The influence an Antwerp port actor has on its suppliers – in this case another Antwerp port actor – is defined by decomposed backward linkages. For Antwerp one thing was very clear: the importance of forwarders. This helps to investigate whether some actors and/or activities are abusing their (potentially) dominant position. Therefore, there is a need to understand the relative importance and the negotiating and market power of the various port actors. One needs to know what their mutual relationships are, whether some actors are dominant, and whether or not they have financial stakes in one another. In a situation where a TOC depends on only one big client (ship owner), negotiations concerning prices and quality of services can/will be different from a situation where that same TOC has several clients, without a dominant one. At the same time the driving forces behind the various forms of co-operation that may emerge (mergers, alliances, participation, etc.) should be made clear.

The average European port as a physical entity is managed by a port authority (PA) which, in turn, is usually partly or wholly controlled and/or regulated by a higher (public or administrative) authority. The PA's major remaining trump card is the allocation of concessions within the port perimeter to terminal operators and industrial and service companies. Normal auction procedures are applied and published. If this process is handled effectively and there is

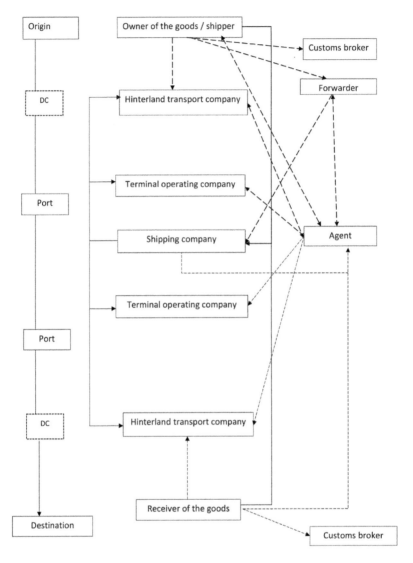

Note: DC = distribution centre.
Source: Based on Meersman, Van de Voorde and Vanelslander, 2010.

Figure 7.1   Structure of a maritime supply chain

real competition for the concessions, then that should ensure efficiency of the various actors within the port. Complaints can result in court procedures.

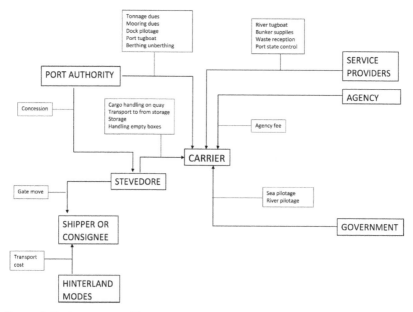

Source: Author's own composition.

Figure 7.2   Pricing and payment of port bills

The major clients of a port are the shipowners and their vessels that call at the port. But the commercial relations are not between the shipowner and the port authority, but between the shipowner (or its agent) on one side, and the terminal operating company and the forwarder on the other. We concentrate first of all on the port authority, the shipowners and the terminal operating company as three of the major port actors.

7.2.2   Port Authority

Port authorities decide on the level of port dues, the price a vessel has to pay to call at the port (Meersman, Pettersen Strandenes and Van de Voorde, 2015). Shipping regulations, contributing to safety, apply in any port. The harbor master enforces international, national and local laws and regulations. International regulations are issued by IMO, the International Maritime Organization (e.g. SOLAS). In some countries or regions, a port commissioner supervises whether port authority decisions correspond with the formal regulation.

Table 7.1   Recent scale increases in the container liner business

Year	Buyer	Company acquired	Amount
2016	CMA CGM	Neptune Orient Lines (NOL)	$2.4 billion
2017	Maersk	Hamburg Süd	$4 billion
2017	Cosco	Orient Overseas Limited (OOIL)	$6.3 billion
2017	Ocean Network Express (ONE)	Merger of 3 Japanese companies: NYK, MOL and "K" Line	n/a

Source: Author's own composition.

Recently, we have seen some port authorities deciding to co-operate with other port authorities. An example is the merger of the ports of Ghent (Belgium) and Sealand port (Netherlands).

7.2.3   Ship Owners

In the past two decades, the container port industry has seen three waves of consolidation, the last one being the most significant. Eight of the top 20 players have disappeared from the market in the last two years. This seems to be the consequence of supply and demand being out of balance, resulting in low freight rates and in a market-share rate war. Table 7.1 shows some of those deals, all of them subject to approval by public authorities in various jurisdictions.

After this move, there will be just seven global carriers with a total capacity of over 1 million TEU (twenty-foot equivalent units). The container shipping industry consolidated into three huge alliances: Ocean Alliance, the Alliance, and 2M. Industry consolidation should raise concerns among the customers of the liners, e.g. the cargo shippers. Can we be sure that the market will remain highly competitive? Antitrust regulators have not intervened yet. No individual carrier will command more than 20 percent of overall market volumes. Consolidation will probably support more stable rate levels. Container liner companies hope to become more profitable and promise their customers less volatile freight rates and better schedule reliability.

7.2.4   Terminal Operating Companies

Container handling has evolved over time from small stevedores, competing with each other at local port level, towards integrated global container terminal operating companies, TOCs. This is the result of the fact that local stevedores were unable to cope with the need for capital investments in new facilities and container cranes. At the same time, the local companies had to negotiate

Table 7.2   *Forecast of global/international terminal operator capacity ranking, 2020*

Operator	Capacity rank	
	2020	Current
Cosco-China Shipping	1st	4th and 8th
APM Terminals	2nd	2nd
PSA International	3rd	3rd
Hutchison Port Holdings	4th	1st
DP World	5th	5th
Terminal Investment Ltd	6th	6th
CMA CGM	7th	9th

Source: Drewry Maritime Research, 2020.

with liner companies working under the umbrella of strategic alliances and/or companies that had recently consolidated or merged.

Table 7.2 gives a forecast of which terminal operator will be number one by 2020, as measured by capacity. The table shows that the merger of China Shipping and Cosco is likely to see it become the world leader in capacity terms. It is also clear that we shall see global and international terminal operators focusing more on merger and acquisition opportunities and less on greenfield projects.

The consolidation of ownership in the terminal operating business should be considered a natural response to the increasing size of liner alliances. The consequence can be that future negotiations between liner companies and terminal operators should be treated as a situation of bilateral oligopolies. However, markets are still contestable. Entry barriers seem to be low, as evidenced by Yilport Holdings, a new entrant, joining the industry (and purchasing the Portuguese group Tertir).

7.2.5   Pilots and Towage Companies

For some ports not located on the coast (e.g. Hamburg and Antwerp), assistance from pilots and towage are needed. We often see that those professions and companies do have a quasi-monopoly concerning the supply of their services.

7.3   THE CHANGING PORT GAME

Liner shipping consolidation, resulting in fewer ship calls with bigger vessels and higher peak handling numbers, also reduces the number of individual customers. However, those customers increase their scale of cargo and become more powerful. They expect, for instance, that terminals will be able to turn around an 18,000 TEU ship as quickly as a 12,000 TEU vessel. That means that container ports and their local actors are being confronted with downward pressure on tariffs and upward pressure on costs. At the level of port authorities, this can lead to more co-operation, for instance, collaboration between neighboring ports.

That also means that the competition game is changing. It starts with fewer container liners, with lower profit margins, deciding to order bigger vessels. As a reaction, port authorities need to invest in the lengthening of quays and deepening of berths and other investments to meet the requirements of ultra-large container ships. Terminal operators have to invest in wider and faster cranes. A much higher peak demand means that there are longer periods when staff are inactive. Moreover, a lot more will need to be done on the land side, such as automatic gates and trucking processes.

As a result, funding becomes a lot more difficult. Governments have already tried to diminish their involvement in port infrastructure investments. But now also infrastructure funds and pension funds are raising questions about whether potential returns in port terminals will be as certain as they used to be. Also, within a port environment, some actors may make mistakes, for instance by investing too much, or not enough. Or one may propose unsuccessful products. Or prices may be fixed at the wrong levels. Until now, the port system has believed that a correction of such mistakes will follow immediately, for instance, through a loss of market share.

Is that reasoning correct? Or does this evolution lead to a need for regulation? Competition rules concerning the container liner companies were drawn up in a very different era from now. Container liner companies were far less powerful than today. Co-operation agreements, such as, for instance, vessel-sharing agreements, were likely to be limited to a specific geographical area. In the meantime, the container shipping industry consolidated. Should these agreements be regulated differently from more traditional consortia agreements?

Although the European Commission recently prolonged the validity of the consortia block exemption regulation (EC) 906/2009 for four years (until April 2024), it can be argued that the current EU regulatory framework on liner shipping consortia agreements is not suitable for the global alliances. The rules should be strengthened to prevent global alliances from abusing their dominant position and market power. Similarly, in the U.S. there is a lively debate on whether now is the time to adjust the maritime antitrust regime, in view of the current round of mergers and acquisition activity, the collapse of Hanjin Shipping, and the concentration of the global trade into the hands of three alliances.

This could become a process that may be the catalyst for regulatory reform, in the sense that the potential consequences of dominant groups negotiating with other actors, like port authorities and terminal operating companies, should be monitored on a continuous basis. At the same time, one should ensure that another customer, being the owner of the goods and/or his forwarder, does not become the victim of this changed power play among port actors and users.

However, these developments may suggest a need to regulate the shipping lines themselves rather than ports. The rising power of the shipping lines should increase the pressure on ports to be efficient.

7.4   THE ACTUAL USE OF PORT BENCHMARKING

7.4.1   Introduction

What is the actual use of port benchmarking by regulators? Are there any benchmarking studies available that can be used? Not only regulators, but also port authorities and other port actors do need to benchmark their activities and performance. A benchmarking process delivers additional information, including about "peers", allows learning by example and adopting best practices, and gives an incentive to make performance step changes. In the end, it is all learning from others. Indeed, a continuous comparison of one's own performance with that of one's peers identifies gaps in performance and creates opportunities to improve that performance and to generate additional benefits.

As usual in benchmarking, questions arise as to comparability. Should studies focus on ports with similar markets, or can differences in traffic be allowed for by the techniques used?

It is clear that benchmarking a port as a whole is of limited value. One should benchmark at the actor's level. Some of those port actors can have and/ or use different benchmarks and indicators, but at some level they also have a joint interest in performance improvements. Even if the focus of the benchmarking activity is on costs, it is clear that a number of quality aspects must also be taken into account.

Table 7.3 gives the example of the relevant concerns of two major clients of a port authority, being a shipping line and a terminal operating company (TOC).

It is clear that, even while using a different set of benchmarking indicators, both major port actors do have common interests and targets, that is, high productivity of the berth, the yard and the loading/unloading and stacking equipment used. High productivity will depend on high reliability. That high reliability can, for instance, be reached by better forecasting of the vessels' arrival times and the hinterland modes' (train, barge, truck, etc.) arrivals, and

Table 7.3   *Potential benchmark indicators for a shipping line and a TOC*

Shipping line	Terminal operator
Total time to service a vessel	Profitability
Level of port dues	Utilization degree of facilities
Level of handling charges	Dwell time
Level of storage charges	Flexibility of the operating system
Flexibility of berthing (and handling) windows	Planning reliability
Availability of feeder services	Distance/time cargo moves to the stacking zone
Access to hinterland infrastructure and modes	

Source: Author's own composition.

Table 7.4   *Models used by Zahran et al. (2017): inputs and output used*

Model (1)	Model (2)
Inputs	
Number of vessels called	Area of open yards (hectares)
Total throughput (x000 tons)	Number of berths
Number of passengers (x1000)	Number of cargo handling equipment
Output	
Total revenues (million $)	Total revenues (million $)

Source: Zahran et al. (2017), p. 526.

by better resource and yard planning. Equally important is the way both actors co-operate to handle exceptional incidents, for instance, when a vessel is delayed due to weather conditions.

The port literature deals with benchmarking port activity, while often making the distinction between port authorities (PAs) and port terminal operating companies (TOCs). The question remains how and in what way regulators are actually using benchmarking as an instrument. Do they benchmark themselves? Or do they use the results of published benchmarking studies?

7.4.2   Benchmarking Port Authorities

Zahran et al. (2017) analyse port authority efficiency while generating revenues using data envelopment analysis (DEA). According to the authors, there has been no study focusing on port authorities and comparing, in terms of efficiency, their revenue-generation mechanisms. Two different modelling approaches are presented: one that relates revenues to the basic throughput and activity of the port and another that takes into consideration land, infrastructure and labor indicators (see Table 7.4).

A sample set of 18 international landlord, multi-activity ports has been used, including Houston (U.S.), Le Havre (France) and Barcelona (Spain). The analysis first discriminates between efficient and non-efficient ports and for the latter it identifies their benchmarks and provides target values for their revenues. In a post-DEA stage the authors examine the relation between efficiency and the size of a port.

A comment to be made is the fact that a landlord port is not in charge of the direct management of the port's facilities. Concessions are one of the few remaining powerful tools, in order to realize the most efficient utilization of terminals and land. Moreover, Goss (1990) stated that revenues by themselves are not a sufficient indicator of efficiency.

Another study, by Tovar and Rodriguez-Déniz (2015), states that while the actual estimation of port efficiency has been extensively studied, the existing literature has paid little attention to developing robust methodologies for port classification. The problem of distinguishing between heterogeneity and inefficiency is widely acknowledged in benchmarking, and aggravated when international datasets are used. From the literature survey it appears that authors using DEA (the vast majority) have tried to solve this problem by splitting the sample into homogeneous groups before the frontier estimation.

The United Nations Conference on Trade and Development (UNCTAD) published a document on port performance, including a section on port benchmarks. An interesting exercise concerns the so-called "port performance scorecard". Table 7.5 gives an overview of the indicators used for the port entity only.

These types of indicators can be collected on a yearly basis. Comparisons can be made for one port over time, and between ports.

7.4.3 Benchmarking Terminal Operating Companies

Pinto et al. (2017) deal with benchmarking operational efficiency of port terminals. In their opinion, the operational data of port terminals is often evaluated by operators and scholars, with the purpose of finding characteristics that lead to superior performance, or identifying the most efficient terminal in a sample. Often methodologies are used that do not allow a distinction between manageable and unmanageable (exogenous) factors, thus often leading to ambiguous results. An example illustrates this: standard high-level indicators, such as throughput and berth occupancy, are also influenced by factors that cannot be manipulated by port managers, such as weather conditions, maritime access channel conditions, external norms and regulations (e.g. work hours) and storage factors of bulk cargoes (Pinto et al., 2017). The authors propose a methodology to overcome this limitation, based on the breakdown of the high-level overall equipment effectiveness (OEE) indicator into a set of indi-

Table 7.5   Indicators used by UNCTAD

Port entity only	Indicators
Finance	EBITDA/revenue (operating margin)
	Vessel dues/revenue
	Cargo dues/revenue
	Rents/revenue
	Labour/revenue
	Fees and the like/revenue
Human resources	Tons/employee
	Revenue/employee
	EBITDA/employee
	Labour cost/employee
	Training costs/wages
Vessel operations	Average waiting time (hours)
	Average overall vessel length per vessel (m)
	Average draft per vessel (m)
	Average gross tonnage per vessel
Cargo operations	Average tonnage per arrival – all
	Tons per working hour, dry or solid bulk
	Box per hour, containers
	Twenty-foot equivalent unit dwell time (days)
	Tons per hour, liquid bulk
	Tons per hectare – all
	Tons per berth metre – all

Source: UNCTAD (2016).

cators, each addressing either manageable or unmanageable factors. Based on this set, it is possible to define achievable efficiency targets for each terminal.

Within the literature, most port terminal efficiency analyses use efficiency frontier methods, using either parametric or non-parametric models (Pinto et al., 2017; Bichou, 2006; Gonzales and Trujillo, 2009). A parametric model relates inputs (time, equipment, costs, etc.) and output. After defining the parameters of the function, the performance of each terminal can be evaluated and compared to its expected value to assess efficiency (see, for instance, Barros, 2005). Non-parametric models identify the most efficient decision-making units of a sample, and evaluate the efficiency gap between top performers and others (see, for instance, Cullinane, Song and Wang, 2004). Most authors here apply the data envelopment analysis (DEA) model. Pinto et al. (2017) state that sophisticated analyses, using parametric and non-parametric models to define efficiency frontiers, often fall into the same trap, this being the contamination of exogenous effects in efficiency calculations.

Table 7.6   *Operational performance indicators commonly used in the port industry*

Indicator	Description
Throughput	Total amount of cargo handled in tons (or containers) in a given period
Load size/tonnage per ship	Average amount of cargo handled per ship call
Ships arrival rate	Average number of ship calls per day
Berth occupancy rate	Percentage of total time with ship alongside berth
Storage occupancy rate	Ratio between total cargo stored (on average) and the rated capacity of the facility
Total time in port	Average time spent by the ships in the port area
Queue time	Average time spent by the ships in the queue
Gross (net) loading/unloading rate	Average amount of cargo loaded/unloaded between the arrival and the departure of ships (excluding non-operational times)

Source: Pinto et al., 2017, p. 507.

Port performance and efficiency can also be measured by using a set of performance indicators that can be benchmarked or compared to theoretical values. It looks simple, but this approach allows the analysis of specific processes of a system. Table 7.6 gives a list of the operational performance indicators commonly used in the port industry.

The indicators listed in Table 7.6 are applicable to the vast majority of ports and terminals, regardless of the types of cargoes and facilities used.

7.5   PORTS: A NEED FOR YARDSTICK COMPETITION?

The former sections clearly show a potential danger that, in some specific relationships, an actor may start to abuse its dominant position. In such a market environment, yardstick competition can offer a solution. It is a specific form of regulation which requires the collecting of information on cost conditions of comparable companies (Bruzzone, 2017). Any remuneration of the regulated undertaking will be linked to the results of the other companies, in order to give an incentive to become much more efficient.

In order to prepare for the application of yardstick competition, one can gather information by following a checklist:

(1)   Is there enough competition, at each level, from shipping companies to TOCs, pilots, towage companies and other service providers? That means the need for information concerning negotiation processes and

results, besides quantitative information concerning market shares, for all actors involved.

(2)   Is there any risk of collusion between actors, both horizontally (e.g. between TOCs) and vertically (between a shipping line and a TOC)? What is the effect of more concentration in the liner business on port competition, e.g. in the case where one liner company dominates the port throughput?

(3)   Are there any barriers to entry and/or exit in the port market (with a reference to contestability theory)? Does the concentration in the TOC business create barriers (cf. those ports with only one TOC)?

Within the maritime logistics chain, we increasingly get forms of co-operation, from alliances between shipping companies to takeovers and mergers in a port context (Heaver et al., 2000; Heaver, Meersman and Van de Voorde, 2001). In some cases there is the risk of a situation where companies start to collude, either horizontally and/or vertically. In some ports there exist joint ventures between the major shipping line and a TOC. That can lead to so-called "dedicated terminals" or "virtual dedicated terminals". In what way is such an agreement blocking normal competitive mechanisms? Collusion between companies can eliminate the incentive to present competitive bids and therefore the information and efficiency-enhancing role of tenders. Fighting collusion remains a crucial task, to be started by checking and comparing the tenders.

Benchmarking also requires the analysis of costs, including the assessment of economies of scale and scope. This is important at each level of port activities, for instance, while tendering for a new concession for a TOC. A port authority of a big port, being aware that oversized concessions should be avoided, will always try to opt for several concessionaires. That creates the possibility to compare the performance of all concessionaires and to develop forms of competition by comparison. An excellent example is the concessions within the port of Antwerp, to PSA and DP World, at the Deurganckdock. Those concession agreements included performance targets. If those contracted targets are not reached, the port authority applies a penalty.

Another issue is that some port authorities are fully or partially controlled by public authorities, e.g. a national or regional government, or a city council. One then may use benchmarking in order to set the proper incentives for the port authority, in terms of both prices (e.g. "port dues") and/or quality.

7.6   THE CASE OF AIRPORTS

There is quite a lot of similarity between seaports and airports, albeit that seaports in the majority of cases deal with freight, while most airports are active in both the passenger and freight markets. Also, airports can be considered a chain of consecutive links, while the airport as a whole also constitutes a link within a global passenger and/or logistics chain. Within the airport, a large number of actors are involved, each of which pursues its own objectives, which gives rise to a considerable degree of heterogeneity. Figure 7.3 gives an overview of these relationships, based on the pricing and payment of airport bills.

There seems to be an important difference between the seaport and airport sector. The potential power of seaport authorities seems to be much lower than the potential power of airport authorities. Although airlines also work together in alliances, their market power seems to be less than that of liner conferences. The reason could be "slot allocation".

In some countries, the airport authority is regulated, whilst the other airport actors are not. In what follows, we shall highlight the most important conclusions of a report on the economic regulation of airports, with specific application to the Brussels Airport Company (Kupfer et al., 2013). The study considered the following aspects: the length of the regulation period; (adjusted) single till versus dual till; tuning of tariffs to those applied at a set of reference airports versus the use of a financial model; the distinction between regulated and non-regulated activities (i.e. the level of economic regulation) and the role of the economic regulator. The purpose of the study was to investigate which type of regulation would be most appropriate for the Brussels Airport Company, taking into account the concepts of natural monopoly and market power.

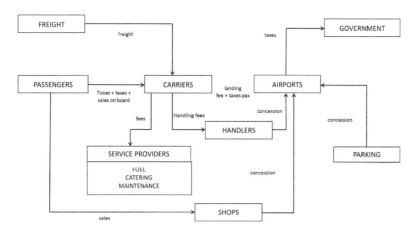

Source: Own composition (Macário and Van de Voorde, 2019).

Figure 7.3   *Pricing and payment of airport bills*

What arguments might justify economic regulation in the airport business? The customary answer, as mentioned before, is the occurrence of market failure. A regulatory intervention for the purpose of introducing a correction is generally regarded as efficient if the costs of intervening will be lower than the cost incurred through market failure. Again, though, no generalization is possible. The market power of an airport will, for example, vary according to the market segment. Larger airports, most of them acting as hubs, may be expected to have some market power over so-called networked airlines, which aim expressly at achieving maximum benefits of scale and scope. There is minimum or even no market power vis-à-vis low-cost airlines, companies specializing in point-to-point services, and charter companies. Invariably, though, the market power of an airport will be largely determined by the presence of nearby competing airports. The likelihood of substitution is crucial, so that a case-by-case assessment is called for.

All this obviously entirely recontextualizes the notion of "regulation" in an airport environment. There can be no doubt that some form of monitoring of airports remains necessary. After all, European Directive 2009/12/EC regarding airport charges (in effect since 15 March 2009) does prescribe explicitly that there should be an independent supervisory authority that safeguards the principles underlying the setting of airport charges (Article 11) and, more generally, to supervise the airports concerned (Article 12). In this context, price cap regulation is a commonly used instrument to discipline private companies with market power, such as airport authorities.

7.7   THE ACTUAL USE OF AIRPORT BENCHMARKING

From a technical point of view one can expect airport benchmarking to be comparable to seaport benchmarking. However, there is one big difference. Quite a lot of airports are privately owned, or in the process of being privatized. The result is that financial indicators get emphasized, together with indicators measuring capacity utilization (e.g. runway slots, parking gates, etc.) and efficiency.

The literature provides quite a number of benchmarking studies. A very important one is the ATRS Global Airport Benchmarking Report, measuring and comparing the performance of several important aspects of airport operations: productivity and efficiency, unit costs and cost competitiveness, financial results and airport charges (ATRS, 2017). Moreover the report also examines the relationships between various performance measures and airport characteristics, as well as management strategies, in order to provide a better understanding of observed differences in airport performance. Being a yearly report, the 2017 version includes 206 airports and 24 airport groups, of various sizes and ownership forms, in Asia Pacific, Europe and North America.

In 2013 the Civil Aviation Authority (CAA) published an *Airport Operating Expenditures Benchmarking Report* (CAA, 2013). This report provides, for 2012, a review and assessment of the airport operating expenditure (opex) benchmarking indicators available to the CAA. This evidence has been used by the CAA to develop benchmarks against comparators for Heathrow, Gatwick and Stansted, based on publicly available data.

The CAA has reviewed several benchmarking studies, each of which has used different data and methods to assess the relative level of efficiency of each airport. The ATRS benchmarking has already been discussed. The Leigh Fisher benchmarking study provides benchmark comparisons of airports across key matrices including opex per passenger. The study is based on financial reporting for 2009, and includes 50 airports (including Heathrow and Gatwick, but not Stansted).

A study of Booz & Company, commissioned by the British Airports Authority (BAA), benchmarks the opex performance of Heathrow against a variety of European comparators, based on 2011 financial account data. The following airports are included: Amsterdam (AMS) (Group); Athens (ATH); Birmingham (BHX); Paris Charles de Gaulle (CDG) (Group); Copenhagen (CPH); Dublin (DUB) (Group); Edinburgh (EDI); Frankfurt (FRA); London Gatwick (LGW); Manchester (MAN); Munich (MUC); and Zurich (ZRH). It is interesting that in addition to the partial productivity metrics, the study also used an econometric model to account for differences associated with uncontrollable factors. This is based on a "residual" approach whereby costs are separated into "Inherent", "Structural", "Systematic" and "Realized" costs, which can then be defined as controllable and non-controllable. The residual productivity analysis, having taken account of these factors, is then used to estimate the relative efficiency gap of Heathrow against the specific comparators.

Building on the evidence and methodologies of the above-mentioned studies, the CAA has undertaken additional analysis on the relative performance of Heathrow, Gatwick and Stansted against comparators. Data has been collected for a sample of 16 airports from 2000 to 2011, subdivided in two sub-samples. Two partial productivity metrics have been used to examine the relative performance of the airports: first, the ordinary opex per passenger (not adjusted to take account of differences in airport activities); second, the adjusted opex per passenger, intended to adjust for airport activities to provide a more consistent estimate of each airport's core operating costs for comparative purposes.

7.8   CONCLUSION

It is clear that both seaports and airports have a lot in common. Both are very competitive sectors, but it remains the case that geographical factors and constraints on development of new facilities may lead to particular ports and airports having some degree of market power. Both are very complex environments, with a multitude of actors influencing each other's behavior and results. That means that there always is the possibility that some actors will start to increase their market power, with a risk that market power will be abused. To a considerable extent, this risk may be reduced by competitive tendering for concessions to provide these services, provided that this process is handled effectively and that real competition emerges.

In short, then, ports and airports raise difficult questions regarding whether regulation is needed and if so where and in what form. Benchmarking, both of ports and airports as a whole, and of individual functions within them, may play a useful role, in the first place simply as a means of monitoring whether there appear to be problems of inefficiency and/or abuse of monopoly power. Where problems are identified, then there may be the need for regulation, based on benchmarking and yardstick competition.

REFERENCES

ATRS (2017), *The ATRS Global Airport Benchmarking Report*, Air Transport Research Society, Embry-Riddle Aeronautical University, Daytona Beach, Florida, U.S.A.
Barros, C.P. (2005), "Decomposing growth in Portuguese seaports: a frontier cost approach", *Maritime Economics & Logistics*, 7(4), 297–315.
Bichou, K. (2006), "Review of port performance approaches and a supply chain framework to port performance benchmarking", *Research in Transportation Economics*, 17(6), 567–598.
Bruzzone, G. (2017), "The role of benchmarking in competition policy and how to use yardstick competition in a procompetitive regulatory strategy", Meeting of the Italian Transport Regulation Authority Advisory Board, Turin.
CAA (2013), *CAA Airport Operating Expenditure Benchmarking Report 2012*, Civil Aviation Authority, CAP 1060, London.
Coppens, F., F. Lagneaux, H. Meersman, N. Sellekaerts, E. Van de Voorde, G. Van Gastel, T. Van Elslander and A. Verhetsel (2007), "Economic impact of port activity: a disaggregate analysis. The case of Antwerp", Working paper document no 110, National Bank of Belgium, Brussels.
Cullinane, K., D.-W. Song and T.-F. Wang (2004), "An application of DEA windows analysis to container port production efficiency", *Review of Network Economics*, 3(2), 184–206.
Drewry Maritime Research (2020), *Global Container Terminal Operators Annual Review and Forecast 2020/21*, Drewry Maritime Research, London.

Gonzales, M.M. and L. Trujillo (2009), "Efficiency measurement in the port industry: a survey of the empirical evidence", *Journal of Transport Economics and Policy*, 43(2), 157–192.

Goss, R. (1990), "Economic policies and seaports: are port authorities necessary?", *Maritime Policy and Management*, 17(4), 257–271.

Heaver, T., H. Meersman, F. Moglia and E. Van de Voorde (2000), "Do mergers and alliances influence European shipping and port competition?", *Maritime Policy and Management*, 27(4), 363–373.

Heaver, T., H. Meersman and E. Van de Voorde (2001), "Co-operation and competition in international container transport: strategies for ports", *Maritime Policy and Management*, 28(3), 293–305.

Kupfer, F., H. Meersman, T. Pauwels, E. Struyf, E. Van de Voorde and T. Vanelslander (2013), "Economic regulation of airports: the case of Brussels Airport Company", *Case Studies on Transport Policy*, 1(1), 27–34.

Macário, R. and E. Van de Voorde (2019), "A Game of Winners and Losers. The Air Transport Casino", lecture at the Air Transport Colloquium, TPR, Antwerp.

Meersman, H., E. Van de Voorde and T. Vanelslander (2009), "The economic fabric of ports", in H. Meersman, E. Van de Voorde and T. Vanelslander (eds), *Future Challenges for the Port and Shipping Sector*, Informa, London.

Meersman, H., E. Van de Voorde and T. Vanelslander (2010), "Port competition revisited", *Review of Business and Economics*, 55(2), 210–232.

Meersman, H., S. Pettersen Strandenes and E. Van de Voorde (2015), "Port pricing", in C. Nash (ed.), *Handbook of Research Methods and Applications in Transport Economics and Policy*, Edward Elgar Publishing, Cheltenham.

Pinto, M.M.O., D.J.K. Goldberg and J.S.L. Cardoso (2017), "Benchmarking operational efficiency of port terminals using the OEE indicator", *Maritime Economics & Logistics*, 19(3), 504–517.

Tovar, B. and H. Rodriguez-Déniz (2015), "Classifying ports and efficiency benchmarking: a review and a frontier-based clustering approach", *Transport Reviews*, 35(3), 378–400.

UNCTAD (2016), *Port Performance: Linking Performance Indicators to Strategic Objectives*, Port Management Series, vol. 4, United Nations, New York and Geneva.

Van de Voorde, E. and W. Winkelmans (2002), "A general introduction to port competition and management", in M. Huybrechts, H. Meersman, E. Van de Voorde, E. Van Hooydonk, A. Verbeke and W. Winkelmans (eds), *Port Competitiveness. An Economic and Legal Analysis of the Factors Determining the Competitiveness of Seaports*, De Boeck Ltd, Antwerp.

Zaharan, S.Z., J. Bin Alam, A.H. Al-Zahrani, Y. Smirlis, S. Papadimitriou and V. Tsioumas (2017), "Analysis of port authority efficiency using data envelopment analysis", *Maritime Economics & Logistics*, 19(3), 518–537.

PART III

Learning from experience: some case studies

8. Rail in Britain

Chris Nash and Andrew Smith

8.1 INTRODUCTION

The experience of Britain in rail regulation is important for a number of reasons. Firstly, Britain took reform of the rail sector further than any other country, with complete separation of rail infrastructure from operations, breaking up and privatisation of rail freight and franchising by competitive tender of almost all rail passenger services, both profitable and subsidised. Secondly, from the beginning, the reform was accompanied by the setting up of an independent rail regulator (ORR) with appropriate powers and responsibilities, not just to oversee non-discriminatory access to the infrastructure, but also to promote the efficiency of the new rail infrastructure company, Railtrack. Railtrack was privatised by the sale of shares, later became insolvent and was replaced by a not-for-profit company, Network Rail, ultimately owned by the government; however, the ORR retained its responsibility in respect of rail infrastructure.

Two principal policy instruments are used in seeking to promote the efficiency of the rail industry in Britain. For train operators, competitive tendering for franchises is the approach, with franchises mostly let and managed by the Department for Transport (DfT) in London. For the infrastructure manager, regulation – including the use of benchmarking – is used.

This chapter will look at the experience of both, with a particular emphasis on the relevance of benchmarking and on encouragement of both investment and quality of service.

8.2 COMPETITIVE TENDERING

Competitive tendering for franchises in Britain was introduced in 1994, and by 1997 virtually all domestic passenger services had been franchised. The details of the franchising process have been revised several times, so current franchises adopt a variety of approaches according to when they were let. Where not otherwise stated, the following description relates specifically to the East Midlands franchise, which is the most recent one to be awarded at the time of writing, but is fairly typical of the most up-to-date situation (pre-COVID-19). It should be noted that a major review of the structure of the rail industry (the Williams Review[1]) has been completed and is awaiting a formal announcement of its findings; and this may lead to a substantial change in the arrangements. It should also be noted that as a result of the COVID-19 challenges, in the spring of 2020 the entire franchised sector was moved temporarily (via a six-month temporary suspension of franchise agreements) to management contracts, for which the government bears all revenue and cost risk.

From the first, great efforts were made to attract sufficient bidders to achieve a competitive price. Thus bidders have access to a data room with extensive data on costs, resources and demand, which the incumbent is required to provide. Existing rolling stock was placed in the hands of leasing companies to make it easier for bidders to obtain access to rolling stock (of course they can also lease from the manufacturer or another leasing company in respect of new rolling stock). Not just the track, but also stations and depots passed to a totally separate infrastructure company to make non-discriminatory access easier. Moreover, the winner takes over an existing company and its staff, avoiding the transition problems experienced in many countries, although this does tend to lock in existing wages and work practices. In Sweden and Germany, entrants were free to recruit their own staff and to set their own wages and conditions, with the existing staff able to stay with the incumbent (this is no longer permitted in Germany); but in Britain the incumbent (British Rail) ceased to exist.

For most franchises, the franchising authority is the Department for Transport (DfT) although a few have been devolved to the national govern-ments in Scotland and Wales or to metropolitan bodies in big cities (in one case a regional body, Transport for the North, works with DfT to manage the franchise, and this model may become more common in the future). Note that England has no regional tier of government, so bodies such as Transport for the North have to be created as combined authorities of the various local authorities specifically to deal with transport.

The process starts with a consultation exercise as to what should be required in the new franchise. As a result of this, an invitation to tender is issued (e.g. DfT, 2018). This specifies the train service requirement, in terms of a minimum number of services to be provided at each station between spe-cific hours, including requirements regarding the time of the first train in the morning and the last train at night. This is specified separately for weekdays, Saturdays and Sundays, and may change during the course of the franchise, for instance, in the light of investment. There are also requirements in terms of maximum journey times, characteristics of the rolling stock to be used and capacity requirements in terms of the number of seats to be provided to and from key stations at peak times.

Bidders, who must have prequalified by showing that they are appropriate organisations to operate a franchise in terms of skills and experience, then submit bids in the form of a series of plans covering, inter alia, franchise management, train service and performance, revenue and customer experience and stations. The precise number and content of each plan varies from franchise to franchise. Of course, a key part of the bid is the required subsidy, year by year, or the premium the bidder is willing to pay each year if the service is profitable. These are in real terms, so, when paid, they are inflated each year by the retail prices index (RPI), and they are also adjusted for any change in track access charges. Otherwise the bidder bears the full risk of any cost increases. There is currently a degree of sharing of revenue risk in some franchises, for instance with the franchising authority bearing the risk of any shortfall in revenue attributed to lower than forecast GDP or employment growth. About a quarter of those let since 2004 have, however, been on a full revenue-risk basis. In the case of the London Overground franchise, where the franchising authority sets the timetable and fares, it bears the bulk of the revenue risk; this is also true of the Thameslink, Southern and Great Northern franchise, where major service changes led to a high revenue risk.

As part of the franchise management plan, some sort of alliance is required with Network Rail, the infrastructure manager, to show how they will work together to achieve the required levels of efficiency and quality of service. The train service plan includes detailed timetables, rolling stock to be used, rolling stock diagrams, crew rosters and forecasts of train loadings. The revenue plan includes proposals regarding fares (some – generally commuter fares and off-peak long-distance fares – are regulated as part of the franchise agreement) and marketing. The customer experience and stations plan covers issues such as passenger information and facilities at stations. An indication of the level of detail expected is provided by the fact that the overall page limit on the bid, including all plans, is 1000 pages.

Bidders must also provide models and assumptions used in forecasting revenue and costs to determine the profitability of the services. This is so that DfT can rerun the model, if necessary, using its own assumptions to provide what it calls a risk-adjusted NPV of the franchise (in other words, what it believes will be the cash flow of the operator). DfT also constructs a comparator model to use in this process. The revenue model is based on the standard industry approach as set out in the Passenger Demand Forecasting Handbook, whilst the cost model is essentially based on a forward projection of the costs of the incumbent. Before the process starts, the comparator model is used to help identify the level and quality of service that is affordable. Parent companies are required to provide a specified amount of support to cover any losses the franchise might make. If this support is exhausted, then the franchise will default and be terminated. If the assessment shows that on the DfT assessment the franchise is likely to default, then the bid is ruled out. If in other respects the bid is non-compliant, DfT may rule it out but is not obliged to do so.

Three specific metrics play an important role in the monitoring of service quality, although the metrics used vary somewhat from franchise to franchise. These are reliability (percentage of trains cancelled), punctuality (minutes of delay caused by the operator) and short formation (percentage of trains running with fewer coaches than in the plan). Benchmarks are specified for these, and if the benchmark is exceeded then the operator is required to prepare recovery plans (for instance, in one recent case the recovery plan required overcoming reliability problems by leasing more rolling stock and recruiting more staff) and may also be required to pay a penalty. If performance remains unsatisfactory, the ultimate penalty is that the franchise may be terminated early.

Existing franchises are typically awarded for a seven-year period, with the possibility of a three-year extension, although in the past franchises of up to 25 years have been awarded where major investment was involved. Because it is recognised that short franchises give inadequate incentive for investments with a longer life than the franchise, mechanisms are in place to correct for this. In the case of rolling stock, franchisees usually lease rolling stock, and if it is considered that leasing rolling stock for a period much less than its life will impose risks on the leasing company, which will then inflate its leasing charges, the government may give a commitment that the succeeding franchisee will continue to lease the stock for a certain number of years, although such undertakings have not needed to be offered in recent years. In the case of investments, for instance at stations, made directly by the franchisee, DfT may agree that these will be designated franchise assets that pass to the next franchisee, and that the residual value of these assets at the end of the franchise may be paid to the investing franchisee. But this happens very rarely because of the challenge of agreeing a valuation for the 'residual value'. Additionally, franchisees are required to establish an innovation fund; use of this fund for specific projects is subject to the agreement of the Rail Safety and Standards Board that this is an appropriate use of the fund.

In the past, franchise contracts were awarded on the basis of the most financially attractive bid. But following the Brown Review (Brown, 2013), points are now allocated for quality of the bid as well and the award criterion is that the franchise should go to the most economically advantageous tender. Scores are attached by industry experts to each of the plans specified above, and a weighted sum of these scores is added to the present value of the franchise payments expected by DfT to be made in practice following risk adjustment. In practice it seems that quality of rolling stock is a key factor in the award of these points, leading to a high (arguably excessive) level of investment in new rolling stock in recent bids. Because these plans are used to help determine the award of the tender, it is considered that the award would be open to legal challenge if DfT did not take steps to ensure that the plan is delivered in its entirety. Thus the plans are contractualised, leading the franchise agreement to impose very detailed obligations on the franchisee (for instance, in the East Midlands case the current franchise agreement stipulates that specific stations should be fitted with closed circuit television, that specific classes of train should have modifications to equipment such as brakes and even that the kitchen at a specific depot should be refurbished). In the case of the timetable, attempts are made to ensure that the way in which it is contractualised does not remove all flexibility; of course the franchisee and DfT may agree a variation, but such negotiations are time consuming and are constrained legally.

DfT has made use of direct awards on a number of occasions, usually for relatively short extensions of existing franchises, for a variety of reasons. These include bringing the end date into line with another franchise with which it is to be merged, or to or from which some services are to be transferred, and most importantly, during the franchising standstill that accompanied the review of franchising that followed problems with the award of the West Coast franchise in 2012 (it was found that DfT had not correctly followed its own process in this award and the award had to be cancelled). In addition, direct awards have been used for some franchises whilst awaiting the results of the Williams Review.

Obviously in the case of a direct award, a key question is whether the bid appears to be value for money compared with the costs and revenue suggested by DfT's own comparator model. If it does not, then DfT may go out to competitive tender even for short franchises. Alternatively, DfT has a contract for provision of an Operator of Last Resort (OLR) which could be brought in under a direct award. The OLR is particularly likely to be involved when a franchise fails, although given sufficient warning of the problem, a direct award to the incumbent or a new franchise competition are also possible outcomes. In the case of direct awards, a check is made that there are no excess profits, as required by Regulation (EC) 1370/2007; this is not in general considered necessary where the award is based on competitive tendering, although it remains a relevant consideration.

Thus in current British practice on franchising, benchmarking as such is not used, but comparisons based on the cost of the incumbent are. It is arguable that benchmarking across all operators should be used, rather than just the costs of the incumbent, in order to ensure that franchise agreements do secure value for money compared with industry best practice and not just the costs of the incumbent. As for other economic regulators in the UK, in sectors such as energy and water, modelling of heterogeneity between operators would be a challenge in obtaining useful results from the benchmarking framework – though with roughly 20 operators, there would be more data to play with than is usually the case for economic regulators in the UK.

Quality of service does play an important part in the franchising process, although that has not prevented great concern about the quality of services, leading to a 'root and branch' review (the Williams Review (report completed but not yet published)), the leader of which has said that franchising in its current form is not working. In particular, reliability of services has plummeted in recent years for a variety of reasons, including late-running infrastructure works and rolling stock deliveries, leading to rushed revisions of timetables to take account of these. But there is also suspicion that fragmentation of the industry, with multiple train operators and a separate infrastructure manager, has hampered the efficient management of these problems.

It will be seen also that the way in which quality is currently managed leads to the franchising authority becoming heavily involved in the intricate detail of management of the franchised services, and to franchise agreements which leave the franchisee very little freedom of action. This has been heavily criticised. For this reason it seems likely, in the opinion of the authors, that franchising will go in one of two ways. Where there is a strong reason for the imposition of public service obligations and particularly where services are subsidised, the train service requirement may be presented in the form of an actual timetable to be run, the actual rolling stock to be used may be specified and so on, and the contract let as a concession to run this service. Where it is felt that market forces are strong enough to dictate quality of service, then the degree of regulation of quality may be much reduced and a much simpler franchise let, or indeed operators may be left simply to run whatever they see as being commercially justified without a franchise. The latter approach – of open access competition – has been promoted by the Competition and Markets Authority for long-distance services (Competition and Markets Authority, 2016).

There are other important incentive mechanisms that should encourage train operators to improve performance. Firstly, passengers are entitled to compensation from train operators for delayed and cancelled trains, this protection forming part of the contract between the passenger and the operator when purchasing tickets. In recent years this scheme has been enhanced to be more transparent and easier for passengers to claim. Increased propensity to claim amongst passengers should further increase the incentives on operators to improve performance, though as with farebox revenue more widely, these incentives may be muted on lesser-used routes.

In addition, operators are also subject to performance incentives within their track access charge contracts (referred to as the Schedule 8 performance regime). These provide for compensation payments to be made between operators and Network Rail and other operators for unplanned disruptions caused by another party. Thus if train operators cause delays to the trains of another operator, then they have to pay compensation equal to the estimated long-term financial impact of the delay in terms of revenue. Similarly, if Network Rail causes delays that impact on an operator then compensation is due from the infrastructure manager (including for delays caused by engineering work beyond that provided for in the base level, compensation for which is paid under the Schedule 4 regime). There are thus incentives for an operator to improve its own performance in order to capture revenue benefits on its own franchise, but also to avoid paying compensation to other operators for loss of revenue due to delays caused to other operators' services. Likewise, Network Rail is incentivised to improve performance: paying penalties if performance is below set levels and receiving bonuses for performance above benchmark levels. These incentives operate in addition to those imposed by specific targets set in franchise agreements.

As a final note, at the time of writing following the COVID-19 developments, all formerly franchised services in Great Britain are being run under management contracts with all revenue and cost risk borne by government, and operators permitted to make a return of 2% of turnover. It may well be some time before operators are in a position to take revenue risk going forward and, as noted earlier, the authors' expectation from the Williams Review is that more services will be let based on concession-based contracts once the rail network returns to some type of 'normality'. Under such a scenario, whilst there will still be a competition to win the concession, benchmarking information on costs could play a more important role because the award process will be solely based on the cost of providing a specified service. Further, the Schedule 8 regime is likely to change, as operators will no longer face revenue risk – and the modelling of the efficient cost of providing a given level of quality could become much more important.

8.3   REGULATION OF NETWORK RAIL

The Office of Rail and Road (ORR) regulates Network Rail essentially on the basis of five-year control periods, with a periodic review before the start of each control period. The periodic review starts with the DfT (or Transport Scotland in the case of Scotland) specifying how much funding is available for rail infrastructure in the coming period (the Statement of Funds Available) and what it expects of the infrastructure in terms of reliability and safety (the High Level Output Specification). Until the current control period, this process also included enhancements, but now these investments are dealt with separately by DfT, which decides which schemes should go ahead and funds them.

The regulator then considers whether the funding is adequate to deliver the targets, including revenue from track access charges, where it considers the appropriate level and structure for the forthcoming control period. If the ORR decides it is not adequate then it must agree with DfT a change, either to the level of funding or to the quality indicators required (in principle some routes could be cut, but it is much more likely that quality would be impacted as service cuts would be politically problematic).

The regulator incentivises Network Rail primarily through setting targets for reductions in cost, which are built into the financial settlement for the forth-coming five-year control period resulting from the periodic review. The regu-lator has used benchmarking in setting these targets. At the time Network Rail was set up, there had been a major expansion of spending on the infrastructure following a fatal accident at Hatfield in 2000. The ORR carried out a review of Network Rail's efficiency performance, in the light of large cost increases, and commissioned a wide range of studies for its 2003 Interim Review of the company's finances. A key weakness of the 2003 review, though, was that the ORR's efficiency determination was ultimately based on two bottom-up consultant reviews of Network Rail's business plan (LEK, Halcrow and TTCI, 2003 and Accenture, 2003). These results were supplemented by internal benchmarking, which indicated the kind of savings that could be achieved if Network Rail implemented its own best practice consistently across the network. But there was no benchmarking against other organisations.

Ultimately then, the 2003 Interim Review was unable to provide a clear, empirically based assessment of Network Rail's relative efficiency position based on hard data from external sources. The ORR nevertheless set a tough efficiency target of 31% over five years (2004–2009). However, costs were starting from a very high base. Thus, although costs then started to fall as Network Rail set about delivering its efficiency targets, by the time of the next periodic review in 2008, the scene was set to take the benchmarking approach a step forward by attempting international comparisons. These studies were described in Chapter 5, and led to the conclusion that there was a 40% effi-ciency gap compared with European best practices. The ORR also gave the company ten years to close the gap, with only two-thirds of the gap targeted to be closed during the immediate control period (control period 4 (CP4), 2009–2014).

During CP4 (to 2014) Network Rail was close to achieving its target, deliv-ering savings of around 18% across operations, maintenance and renewals, compared to a target of 21%. However, during CP5 efficiency performance worsened. Instead of efficiency continuing to improve towards meeting the overall gap identified in 2008, efficiency performance deteriorated by around 12% (see ORR, 2018). The regulator identified a number of reasons for this worsening performance, including a lack of planning which meant that Network Rail was not well set up to deliver planned renewals at the start of CP5, which reduced productivity. In addition, part way through CP5 the government imposed strict cash limits on Network Rail, when the company was formally reclassified as a state-owned company, which meant that the company's borrowing would be classed as government borrowing. This led to a reprofiling of work that further exacerbated the situation. It was also argued that the company was too centrally driven and therefore there was not enough substance behind the planned efficiency targets; and access to the network was becoming an increasing problem given growing traffic, causing costs to rise.

During the 2018 regulatory review – to set targets for CP6 (2020–2024), the efficiency challenge from the regulator was largely based on bottom-up studies and challenges of Network Rail's plans, but was supplemented by econometric benchmarking using data for Network Rail's geographical routes (and a further disaggregation beneath that). This benchmarking exercise used route level data (ten routes at the time) over five years; thus making it comparable in terms of datasets for other regulated utilities (e.g. the water and sewerage business). The analysis was supplemented by data for 37 maintenance delivery units (MDUs; covering maintenance costs only), based on two years' data.

In line with other regulators, the range of explanatory variables, given the sample size and data availability, is relatively small and does not extend to the inclusion of quality variables. The MDU dataset did include a wider range of variables, helped by the larger cross section (37 MDUs), such as line speed, measures of electrification and criticality (this relating to the importance of the route in terms of how costly a delay would be). These additional variables, though, are more to do with the characteristics of the infrastructure and the nature of the services running than on directly trying to incorporate measures of quality into the cost function. The analysis indicated an efficiency gap, if all parts of the network could achieve an estimate of best practice, of around 16% (having made an assumption that part of the cost gap was due to random factors).

Overall, however, the ORR determined that the econometric modelling was not sufficiently robust to be used on its own, but it formed confirmatory evidence to their other studies. Still, the exercise is a good starting point in the view of the authors and we would expect this work to take on increased importance in future reviews, particularly given the enhanced devolution within Network Rail. International benchmarking was not used because of perceived data comparability issues. As noted, quality measures were not included within the econometric framework. Clearly, in the absence of other measures, this approach of setting cost targets could therefore threaten quality of service and investment. But there is also a set of quality targets in terms of delays for which Network Rail is responsible, as well as asset condition. The overall target set by the ORR for CP6 was an efficiency gain of around 10%, which, if achieved, would broadly offset the deterioration in efficiency seen during CP5.

There is also a licence condition requiring Network Rail to 'meet the reasonable needs of its customers'. These are set out in a 'balanced scorecard' listing key performance indicators that are crucial to each train operator, as well as targets at the level of the Network Rail route, and the regulator may impose penalties if these targets are not reached (although the effectiveness of financial penalties on a nationalised industry is open to debate). Specifically, the ORR is increasing the emphasis on Network Rail focusing on the impact it has on the passenger, through targeting measures such as the company's contribution to the delays that passengers experience. The scorecard targets were intended to be agreed between Network Rail and the train operating companies, but in the majority of cases agreement was not reached in the current control period. Alongside these targets and penalties there is the Schedule 4 and 8 performance regime that additionally incentivises improved performance (see section 8.2 above).

The regulator reviews the adequacy of Network Rail business plans, including how it proposes to achieve the targeted quality of service, and its plans for investment (although as noted above in respect of enhancements, these are largely determined by funding decisions taken by the Department for Transport outside the periodic review process). Investment is also encouraged by the fact that the regulator examines asset management plans, including estimated life cycle costs, rather than just cash flow. However, the ability to optimise life cycle costs has been limited in recent years by a financial crisis in Network Rail caused by the imposition of cash limits at a time of rising costs (as noted above, this coincided with Network Rail being formally classified as a state-owned company). As a result, some renewals have been postponed even where this is estimated to raise life cycle costs. For the current control period, the regulator required Network Rail to increase its level of renewals in order to improve asset sustainability.

One innovation in the current control period (CP6) is that targets are being set separately for the eight geographical Network Rail routes and also for the 'systems operator' function. This is intended to benefit implementation by making the targets more directly relevant to managers taking decisions at the route or headquarters level. It will also permit a degree of benchmarking of routes against each other, in terms of both costs and performance on quality. Network Rail has also more recently divided its network further into 14 routes, grouped into five regions. Thus the scope for benchmarking is increased (or will be over time) with the availability of a larger cross section of routes (though routes within the same region may not be seen as totally independent observations for econometric work). By way of comparison, in its gas distribution benchmarking approach, Ofgem benchmarks eight firms, some of which have common ownership.

It was noted above that enhancements were taken out of the regulatory framework, with DfT taking direct responsibility. As discussed above, recent years have seen significant problems of underperformance against efficiency targets within Network Rail. During the previous control period (CP5),

Network Rail was targeted with a substantial improvement in efficiency performance but in fact delivered a substantial deterioration in efficiency. This applied across different cost categories but has particularly impacted on capital expenditure (renewals and enhancements). There appears to be no formal benchmarking regime for enhancements, though a new initiative, entitled the Transport Infrastructure Efficiency Strategy (TIES), is seeking to develop a benchmarking framework and other initiatives to bring about efficiency improvements across transport infrastructure projects (including identifying commonalities between modes for similar types of project). A renewed focus on benchmarking the efficiency with which projects (enhancements and renewals) are carried out could potentially deliver substantial savings, and there are lessons that can be learnt from both other transport infrastructures and other sectors (see for example, Smith et al., 2019).

8.4   VERTICAL SEPARATION

There has long been concern that the separation of infrastructure from operations has resulted in inflation of costs, since neither the train operator nor the infrastructure manager is incentivised to optimise the system as a whole (McNulty, 2011). Thus Britain has experimented with alliances between the train operator and the infrastructure manager, in which they work closely together and in one case actually shared changes in costs and revenues from the base position. This should fully align incentives between infrastructure manager and train operator. However, this arrangement only lasted for three years and it has been impossible to negotiate such an arrangement again, as the infrastructure manager does not wish to bear the revenue risk and the train operator does not wish to bear the increasing cost of infrastructure. Moreover, alignment of incentives is only the case for the main user of the infrastructure in question. In Britain the franchising system means that much track is used solely or mainly by one operator, with some degree of use by other franchises with overlapping services and by freight operators. However, the key main lines are used by a variety of operators as often suburban, regional and intercity services are under separate franchises, and there are also freight operations and, on one main line, some open access passenger operations as well. Nevertheless, as noted above, some form of alliance is required by current franchising arrangements; such alliances include arrangements for regular meetings and exchange of information, joint training programmes and secondment of staff.

One issue the Williams Review is considering is whether a closer relationship between the infrastructure manager and the train operator is required. There are alternative ways in which this might be achieved, perhaps by leasing infrastructure to the leading train operator on a particular route, establishing a state-owned holding company for a particular route (which might still contract out train operations and track maintenance) or even by a return to totally vertically integrated companies. Although the Williams Review findings have not yet been published, it appears from statements by Keith Williams himself that it will recommend establishing a new strategic body responsible both for the infrastructure and for concession operations. Such a body would be better placed to coordinate planning of infrastructure and services; it would also place concessions at one remove from direct political control. However, whilst the government has announced its intention of moving towards more concessions (i.e. retaining revenue risk itself) when the current arrangements for dealing with the coronavirus end, it has remained silent on the issue of creating a new strategic body.

8.5   CONCLUSION

It would be expected that competitive tendering should ensure value for money for rail passenger services, without extensive need for benchmarking. But in practice train operating costs in Britain have increased whilst there has been concern over service quality, so perhaps there should be a greater role for benchmarking in checking the value for money achieved by franchises in practice. In Britain there has almost invariably been strong competition for franchises, with several shortlisted bidders, so the measures adopted to encourage competition appear to have worked, even if this has not led to a good outcome in terms of costs. The expected move to more concession-based gross cost type contracts (as used widely in Sweden and Germany) could lead to greater focus on cost reduction, and perhaps an increased role for benchmarking to inform the assessment of bids. Obviously, in cases where there is only a single bid, or a very small number of bids, benchmarking to check value for money becomes more important, as it does in the case of direct awards. However, currently, as has been seen, a comparator model based on the costs of the incumbent is used rather than a model based on industry best practice.

Benchmarking is more important in the case of the infrastructure manager, which is essentially a monopoly. As has been seen, benchmarking of Network Rail against rail infrastructure managers in other European countries has been used to assess the scope for cost reductions by the British infrastructure manager, but there are concerns as to comparability of data and as to whether it is possible to adequately allow for heterogeneity of circumstances. Currently, in terms of econometric benchmarking techniques, more emphasis is being placed on internal benchmarking within Network Rail, a process which should be furthered by the reorganisation of Network Rail into regions and lines, with much more autonomy than in the past. Greater emphasis is also being placed on bottom-up approaches.

It will be seen that there are detailed measures for ensuring quality of service in both the franchising process and the regulation of the infrastructure manager in Britain, but how successful these have been is open to doubt, given dissatisfaction with service quality in recent years. To a large extent, these measures rely on DfT taking detailed decisions about investment, what services should be delivered and even how they should be delivered. Significant funding has been available for rail infrastructure since Network Rail's creation in 2002, partly because the company's debt was not part of the government's balance sheet, a situation that has now changed. It has, however, been very problematic to ensure that Network Rail used this money wisely and indeed the company's efficiency performance has been far worse than expected in recent years. The failure to get a grip on costs remains an issue and potentially undermines the ability of Network Rail and funders to justify future investments, and risks diluting the available funding more than would be necessary if the company were operating more efficiently. Recent reforms to devolve greater powers to Network Rail regions and routes, supported by yardstick competition, could have an important role to play in future. However, the Williams Review is expected to suggest substantial changes both in the franchising process and in the regulation of Network Rail. It is expected that a new strategic body will take responsibility for both infrastructure and planning operations, with use of concessions on the basis of gross cost contracts to perform the actual operations.

ACKNOWLEDGEMENTS

We are very grateful to Richard Davies and Neil Fleming of the Department for Transport, London, for comments on an earlier draft. We are solely responsible for any remaining errors and for any opinions expressed.

NOTE

1. Since this chapter was written, a White Paper resulting from the Williams Review has been published (see Great British Railways – publishing.service.gov.uk). It confirms the proposal to create a new railway authority (Great British Railways) to absorb both Network Rail and much of the rail work of the Department for Transport. It will be responsible for planning both infrastructure and passenger services, with the latter being operated as concessions by private operators, except that it is stated that operators of more profitable services may have more commercial freedom and a degree of revenue sharing. Freight will remain the responsibility of commercial private operators.

REFERENCES

Accenture (2003), *Review of Network Rail's Supply Chain*, London.

Brown, R. (2013), *The Brown Review of the Rail Franchising Programme*, Cm 8526: London.

Competition and Markets Authority (2016), *Competition in Passenger Rail Services in Great Britain: A Policy Document*.

DfT (Department for Transport) (2018), East Midlands franchise 2018: invitation to tender.

LEK, Halcrow and TTCI (2003), Report to the Office of the Rail Regulator, Network Rail and SRA: International benchmarking, London.

McNulty, R. (2011), *Realising the Potential of Rail in Great Britain – Final Independent Report of the Rail Value for Money Study*, London: Department for Transport.

Office of Road and Rail (ORR), (2018), *Periodic Review Final Determination, Summary of Conclusions for England & Wales*, October 2018.

Smith, A.S.J., P.E. Wheat, J.-C. Thiebaud and A. Stead (2019), *Capex Bias and Adverse Incentives in Incentive Regulation: Issues and Solutions*, International Transport Forum Working Group Paper (www.itf-oecd.org/sites/default/files/docs/capex-bias-adverse-incentives.pdf).

9.   Belgian ports and airports

Eddy Van de Voorde

9.1   INTRODUCTION

Although the seaport and airport sectors are both highly competitive, geographic factors and constraints on the development of new facilities may result in monopoly power for particular ports and airports (Chapter 7). In practice, there is always a possibility that some actors will increase their market power, thereby creating a risk that such power will be abused. At that time, the benchmarking of ports and airports as a whole, as well as of individual functions or actors within them, could be useful as a means of identifying potential problems of inefficiency and/or abuses of monopoly power.

In this chapter, we use benchmarking and yardstick competition to identify potential problems and the resulting need for regulation, based on two specific cases concerning, respectively, the Antwerp seaport and Brussels Airport Company. The underlying idea is that each case and the corresponding learning process can offer potential input for similar situations in other countries, for instance with respect to the types of incentive schemes that could be adopted, the ways in which quality levels are measured and the means of coping with concessions and penalties. This chapter is intended to direct special attention to the generalization of case study results to an environment that differs in terms of both geography and economics.

The first case addresses the discussion concerning the application of penalties, as provided for in the concession agreement between the Antwerp Port Authority and major international terminal operating companies. The case is considered from several perspectives, including the extent to which these penalties can be enforced by third parties and the extent to which competing companies are disadvantaged by the Port Authority not collecting the penalties. The analysis corresponds closely to developments in port governance.

The second case concerns the regulation of the airport in Brussels, with special attention to certain aspects including the duration of the regulated period, the issue of adjusted single-till or dual-till systems, the question of whether tariffs should be based on reference airports or on a financial model, the distinction between regulated and non-regulated activities, and the role of the economic regulator. One interesting issue is that the regulatory process applied in this case has also been linked to airports of the size of Copenhagen, Lisbon, Madrid and Rome Fiumicino.

The output of these two cases can be used for two purposes. First, it provides an overview of crucial points of discussion in the debate concerning benchmarking and regulation. Second, the outcomes also make it possible to determine the extent to which quantitative (or other) benchmarks can be generalized.

9.2   A SEAPORT CASE: COPING WITH CONCESSION (OR OTHER) PENALTIES

9.2.1   Seaports: The Regulatory Framework

Relatively few scientific studies have addressed existing regulations on port authorities and port-related activities. One exception is the topic of 'port governance' (see e.g. Van de Voorde and Verhoeven, 2017). The topic itself provides evidence of the limited presence of regulations.

International regulations do exist for a port's most important customers, and particularly for shipping companies relating to worker protection, safety and environmental considerations. These regulations primarily concern the requirements for marine fuel. In this regard, since 1 January 2015, an allowable sulphur content of 0.10 per cent m/m (by mass) has applied to marine fuel used within the emission control areas (ECAs). The ECAs include the Baltic Sea area, the North Sea area, the North American area and the United States Caribbean Sea area. Outside these ECAs, an allowable sulphur content of 3.5 per cent m/m will apply until 1 January 2020. Thereafter, the maximum allowable sulphur content outside the ECAs will be 0.5 per cent m/m (IMO MARPOL Annex VI Reg. 14). Since 2010, vessels moored in ports within the European Union have not been allowed to use any marine fuel with a sulphur content of more than 0.1 per cent m/m (Directive 2005/33/EC). Another convention from 2004 requires the signatory flag state to ensure that vessels registered in that state conform to the standards and procedures for the management and monitoring of ballast water and sediment (International Convention for the Control and Management of Ships' Ballast Water and Sediments – Ballast Water Management Convention). This is intended to prevent the spread of hazardous aquatic organisms from one region to another through the release of ballast water. More specifically, this means that, beginning in 2024, all vessels will be required to have an approved Ballast Water Management Treatment System on board.

Even within a specific port environment, however, certain regulations apply to these shipping companies and their vessels. One typical example is provided by the Port State Control, which is used to inspect foreign vessels in national ports with regard to safety and the environment, the qualifications of the crew and on-board working and living conditions. The primary goal is to eliminate substandard vessels. It amounts to a reaction to the deficient inspections of the flag states, and particularly those of the least wealthy states, who have delegated these inspections to classification agencies.

Moreover, the regulatory framework includes measures focusing on the safety of ports, ranging from the protection of the actual seaports up to and including the protection and inspection of cargo. The International Maritime Organization (IMO) plays an important role in this regard as well. Some countries (e.g. the United States) have specific programmes that have global consequences for the entire maritime and port network. Typical examples include the Container Security Initiative and the Customs Trade Partnership against terrorism.

Questions remain concerning the necessity of additional regulations within a port context. Ports in nearly all countries are subject to at least partial governmental control, whether direct or indirect. In contrast to the aviation sector, however, there is hardly any control over the published prices in ports (e.g. port dues), to say nothing of the prices that are actually applied. Ports are also not usually subject to benchmarking. Does this mean that it is assumed that there is no excessive concentration of power in port contexts and/or that there is no risk that any position of power that might exist will be abused? With regard to concessions, there is a common preference for competitive tendering as a tool which should ensure effective competition.

Nevertheless, things are changing within the port landscape. These changes are related to one of the last true assets at the disposal of port authorities, i.e. the award of concessions. It seems self-evident that, when awarding a concession, a government would monitor the proper observance of all applicable legal rules. Even after the fact, however, close monitoring is needed in order to determine whether the concession terms specified in the contract are being respected. If this is not the case, there is a chance of commercial damage to third parties.

9.2.2   Uncertainty for Port Authorities

Port authorities and port companies are often confronted with risks and uncertainties. One typical example involves the need to respond to a development in legislation concerning spatial planning and the delineation of the seaport area, which is sometimes referred to as the port perimeter. In addition, changes are occurring throughout the world with regard to the tax regimes to which port companies are subject. For example, in 2013, the European Commission launched an official investigation to determine whether the state of corporate taxes for ports in certain countries is compatible with European rules on state aid and whether the ports in those countries should be subjected to corporate taxing as well.

Another sensitive issue has to do with the application of and developments in environmental legislation. In many cases, there are also several ongoing lawsuits, each with its own risks, and many that could have an important financial impact.

In the following sections, we provide a detailed examination of a concrete case within the port of Antwerp. More specifically, it involves the question of whether the port company should collect fines specified in a concession agreement linked to tonnage obligations. The learning process linked to the concrete steps taken by all of the actors involved, along with the legal arguments adopted in this regard, can undoubtedly provide more general insights for the global port sector.

9.2.3   Concession Agreements and Transshipment Obligations

Within the port perimeter, several companies work at terminals that have been given in concessions by the port authorities. This is done according to concession agreements, which specify aspects including the corresponding concession payment. In many cases, these payments are also linked to transshipment obligations (i.e. each year, the companies must process a certain tonnage of freight that has been agreed upon with the port administration in advance). The contract indicates that failure to meet these objectives constitutes cause for fines.

In 2012, the Antwerp Port Authority announced that, of the 148 concession agreements that it had concluded with companies in the port at that time, 15 included volume obligations. Six of these 15 agreements gave cause for collecting fines. One can raise the question whether these are sensible incentives. How far can the Terminal Operating Company control how much it handles? But presumably firms are willing to bid on this basis. As such, it is a purely commercial transaction.

Based on the concession agreements that had been concluded, the two largest container handling agents, PSA and DP World, were required to pay fines amounting to €51 million in 2012, because they had not met their transshipment obligations in the 2008–2011 period. The total fines of €51 million were broken down into €35.5 million for PSA and €15.6 million for DP World. In November 2012, the Antwerp Port Authority indicated the desire to reduce these fines drastically, or even to waive them. One important argument was that the strict fine clauses from 2004 were outdated, due to the economic crisis. Future business should take precedence over short-term fines. The Port Authority had not booked the fines as future income.

The port company's attitude was the subject of strong criticism. Other companies within the port perimeter were required to pay their fines. The Katoen Natie company had to pay a fine of €326,000 for one of its terminals, as the transshipment obligations for 2010 and 2011 had not been met. Although the company paid the fine, the port company refunded the amount due to a 'material error'. Katoen Natie then retransferred the amount to the Port Authority. Moreover, it is uncertain whether waiving fines would be effective in generating more traffic and/or anchoring PSA and DP World more firmly in the port, assuming that the shipping companies – and not the terminal operators – are the most important decision-makers in the selection process within a port (Meersman et al., 2010b).

On 14 December 2012, Katoen Natie filed a complaint with the European Commission (DG Competition) about unlawful state aid and the violation of the principle of equality. The same company also declared that the Port Authority's auditors were in default, as they had not booked the fines as potential income.

In late December 2012, the Port Authority's supervisory board announced that a new decision would be taken in accordance with the principle of equality and legally tested against the anti-trust law and the allocation of governmental support. Explicit reference was made to the concession conditions of 2004, which stated that the fines could be adjusted in the interest of the commercial and competitive environment and after benchmarking with comparable terminals in north-western Europe.

In January 2013, the Belgian Competition Council launched an investigation into the manner in which the Antwerp Port Authority was collecting fines from companies that had not met their transshipment obligations. The investigation was also intended to determine whether any unauthorized discrimination had occurred. The application of unequal conditions to competing companies for equivalent performance is potentially problematic. Pursuant to Article 102 of the Treaty on the Functioning of the European Union (TFEU), applying dissimilar conditions to equivalent transactions with other trading partners, thereby placing them at a competitive disadvantage, when carried out by an undertaking holding a dominant position, is considered an abuse of dominance and therefore is prohibited.

In addition, on 7 March 2013, Katoen Natie and Seaport Terminals subpoenaed the Flemish Region for its alleged refusal to exercise administrative oversight on the Antwerp Port Authority, including the payments to be charged due to unmet tonnage obligations. On 12 February 2015, the court declared the claim admissible, albeit unfounded across the board. Katoen Natie filed an appeal against this decision on 21 May 2015.

In early March 2013, the Port Authority sent a proposal to its supervisory board to file a claim against the PSA and DP World companies in the amount of €15 million for not meeting the tonnage obligations in the 2008–2012 period. This amount was considerably lower than the original fine of €67 million. An additional motivation had to do with the fact that, in recent years, no fines had been collected in the German ports either. In Rotterdam, no penalty clauses were included for Maasvlakte 1, while those for Maasvlakte 2 were substantially adjusted.

On 10 April 2013, preliminary relief proceedings were launched with the president of the commercial court in Antwerp. In preliminary relief proceedings, this court declared itself as having no jurisdiction on 1 July 2013. An appeal was also declared unfounded in a decision of the Court of Appeals on 2 April 2014.

The case proceeded. On 15 January 2016, the European Commission announced that it would launch an in-depth investigation into two potential state aid measures. The first was the decision of 26 March 2013 on the reduction of fines for the 2009–2012 period for PSA and DP World, as motivated by the economic crisis. The second was the enforcement of the reduced payment for Antwerp Gateway NV, a subsidiary of DP World, based on a decision of 21 May 2014. In February 2016, the Brussels court of first instance ruled against Katoen Natie in the case of the Antwerp port fines.

In March 2016, the European Commission published a report that followed the arguments of Katoen Natie on a number of points concerning the potential infringement of the rules on state aid. An important point in this regard is that government funds were involved, as the Port Authority was not a private company (the conditions under which the use of resources of a public body or a publicly controlled company is considered state aid are illustrated in the European Commission's Notice on the notion of state aid, analysed in Chapter 10 of this volume).[1] As to the controversial measures, the Commission found that a long period of time had passed between the beginning of the economic crisis (late 2008, early 2009) and the decision taken in 2013 to waive a portion of the fines. In addition, the report stated that the waiving of a portion of the fines was disproportional, given that transshipment had declined by 38 per cent, while the fines had been reduced by approximately 80 per cent. Moreover, the measure seemed to be of a selective character, as it applied to only two companies. This was followed by a period of mutual conclusions, in anticipation of the final decision by the European Commission pursuant to the EU rules on state aid.

A ruling would ultimately come about three years later. In December 2018, the European Commission ruled that the reduced fines for failing to meet the tonnage obligations did not constitute illegal state aid. The Port Authority's decision could be defended within the broader framework of the economic crisis after 2009. At that point, PSA and DP World were still in the start-up phase, and they were important players within the port. Although the Port

Authority was indeed a governmental actor, the intervention was in line with what a private company would have done and thus satisfied the so-called 'market economy operator principle', which allows the exclusion of state aid.

9.2.4 The Learning Process

The port and maritime sectors have relatively few characteristics that could lead to possible abuse of a monopoly position. This applies to all actors. In virtually all sub-markets, so many players are operating that there is little chance that a monopoly situation could emerge, let alone be abused.

The Port Authority constitutes a possible exception. It has less influence over the operations of the port than was previously the case, however, and it has access to fewer economic incentives. One exception has to do with concessions, which constitute one of the few remaining assets at the disposal of a port authority. It would be reasonable to assume the existence of regulations and oversight with regard to the auctioning process associated with the allocation of concessions. As illustrated in the case presented here, monitoring and regulations are sometimes needed even with regard to the application of contractually established clauses – if only to avoid the necessity of contesting legal procedures at various levels.

This provides an incentive to conduct a detailed analysis in the initial phases (i.e. the research phase) with regard to all concession agreements that have been established up to that point. This would undoubtedly yield many good comparisons, including between terminal operators, in addition to providing an idea of the diversity of penalty (and other) clauses.

9.3 AN AIRPORT CASE: THE ECONOMIC REGULATION OF BRUSSELS AIRPORT COMPANY

9.3.1 Introduction

This section is based on the results of a study on the possible revision of the existing regulation of the Brussels Airport Company (BAC), which expired in 2011 (Meersman et al., 2010a).

Brussels Airport Company (BAC) was privatized in 2004. After a few financial movements, this process resulted in 75 per cent of the shares being in the hands of a private investor, with 25 per cent remaining in the hands of the Belgian state. From that time on, the operations of BAC were subject to a new regulatory framework consisting of two Royal Decrees. One was the Royal Decree of 27 May 2004 concerning the conversion of Brussels International Airport Company (BIAC) into a publicly traded company under private law and relating to the airport facilities. The other was the Royal Decree of 21 June 2004 relating to the allocation of the exploitation licence of the Brussels National Airport to the publicly traded company BIAC NV, which was renamed 'The Brussels Airport Company NV' (BAC) during the general shareholders' meeting of 4 October 2006.

The economic regulations applying to BAC at that time contained several important principles. They drew a distinction between regulated and non-regulated activities. The adjusted single-till principle applied, in which income from the non-regulated activities could be used to subsidize the regulated activities under certain conditions. The regulations provided for a transition from an adjusted single-till system to a dual-till system (without cross-subsidy) by 2026. Reference airports are used with regard to fees and the quality of services. The fees for regulated activities are set according to a formula for a period of five years, with indexation. The fees should guarantee a fair profit margin for the regulated activities, and they are coordinated with the fees of the reference airports. The users are consulted about the fee formula and any adjustments during the regulated period. The operations of BAC are subject to adherence to conditions in several areas, including the quality of services, capacity guarantees, safety and security, and the environment. An economic regulator oversees the proper application of the prevailing regulatory framework and approves the fees for the regulated activities.

The most important objective of the first economic regulations through 2011 was always to minimize or eliminate the negative effects of a 'natural monopoly' and the associated risk of abuse of the dominant position. This essentially amounts to preventing a situation in which the pricing would not be related to costs, by returning excessive profits compared to the level of competitive markets (avoidance of overcharging). This is done by identifying 'acceptable' costs based on the value of the regulated activities (regulatory assets base). In addition, an incentivizing system is provided, which urges the airport operator to work in an efficient (and cost-efficient) manner (e.g. by establishing a fixed price for a multi-year regulated period, with the airport operator retaining the benefits of successfully limiting costs). This leads to a greater profit margin for the operator. Moreover, the airport operator is encouraged to carry out timely, efficient investments by guaranteeing an appropriate return on the invested capital and by monitoring and ensuring that the proposed model of economic regulation can be funded. One can raise the question, what is an appropriate return? This is a very contentious issue in the literature (e.g. the Averch-Johnson effect). Finally, a general balance must be provided between economic and societal interests.

In 2010, the category of 'regulated activities' included the landing and take-off of aircraft, the parking of aircraft, the use of facilities by passengers, the provision of fuel for aircraft through centralized infrastructure and the operations aimed at ensuring the safety of passengers and the security of airport facilities.

The following sections provide an in-depth examination of a detailed proposal for an adjusted set of regulations. Explicit consideration is given to the European framework leading towards a uniform European regulatory scheme on the levying of airport charges and an accompanying system of economic regulation, based on Directive 2009/12/EC.

The key aspects of the Directive can be clustered into the following elements: regular consultation between the airport managers and the airport users with regard to airport charges, transparency, non-discrimination, differentiation and independent oversight by a regulator.

9.3.2　Length of the Regulated Period

One area of attention concerns a possible reduction in the length of the regulated period from five years to one year, with the fees being established annually after consultation with the users and after approval by the economic regulator. The issue emerges from Directive 2009/12/EC on airport charges, which foresees regular consultations on the determination of fees. It thus concerns the length of the regulated period, taking into consideration the economic context, including the market relationship between the parties and the stability (or instability) of the sector. What impact does the length of regulated period have on the incentives for the airport operator to work in a cost-efficient manner? If the multi-year determination of fees is favourable for the economic development of the airport, the users and the airport operator must have arrived at an agreement to this end, in accordance with the European Directive. Another possible solution would be to allow the regulated period to be longer than one year (with a fixed fee), but with annual consultation between the users and the airport operator concerning other elements (e.g. quality level, investments). Which risks are borne by the airport operator and users within a system of annual consultation? If a multi-year system is retained, would it be advisable to have an adjustment mechanism in case of unexpected external shocks (e.g. the attacks on 11 September 2001 in the USA)?

The arguments can be summarized as follows. In the existing system, the five-year period of regulation poses less of a problem than does the fact that the fees are fixed and usually unable to be changed. Regulators argue that a price regulation for long periods is based on prognoses that might be distorted. The airport's products change regularly, and the annual revision of the regulations ensures that parties will never be bound by conditions that are outdated. European Directive 2009/12/EC on airport charges does require regular consultation on airport charges. In Belgium, this is stipulated as being once per year. Annual price-setting nevertheless does require a great deal of negotiation. The length of negotiations has been estimated to be at least 6.5 months per year. Annual price-setting can lead to volatility. In the literature, one argument that has been advanced for a five-year regulation period is that the airports should also have the opportunity to adapt to new prices (Niemeier 2009, p. 20).

Given that all parties have an interest in stability, it has been proposed to adopt a 'step-wise' system in the future. This suggestion assumes a system in which fees are set for a period of five years. These fees would be determined in negotiations between BAC and the airline companies. Annual consultations would be organized with the same actors. Previously agreed-upon fees could be adjusted in case of clear deviations between the traffic prognoses adopted before the fees were set and the traffic figures that are actually realized. This adjustment would occur in two directions (i.e. in case of either under-estimation or over-estimation of the prognoses). Adjustments would be made according to the extent by which a previously agreed-upon threshold is exceeded (e.g. 10 per cent). The regulator would follow and monitor the consultations, in additional to actually intervening if requested by market parties.

This proposed system would fulfil the regular consultation requirement specified in the European Directive, and it would allow reaction to incorrect estimates of future traffic, avoiding excessive annual volatility and avoiding situations that would require directing excessive resources towards potentially unproductive annual negotiations. The proposed system of price-setting and annual consultation does not impose any specific risks to the airport operator and users. The only exception would be unexpected external shocks (as with the attacks on 11 September 2001). Exceptional situations would be subject to exceptional measures, however, in which the responsible governmental authority could take its own specific initiatives.

9.3.3   Adjusted Single-Till or Dual-Till Systems

A second area of attention has to do with a possible shift towards a dual-till system, which would not allow any cross-subsidization for the regulated activities using the income from non-regulated activities. In a dual-till system, the airport operator receives a fair profit margin on the regulated activities as a return on invested capital. In an adjusted single-till system, the airport operator is guaranteed a fair profit margin, due to partial subsidization through the income from non-regulated activities in some cases. According to the current economic regulations, the adjusted single-till system should be used if, when setting the fees for the regulated activities for a given regulated period, the fees at Brussels Airport exceed the average of the fees of the four most expensive reference airports. The adjusted single-till system is not applied in the current system, as the conditions have not been met.

What would be the consequences of a shift from the adjusted single-till system to a dual-till system? Which system would make the best contribution to strengthening the competitive position and sustainable economic development of BAC relative to the surrounding airports? What would be the potential advantages and disadvantages of such a shift to the airport operator and to the users?

The existing system amounts to a diminishing 'adjusted single-till system', in which some of the proceeds from commercial activities can be used to fund regulated activities. The regulator has advocated eliminating this system in the future and replacing it with a dual-till system, in which there is no cross-subsidization of regulated activities through commercial activities. To this end, the regulator applies the following arguments. According to the regulator's own calculations, BAC is already applying the dual-till model in practice: the level of subsidy in the adjusted single-till system is already 0 per cent. The relationship between the proceeds from regulated activities and non-regulated activities is of such magnitude that there would be little cause to use the non-regulated activities to subsidize the regulated activities. Given that the management of the airport in Brussels is privatized, the government cannot simply intervene with regard to the commercial proceeds. The reference airports with the least expensive fees (e.g. Frankfurt and Vienna) use dual-till systems. It is thus not the case that airports with single-till systems (e.g. London Heathrow) are less expensive. A dual-till system is objective, and it is not open to discussion about its implementation. A single-till system requires complex systems for analysis and monitoring, which may be controversial (e.g. concerning the level of subsidization).

A second stakeholder, the government, has expressed a preference for using the current adjusted single-till system to keep the fees at BAC as competitive as possible relative to those of competing airports. Moreover, the proceeds from commercial activities are made possible by the activities of the airline companies. It would thus seem logical for the proceeds from these activities to contribute to subsidizing the regulated activities.

The third stakeholder, BAC, states that the dual-till system is not applicable unless the ROC (return on capital) corresponds to the WACC (weighted average cost of capital). Cross-subsidization should occur as long as the level of the WACC has not been reached. In this respect, BAC is developing along a linear path towards the WACC, depending on the market data, and it can therefore achieve the level of having 'ROC equal to WACC' without drastically increasing the fees. The linear development is intended to avoid snubbing the airline companies with higher fees. It is hoped that the gap will close over time, in part due to improved performance.

Although each stakeholder has its own arguments, each remains only a partial argument. The government should ensure that the proper incentives are offered to BAC. At the same time, it is important to avoid turning the choice between an adjusted single-till system and a dual-till into an ideological discussion. In this respect, it can be established that the existing regulations, in one way or another, impose an obligation on BAC to switch from an adjusted single-till system to a dual-till system by 2026. At present, there is no cross-subsidization (measured as income from commercial to non-commercial activities). For its part, BAC has opted for a gradual alignment of its ROC with the WACC, which will take several years.

For these reasons, a proposal has been made to retain the adjusted single-till system within the framework of the existing regulations (i.e. shifting to a dual-till system within the originally specified period). To provide a meaningful reaction to the regulator's argument that the system is 'too vague', it has been explicitly proposed that BAC should report figures each year at a level of detail that would make it possible to gain insight into the extent of cross-subsidization (either explicit or implicit) and the timeline to be followed in moving towards the dual-till system.

9.3.4   Coordination of Fees with Those of Reference Airports

The existing tariff formula provides for fees that guarantee a fair profit margin as return on invested capital. These fees must be coordinated with the fee practices of the reference airports. The coordination of the fees of Brussels Airport with those of the reference airports is used as an indicator for whether the adjusted single-till principle should be applied. The coordination of fees is also used for coordinating the performance of Brussels Airport with that of the reference airports with regard to various 'key performance areas', including cost-efficiency, quality of services (e.g. to users, passengers, ground handling) and the environment.

Consideration is being given to discontinuing the coordination of fees with the fee practices of the reference airports. Instead, the level of the fees would be assessed according to a financial model that clearly indicates what a fair profit margin on the regulated activities (i.e. the *regulatory assets base*) would be. The weighted average cost of capital (WACC) method has been proposed, in addition to imposing its components (e.g. the risk-free interest rate, the relationship between debts and shares, the equity risk premium and the equity beta). This method would replace the current method, which is described in Article 50, §1 of the aforementioned Royal Decree of 21 June 2004:

> The profitability of the regulated activities ('ROC') is measured according to the income before financial expenses and taxes for the regulated activities after subsidization ('EBIT'), divided by the sum of the net fixed assets and floating assets that are intended for these regulated activities. For the first full calendar year of the first

period, such profitability shall not be less than zero. It can be greater than zero if, at the time that the tariff formula is established pursuant to Article 7, §7, the average income from the regulated activities for each unit of traffic at the Brussels National Airport is less than that of the average for the similar regulated activities of the reference airports. Such profitability will then develop in a linear manner in order to guarantee a fair profit margin as return on invested capital at the time that the 'dual-till' mechanism is implemented. The fair character of the return on invested capital shall be assessed based on the market references and according to the method of the weighted average cost of capital ('WACC').

In effect, the regulator has thus proposed abandoning the fee-determination mechanism based on reference airports and replacing it with an alternative financial model based on objective financial parameters. The problem has two dimensions. In the current system, the fees must be established in a manner that guarantees a fair profit margin as return on invested capital. At the same time, however, the tariff practices are coordinated with those applied at the reference airports.

What is the possible impact of eliminating the principle of coordination with the reference airports and of the prior determination of the value of the components of the WACC on the competitive position of the airport and its economic development?

The regulator has advanced meaningful arguments with regard to the existing system of reference airports. Proper benchmarking cannot be done unless all parameters from the reference airports are identical, or a statistical model is used to allow for the differences. Such is not the case. The airports differ with regard to the services that are and are not included in a given regulated activity. This makes it difficult to make any objectively verifiable fee comparisons. Moreover, any benchmarking exercise entails the possibility of discussions concerning which airports should or should not be included in the reference group. For example, the coordination of fees with those of airports with infra-structure suitable for accommodating A380 aircraft could result in perverse incentives. It is thus highly important for Brussels Airport to be compared to a proper set of comparable airports.

Any benchmarking exercise would be useful, however, if only because of the information that it would yield with regard to the relative position of the airport in question. One solution could be to expand the array of reference airports and use the results in a different way. An accurate benchmark requires the use of airports serving markets that are comparable to those served by Brussels Airport. In other words, they should be true 'peers'. The following criteria can be used in the selection of reference airports: geography (e.g. airports in western Europe); number of passengers (e.g. a minimum of 10 million); type of aircraft that can be accommodated by the airport; provision (or potential to provide) activities of a similar nature (e.g. presence of legacy carriers and

Table 9.1   Subsets of reference airports

Broad array of West European airports	Subset 1: Reference airports used thus far	Subset 2: Other reference airports
Amsterdam – Schiphol	Amsterdam – Schiphol	Copenhagen
Frankfurt	Frankfurt	Lisbon
Copenhagen	Paris – Charles de Gaulle	Madrid
Paris – Charles de Gaulle	London – Heathrow	Milan Malpensa
Lisbon		Rome Fiumicino
London – Heathrow		Vienna
Madrid		Zürich
Milan Malpensa		
Rome Fiumicino		
Vienna		
Zürich		

low-cost carriers); urban or regional function of the airport; whether the airport serves as a hub.

It has been proposed to work with a broader array of reference airports, based on two subsets of airports, i.e. those used thus far and additional ones (see Table 9.1). This would allow an accurate analysis. Differences between the two subsets would indicate that there are specific elements that cause the reference airports that have been used thus far to be more or less expensive than the other airports. This would subsequently enable a precise analysis of where Brussels Airport is positioned and why.

The financial model that is used is even more important. The model must indisputably be based on objective, transparent, consistent and verifiable parameters. It is nevertheless important to consider whether the financial model should or should not be imposed by the regulator. Another potentially acceptable option would be to work in a graduated manner in this regard. In calculating its costs, BAC uses the 'activity-based costing' (ABC) method. These costs form the foundation for fee negotiations with the airline companies. The regulator follows and monitors the consultations, in addition to actually intervening if requested by market parties. The regulator can select a model to use as a test for the fees negotiated by BAC and the airline companies. This model is not imposed, but only used for assessment purposes. If the negotiated fees exhibit major differences relative to the results of the benchmarking exercise and those of the model used by the regulator, consultation is planned, in dialogue with the competent authority. Such consultation could also occur following a complaint by an airline company.

In a highly competitive environment, BAC should obviously have every interest in fees that are competitive, thereby guaranteeing sufficient traffic, income and profit. In this regard, the task of the regulator should not necessarily involve determining these fees, but rather verifying that any possible position of dominance is not being abused.

9.3.5   Level of Economic Regulation

The underlying principle is that economic regulation is motivated by the existence of a natural monopoly. As a result of this underlying principle, several activities are regulated. The necessity of economic regulation can also be justified according to the existence of a certain determinable form of market failure. The abuse of a position of dominance could fall within this category. It is therefore important to consider whether, within the current economic environment, it can be deemed that BAC holds monopoly power or at least a dominant position and is capable of abusing its position of dominance, thereby necessitating stricter control and economic regulation.

The argument that an airport has the character of a natural monopoly is no longer tenable. It is no longer self-evident that airports are characterized by decreasing average costs. As to whether the risk of abuses of dominance justifies a stricter regulation, the assessment of the competitive framework within which BAC operates indicates that the company is subject to strong competitive pressures. In particular, with regard to low-cost companies, as well as companies specializing in point-to-point services and charter companies, BAC holds the least market power, if any at all. Moreover, the presence of nearby competing airports creates a significant likelihood of substitution.

Given the strong competition it faces, even from other modes, for BAC there seems to be no justification for stricter economic regulation. The elements that are currently regulated are also not disputed. Some level of dispute is possible, however, with regard to implementation: would a new initiative (e.g. a 'fast lane' to avoid waiting at security) fall under the regulated or non-regulated category? It would be advisable to increase the transparency and stability of the system.

9.3.6   The Role of the Economic Regulator

A final question concerns the extent of independence that the economic regulator of the operations of BAC should have. The economic regulator has requested reinforcement of the role and powers of this position. The intervention of the minister would be restricted or even eliminated. Does the current position of BAC justify reinforcing the role of the economic regulator? How likely is BAC to abuse any position of dominance that it might have to the detriment of the public interest (e.g. users, passengers, airport development)?

The necessity of oversight of BAC is beyond dispute. European Directive 2009/12/EC on airport charges explicitly prescribes that there must be an independent supervisory authority to maintain oversight of the principles for determining airport charges (Article 11) and, more generally, of the airports that are subject to these principles (Article 12). In the case of BAC, the issue to be addressed is whether, in light of the competitive pressures which make the scenario of abuse of dominance unlikely, the current *ex ante* regulation of BAC continues to be necessary, or would *ex post* regulation suffice, in combination with the possibility of competition law enforcement.

Ex ante economic regulation is relatively complex and expensive and therefore would be justified only when the negative economic consequences of abuse of market power are significant and of a magnitude that exceeds the costs associated with the actual regulation. If *ex ante* regulation is no longer justified, a different positioning of the regulator relative to BAC, the airline companies and the government should also be considered. Currently, the regulator is positioned between BAC and the airline companies. This does not seem necessary. In contrast, the regulator should be positioned between the market actors, intervening in case of complaints or irregularities and reporting to the government.

The intervention of the regulator should be restricted to cases in which the users and the airport operator have failed to reach an agreement or when there is a supported complaint from one of the parties. The intervention of the economic regulator should also be restricted to purely economic matters (e.g. the determination of the fee system, tariff controls and the processing of complaints about the fees). The intervention should not be expanded to other possible aspects of economic regulation (e.g. the quality of services, in the absence of a demonstrable connection with fee-setting).

9.3.7   What Can We Learn from This Analysis?

As indicated by the preceding analysis, for BAC there is no evidence that any natural monopoly exists. Moreover, BAC is subject to such a degree of market pressure that makes the scenario of abusive exploitation of market power highly unlikely.

This obviously places 'regulation' within a completely different context. Without a doubt, however, oversight on BAC and airport operators will continue to be necessary. European Directive 2009/12/EC on airport charges explicitly stipulates that there should be an independent supervisory authority to maintain oversight on the principles for determining airport charges and, more generally, on the airports that are subject to this authority. The regulation could be interpreted in a different manner.

In summary, this means that, in this case, the powers of the regulator should not be expanded. The intervention of the regulator should here be restricted to cases in which the users and the airport operator have failed to reach an agreement or when there is a supported complaint from one of the parties.

9.4 WHAT CAN OTHER COUNTRIES LEARN FROM THESE CASE STUDIES?

Case studies provide an important source of information, including with regard to arguments that have been used and decisions that have been taken. At the same time, however, these case studies should always be interpreted within their economic and geographical frameworks. The results and findings are primarily suited for use in their own environments. The results cannot be automatically extrapolated to other environments.

At the same time, however, cases largely pinpoint specific areas of attention. This is also the intent of the cases presented here: to direct attention to specific problems linked to seaports and airports. The existing regulation of Brussels airport focuses on several areas of attention that are (or could be) crucial for other international airports as well. The issue of whether to require the application of penalty clauses for Belgian seaports can be easily translated to other international port environments.

The following research steps would seem obvious in responding to another working environment. To what extent does a situation differ from the situation in Belgium, as presented in these two cases? This question primarily calls for the elaboration of several micro-studies, including, for seaports, a detailed analysis and comparison of the concession agreements that have been applied. The analysis of the possible consequences of differences identified in such cases could be used to establish a broader research framework.

ACKNOWLEDGEMENT

The author would like to thank Ginevra Bruzzone and Chris Nash for their helpful and constructive comments and suggestions to help improve the quality of this chapter.

NOTE

1. In early 2016, the Antwerp Port Authority was converted into an autonomous municipal company, with the City of Antwerp as a shareholder. The supervisory board would have fewer politicians and more external administrators.

BIBLIOGRAPHY

Gillen, D. and H.M. Niemeier (2008), 'The European Union: evolution of privatization, regulation, and slot reform', in C. Winston and G. de Rus (eds), *Aviation Infrastructure Performance: A Study in Comparative Political Economy*, Brookings Institution Press, Washington DC, USA.

Marques, R.C. and A. Brochado (2008), 'Airport regulation in Europe: is there need for a European Observatory?', *Transport Policy*, 15, 163–172.

Meersman, H., T. Pauwels, E. Struyf, E. Van de Voorde and T. Vanelslander (2010a), *De economische regulering van Brussels Airport Company*, Eindrapport, Universiteit Antwerpen, Antwerp, Belgium.

Meersman, H., E. Van de Voorde and T. Vanelslander (2010b), 'Port competition revisited', *Review of Business and Economics*, 55(2), 210–232.

Morrison, S.A. and C. Winston (2000), 'The remaining role for government policy in the deregulated airline industry', in S. Peltzman and C. Winston (eds), *Deregulation of Network Industries. What's Next?*, Brookings Institution Press, Washington DC, USA.

Niemeier, H.-M. (2009), 'Regulation of large airports: status quo and options for reform', International Transport Forum 2009, Challenges and opportunities in the downturn, Leipzig.

Odoni, A.R. (2016), 'Airports', in P. Belobaba, A. Odoni and C. Barnhart (eds), *The Global Airline Industry*, Wiley, Chichester.

Port of Antwerp (several years), *Annual Report*, Antwerp, Belgium.

Starkie, D. (2002), 'Airport regulation and competition', *Journal of Air Transport Management* 8(1), 63–72.

Starkie, D. (2008), *Aviation Markets. Studies in Competition and Regulatory Reform*, Ashgate, Aldershot, UK.

Van de Voorde, E. and C.A. Nash (2018), 'Seaports and airports', in Autorità di Regolazione dei Trasporti, *Benchmarking and Regulation in the Transport Sector. Report of the Advisory Board*, ART, Italy.

Van de Voorde, E. and P. Verhoeven (2017), 'Port governance and policy changes in Belgium 2006–2016: a comprehensive assessment of process and impact', *Research in Transportation Business & Management*, 22, 123–134.

Winston, C. and G. de Rus (eds) (2008), *Aviation Infrastructure Performance: A Study in Comparative Political Economy*, Brookings Institution Press, Washington DC, USA.

PART IV

The interplay with competition policy

10. The interplay of regulation and State aid control in the transport sector

Ginevra Bruzzone

10.1   INTRODUCTION

Although in Europe significant privatization processes have taken place in the transport sector over the last decades, public funding is still widespread, both for the construction and operation of infrastructure (airports, ports, rail, roads) and for the provision of public transport services. At the same time, notwithstanding liberalization processes which have gradually opened several markets to competition, there remain several situations of significant market power.

In such an environment, both economic regulation and the control of State aid play an important role. The goal of this chapter is to outline the main features of their interaction and point out whether there is room for streamlining the use of the different policy tools.

10.2   STATE AID CONTROL VERSUS REGULATION: OBJECTIVES AND SCOPE OF APPLICATION

The necessary starting point is acknowledging the differences in the objectives and the scope of application of economic regulation, on one hand, and of State aid control, on the other.

The main objective of economic regulation is efficiency. Economic regulation is typically used to correct market failures, including the inefficiencies which may result from the lack of competition. Some efficiency-enhancing mechanisms can also be useful in the design of long-term contracts between public authorities and undertakings, both in case of direct award and in the case of tenders. In the transport sector, long-term contracts may relate, for instance, to the management of infrastructure or to the provision of public transport services.

Economic regulators typically focus on fair access conditions to infrastructure and, when necessary in the light of the market conditions, on criteria for the establishment of tariffs, as well as on the design of price or subsidy caps in long-term contracts. As discussed in the previous chapters of this volume, benchmarking may be useful in all these respects.

For the control of State aid (Arts 107–109 of the Treaty on the Functioning of the European Union (TFEU)), the direct objective is not to enhance efficiency but to minimize distortions of competition resulting from the use of public resources.

Pursuant to Art. 107(1) TFEU, State aid, that is, the use of public resources to provide a selective advantage to undertakings or groups of undertakings which can distort competition and have an impact on trade between Member States, is in principle incompatible with the common market. However, the prohibition of State aid is far from absolute: other complementary EU rules provide that State aid may be considered compatible with the internal market when it is necessary and proportionate to pursue well-defined public interest objectives.

For the transport sector, there are three main different legal bases in the TFEU which can be used to justify State aid as compatible with the common market: Art. 107(3), Art. 106(2) for the compensation of public service obligations and Art. 93 within the framework of the common transport policy, with its implementing Regulation 1370/2007 for public passenger transport services by rail and road.[1]

The European Commission has exclusive competence to assess whether State aid is compatible with the Treaty, pursuant to one or the other of the relevant legal bases. Notably, since the adoption of the State aid action plan in 2005 and especially with the so-called State Aid Modernization (SAM) initiative launched in 2012, the Commission has made significant efforts to clarify its approach, so as to distinguish good aid from bad aid, and to ensure that such criteria are applied consistently in the different areas. The Commission's general view is that any aid measure must respect seven principles:

i.   It must pursue an objective of common interest.
ii.   It must be necessary to this aim, i.e. bring about a material improvement that the market cannot deliver itself, for example remedying a market failure or addressing an equity or cohesion concern.
iii. It must be an appropriate policy instrument to pursue the objective.
iv.   It must have an incentive effect, i.e. change the behaviour of the beneficiary and not simply crowd out private investments.
v.   It must be limited to the minimum needed to induce the additional investment or activity.
vi.   Negative effects on competition and trade should remain limited.
vii. Information about the aid measure should be transparent.

The general approach is further specified in the different sectoral guidelines issued by the Commission, such as, for instance, the Guidelines on State aid to airports and airlines[2] or the Guidelines on the interpretation of Regulation 1370/2007.[3]

These principles are clearly based on an economic perspective, thus making it easier to assess the interplay of State aid control and economic regulation. For State aid control, the main idea is that public resources, when used to provide an artificial selective advantage to an undertaking or group of undertakings, should pursue clearly defined public interest objectives (including in particular, efficiency-enhancing corrections of market failures) and be designed in a way which takes into account the need to maintain incentives to invest and to adopt efficiency-enhancing conduct in the market, both with reference to beneficiaries of the aid and to other undertakings.

Importantly, in State aid control the assessment of whether State aid entails distortions of competition is made at all levels of the value chain, not only with respect to the direct beneficiaries of the aid measure. Thus, for infrastructure, State aid control considers whether public funding results in a selective competitive advantage either for the developer/first owner of the infrastructure, for the manager/operator of the infrastructure which provides services to users (when different from the developer), for direct users of the infrastructure or for their business customers. Similarly, aid to service providers may provide a selective advantage also for the direct or indirect business users of such services.

On the other hand, the scope of State aid control is significantly different from the scope of economic regulation. The Commission may intervene only when all the conditions provided by Article 107 TFEU are met. In particular, State aid control is applicable only to measures entailing the direct or indirect use of public resources, imputable to public authorities, and providing a selective advantage to an undertaking or a group of undertakings which they would not have received from market economy operators.[4] A measure does not involve an economic advantage if the State acted under the same terms and conditions as a commercial investor when providing the necessary funding. The Commission suggests that this can be demonstrated "by significant pari passu co-investments by commercial operators on the same terms and conditions, and/or by an ex ante sound business plan (preferably validated by external experts)" showing that the investment provides an adequate rate of return for the investors. The rate of return should be in line with the normal market rate of return that would be expected by commercial operators on comparable projects, taking into account all relevant circumstances. In the NoA Notice the Commission stresses that for the developer/owner of the infrastructure the advantage cannot be excluded by a tender: a tender only minimizes the amount of the aid.[5]

Moreover, State aid control intervenes only when such advantage may distort competition. Since the focus is the protection of competition, the relevance of State aid control in the transport sector has increased with liberalization and the resulting increase in competition in the relevant markets (airlines etc.).

As to the construction and management of infrastructure, even in 1995 the Commission argued that as long as access and usage remained public and general, the public funding of infrastructure would not constitute State aid and, at the same time, would normally be regarded as being in the public interest.[6]

The competitive evolution of air transport markets in the 1990s and the ensuing impact on airport strategies led the Commission to change its view. By 2012, with their judgments in *Aéroports de Paris* and *Leipzig Halle*, initially the General Court and later the European Court of Justice had clarified that when airport infrastructure is used to carry out a commercial activity, its operation and also its construction are to be considered economic activities and any public funding, when given on conditions different from those which would have been followed by a market economy operator, may fall into the scope of application of State aid control.[7]

The Commission took this case law concerning the airport sector as a basis for unfolding a systematic approach to infrastructure financing under State aid rules, also in other sectors in which liberalization, privatization, market integration and technological progress were increasingly leading to a commercial exploitation of infrastructure.

On the other hand, in those markets in which there is no actual or potential competition, either in the market or for the market, and which therefore are the typical target of regulatory measures, State aid control is not applicable since such markets are not a concern from the point of view of the rules which aim at avoiding "distortions of competition" resulting from the use of State resources. As we shall see in later paragraphs, this is still currently the case for most rail infrastructure.

Summing up, the main areas of potential overlap between the two sets of policy tools include:

a. public transport services when efficiency-enhancing mechanisms are included in contracts and State resources are used to compensate for public service obligations;
b. publicly funded infrastructure when economic regulation has the task of ensuring fair access conditions and, at the same time, there is some competition in the market which justifies the application of State aid control, or the selective advantage may distort competition among the direct or indirect users of the infrastructure.

A final general remark is that, for economic activities which fall outside the scope of EU Directives, for instance because of their small size or local nature, by means of State aid control the European Commission can set some common rules aimed at ensuring an efficient use of public resources. The requirement, set by Art. 107(1) TFEU, that EU rules apply only to measures having an impact on trade has been interpreted broadly by the European Court of Justice, so as to cover also local transport services and local infrastructure.[8] In principle, an impact on trade can be excluded only when the economic activity involved is of no actual or potential interest either for users or for competitors from other Member States and therefore the measure has no direct or indirect cross-border impact on undertakings or customers. As a result, the State aid discipline may interact not only with regulation based on EU legislative acts, but also with national or regional regulatory measures not rooted in EU provisions.

This conclusion remains broadly valid, although recently the Commission showed willingness to follow a "big on big, small on small" approach, whereby it intervenes only in significant cases. A clear example is provided by the decision of 20 July 2017 in the *Marina di Isola* case. The case was brought by two Slovenian companies, controlled by an Italian undertaking that managed the Marina di Isola tourist harbour, in respect of the tax advantages granted by the Isola municipality to another undertaking, Komunala Izola, owned by the municipality, which managed another marina nearby. The Commission decided that the tax advantages did not affect trade between Member States and therefore fell outside the scope of application of State aid control. The Commission stressed in particular that only 37 berths managed by Komunala Izola were available to non-residents, i.e. 1.07 per cent of available yacht berths in Slovenia and 0.05 per cent of those available in the Adriatic area.[9] In 2019 the *Marina di Isola* decision was upheld by the EU General Court.[10] The Court argued that, for the application of Art. 107(1), it is not necessary that the distortion of competition or the impact on trade be appreciable or substantial, but only potential, provided that it is not merely hypothetical or presumed. However, such impact must be demonstrated. In light of the very small market share of Komunala Izola, it could not be reasonably expected that the tax advantage would produce more than a marginal effect on trade and cross-border investment, even if a (marginal) distortion of local competition could not be excluded.

10.3   THE TWO-WAY INTERPLAY OF REGULATION AND STATE AID CONTROL

The interaction between regulation and State aid control goes in both directions. On one hand, the profitability of a regulated economic activity, including related investments, affects whether private resources are sufficient or, instead, some public support is needed on more favourable conditions than the ones which would have prevailed in a market economy. Thus, taking the public policy objectives pursued by the government as a given (e.g. the availability of infrastructure or a public service at the envisaged quality conditions), regulation has an impact on whether State aid is needed. On the other hand, efficiency-enhancing regulation and regulatory accounting may facilitate the control of State aid.

Primarily, in order to be considered compatible, State aid should not overcompensate beneficiaries, that is, it should not go beyond what is strictly justified. In this perspective, if regulation (or the conditions of a tender) ensure that the beneficiary is efficient, and in particular that costs are minimized, then the task of controlling the compatibility of State aid measures is simplified. In other words, under appropriate regulatory conditions, efficiency may be presumed.

Furthermore, when the beneficiary of the aid measure operates in several markets, accounting separation may be required in order to ensure the compatibility of State aid. For services of general economic interest, a specific Commission Directive sets basic rules for separation of financial accounts between services of general economic interest (SGEI) and other activities performed by the same undertaking, unless compensation is granted by means of a public procurement procedure.[11] Also in this respect, when stricter separation requirements are mandated by regulation, the task of controlling State aid is simplified.

As to benchmarking, the previous chapters of this volume illustrate how it can be used in the transport sector in order to promote the efficient operation of regulated undertakings. In State aid control, benchmarking is typically used in two different steps of the evaluation. Firstly, it can be employed to assess whether a measure entails State aid, that is, whether the use of public resources is different from the market economy operator benchmark.[12] Secondly, once the existence of State aid has been ascertained, benchmarking with efficient providers can be used to ensure that the aid measure does not entail overcompensation of the beneficiary of the aid measure.

The way in which the compatibility of State aid is assessed by the Commission also matters to the interplay of State aid control and regulation. Whereas in the past all measures had to be notified *ex ante* to the Commission pursuant to Art. 108 TFEU and were assessed on a case-by-case basis, the modernization of State aid control entailed the adoption of a number of block exemption regulations and regulatory decisions identifying sets of conditions which, when they are met, entail the presumption that the aid measure is either de minimis[13] or compatible, with no need to notify it to the Commission.[14] This is a kind of regulatory approach to State aid, which encourages Member States to follow the model provided *ex ante* by the Commission.

Moreover, even if the Commission guidelines are not legally binding on national authorities,[15] from the point of view of Member States it is practical to follow them when designing aid measures still subject to notification, so as to ensure a rapid assessment of their compatibility by the Commission. The main references for the transport sector are the Community Guidelines on State aid for railway undertakings (2008/C 184/07), the Guidelines on State aid to airports and airlines (2014/C 99/03), the Framework communication for State aid in the form of public service compensation (2012/C 8/15), the Analytical Grids published on the DG Comp website for the assessment of State aid to other infrastructures,[16] and the Communication on the interpretation of Regulation 1370/2007 (2014/C 92/01).

In the light of this general framework, the following paragraphs will focus on the interplay of State aid control and regulation with specific reference to airports (section 10.4), seaports (section 10.5), rail infrastructure (section 10.6) and public transport services by road and rail (section 10.7).

10.4 AIRPORTS

10.4.1 Regulation versus State Aid Control

For airports, the main task of economic regulators in EU Member States is defining models for the adoption of airport charges which are cost-oriented, promote efficiency and are capable of incentivizing investments so as to foster innovation, security and quality of services.

Directive 2009/12 sets a common set of rules for airports with traffic above 5 million passengers, with no prejudice to the right of each Member State to apply additional regulatory measures consistent with EU law. Public authorities may also be entrusted with the task of monitoring that charges for the use of infrastructure and services provided on an exclusivity basis comply with the principles of cost-orientation, transparency and fairness.

When performing these regulatory tasks, benchmarking can play an important role. In Italy, for instance, national legislation expressly requires that the managing body of the airport, when setting charges for the use of infrastructure and services provided on an exclusivity basis, takes into account the EU average level of airport charges in comparable airports. The models for the adoption of airport charges may refer to benchmarks and in particular be based on an estimate of efficient conditions.

While public support has always played an important role in the airport sector, even in 1994 the Commission Guidelines on the application of State aid control to the aviation sector focused only on restructuring aid to flag carriers and compensation for the public service obligations of transport services. As already illustrated in the introduction, public support for airport infrastructure and operations was considered to fall within the remit of general economic policy, and not of economic activities.

The importance of State aid control to airports increased with the liberalization of air transport in the 1990s, the rising role of low-cost carriers and the resulting competition between airports to attract air traffic and thus spur regional economic growth. In light of the more commercial attitude of airport business models, the Commission revised its approach to State aid control in the sector and the European Court of Justice soon confirmed that not only the management and operation of airports, but also the construction of airport infrastructure which is intended to be exploited for commercial use, may be an economic activity and therefore be subject to State aid rules.

The current approach is outlined by the Commission's 2014 Aviation Guidelines to airports and airlines, which address how the Commission assesses, respectively, investment aid and operating aid.[17]

10.4.2   Investment Aid

As to the public funding of airport infrastructure (e.g. runways, terminals, enhancement of access modes, etc.), the assessment of whether it entails State aid focuses on whether the same choice would have been made by a private market economy operator (the so-called market economy operator principle – MEOP). Regulation may affect whether it would be possible for a market economy operator to cover the costs by means of access charges.

If public funding does not respect the MEOP and is thus State aid, the Commission may consider it compatible if it pursues a well-defined objective of public interest, it is necessary and appropriate to pursue it, it has an incentivizing effect (does not entail a mere crowding-out of other investments but results in more investment than in the absence of aid), and it is proportionate and minimizes negative effects on competition and trade. With respect to aid to investment in airport infrastructure, the Commission argues that objectives of common interest include increasing the mobility of citizens and enhancing connectivity within the EU, reducing air traffic congestion in the main hubs, and fostering regional development. It stresses that the need for public support is linked to the size of the airport and, in order to ensure that State aid is an adequate instrument, invites Member States to elaborate national strategic plans for airport infrastructure, so as to increase the coherence of public measures. As to distortions of competition, the Commission in principle will not approve State aid if within the catchment area of the airport there are competing airports with unexploited capacity.[18] The absence of a business plan is taken as an indication that the MEOP test is not satisfied. Aid will be considered proportionate if it just covers the funding gap of the project determined on the basis of an *ex ante* business plan (net present value of the difference between expected costs, including investment costs, and revenues over the lifetime of the investment). Moreover, in order to avoid undue distortions of competition, access to the infrastructure should be open and not dedicated to a specific user. In the presence of physical constraints, the Commission requires that access to the infrastructure be granted on the basis of objective criteria.

The same approach is used to assess whether the conditions applied by airports to air carriers entail State aid for airlines: the criterion is whether the same conditions would have been deemed acceptable by a market economy operator. In the 2014 Guidelines the Commission looks sceptical about the usefulness of considering the conditions applied in other airports as a benchmark. The reason, in the Commission's view, is that public support is so widespread that conditions in other airports do not represent how a market economy operator would act.

Thus, unless the comparison is corrected by eliminating the bias resulting from public support, the methodology to assess whether the conditions applied to airlines entail State aid is based on ascertaining whether the expected incremental revenues of the deal cover at least its incremental costs and, more generally, whether the airport strategy is such as to achieve profitability in the long run. Importantly, the circumstance that the fees paid by users may not cover all the costs incurred in the construction of the infrastructure is not seen as entailing, as such, an economic advantage for users. Indeed, if users were able to pay the full cost of the infrastructure, it would not be necessary to support it by means of State aid.

10.4.3   Operating Aid

In contrast to investment aid, operating aid is usually considered incompatible with the Treaty, except when it can be viewed as the compensation for a public service obligation in respect of a service of general economic interest.

In the 2014 Guidelines, however, the Commission has introduced, on a temporary basis, a more flexible approach aimed at taking into account the situation of several smaller airports which would otherwise be inconsistent with State aid rules. For smaller airports (with fewer than 3 million passengers), the Commission commits to considering business plans ensuring a gradual elimination of operating aid in ten years' time as compatible pursuant to Art. 107(3). After the transitional period, airport charges, including in smaller airports, should be sufficient to cover all operating costs, with the only exception being services of general economic interest.

10.4.4   Safe Harbours

In addition, the General Block Exemption Regulation sets specific conditions under which investment and operating aid to airports is presumed to be compatible and should not be notified.[19]

Moreover, when airport services can be considered services of general economic interest, the SGEI Decision 360/2012 exempts from notification aid to airports with yearly traffic of fewer than 200,000 passengers, provided that the public service obligation is clearly defined, compensation does not exceed the net incremental costs incurred in discharging of public service obligations, accounting separation is complied with, the Member State carries out checks of the absence of overcompensation every three years and ensures that the undertaking will repay any overcompensation.

10.4.5   Some Remarks

The current approach of the European Commission to State aid control in the airport sector, illustrated above, is clearly pursuing two main objectives. First, it aims to avoid public resources being used to support competition between airports when there is no clear positive impact on a common interest objective. Second, it aims to ensure that airport business plans, even when supported by public resources, are sustainable and, in the foreseeable future, will not require operating aid, with the only exception being compensation for properly defined public service obligations. An interesting consequence is that, whilst marginal cost pricing is permitted (even encouraged) for rail infrastructure, beyond the transitional period it may not be permitted for airports if it fails to cover total costs.

Further notable features are that the Commission encourages national planning of airport infrastructure and that for airports the Guidelines suggest that benchmarking may lead to biased results if it does not properly take into account the existence of widespread public support in comparable markets.

10.5   SEAPORTS

10.5.1   Regulation versus State Aid Control

As illustrated in Chapter 7, the port sector is undergoing major transformations and most seaports, like airports, have to meet fierce competition.

On the other hand, along the value chain there are activities which, because of economic features or exclusive/special rights, entail some market power which may justify the introduction of efficiency-enhancing mechanisms.

Common rules at the EU level, such as Regulation (EU) 2017/352, acknowledge the importance of promoting efficiency and an environment favourable to investment for the development of ports in line with current and future logistics requirements. Regulation 2017/352 provides that qualitative requirements and any limitation on the number of providers of port services should be strictly justified and the procedure for granting the right to provide services must be transparent and non-discriminatory. If the activity is directly exposed to competition, no further constraint is required. As to access to port facilities, the charging system should be transparent and non-discriminatory and contribute to the maintenance and development of infrastructure and the efficient provision of services. Specific rules on accounting separation are provided.

Such rules apply only to maritime ports of the Trans-European Transport Network (TEN-T) and a subset of services, although Member States are free to apply the same approach or further regulatory constraints to other ports and services. Moreover, Regulation 2017/352 expressly refers to the application of State aid control both for investment aid and for compensation for public service obligations.

10.5.2   The Current Approach of the European Commission

As for airports, so also for ports; in the State aid perspective there is a concern that public resources may be unduly used to distort competition at the different levels of the supply chain (the owner or manager of the port, operators using the port infrastructure to provide services, end-users of the port facilities).

Thus, in order to avoid the application of State aid control, any public funding of seaports should be consistent with the market economy operator principle.

When a support measure is State aid, it is deemed compatible only when necessary and proportionate to achieve objectives of common interest (e.g. facilitating trade and connectivity, improved intermodal links, etc.) and distortions of competition are kept to a minimum (e.g. access is provided on non-discriminatory terms). So far, the Commission has not published sectoral guidelines on how it assesses whether State aid to ports is compatible with the Treaty, therefore enforcement criteria should be taken from the Commission's decisions.

For instance, aid for renewal of the Italian port of Salerno was deemed compatible because, on the one hand, it was not deemed to have a significant impact in terms of attraction of commercial traffic from other ports and, on the other, access to the infrastructure would be provided on the basis of competitive tenders.[20]

As to the economic conditions applied to users of the port infrastructure or users of port services, compliance with the MEOP is usually assessed by taking as a benchmark the conditions applied in comparable ports. For instance, in 2014, in the assessment by the European Commission of public funding of the Liverpool City Council Cruise Liner Terminal, an artificial advantage for cruise companies was excluded since all ships would have been given access on equal and non-discriminatory terms, and charges would have been established on the basis of an annual market analysis of the fees charged in other UK ports.[21] In the already mentioned port of Salerno case, the Italian authorities not only committed to provide access on the basis of tenders, but also to cross-check the concession fees resulting from the tender (and thus presumably in line with "market prices") with fees paid for similar concessions in comparable Italian and foreign ports.

10.5.3   Safe Harbours

Some categories of aid to investment and dredging for maritime and inland ports are block exempted by the General Block Exemption Regulation (GBER), as revised in 2017, pursuant to Art. 107(3), with no need for an *ex ante* notification to the Commission.[22] Moreover, when ports with an annual traffic not exceeding 300,000 passengers are entrusted with the fulfilment of a clearly defined public service obligation, compatibility of public service compensation pursuant to Art. 106(2) is presumed, with no need for notification, if the conditions set by Decision 360/2012 (already illustrated with reference to airports) are met (including accounting separation and regular checks of the absence of overcompensation). As already seen, for very small ports, the recent approach of the Commission in the *Marina di Isola* case signals the willingness to focus enforcement on cases which may entail a significant distortion of trade.

10.5.4   Some Remarks

For ports, benchmarking is often used by the European Commission to assess whether public support results in aid, that is, in an artificial advantage for beneficiary companies which would not have existed in normal market conditions. Some authors raise the question whether the asymmetry with the approach followed by the European Commission for airports, whereby benchmarking is considered unreliable because of widespread public intervention, is justified (Woll and Meaney, 2017).

10.6   RAIL INFRASTRUCTURE

10.6.1   The Current Approach to the Assessment of Public Funding

Public resources are the main source of funding of rail infrastructure; however, by contrast to the approach adopted for airports and seaports, so far the Commission has been reluctant to include it in the assessment of State aid. The main reason is that national rail infrastructure is seen as a natural monopoly and therefore, provided that specific conditions are met, public funding is not capable of distorting competition.[23] Competition between different transport modes (and the related infrastructure) is traditionally considered too indirect to justify a different solution.

The approach followed by the Commission is illustrated in the Guidelines on State aid for railway undertakings of 2008. As to users of rail infrastructure, in the Guidelines the Commission argues that, as long as the network is open to all potential users on equal and non-discriminatory terms, the risk of distorting competition between transport companies is avoided.

The 2008 Railway Guidelines are currently being revised within the fitness check of State aid rules. The latest official statements by the Commission on the subject matter can be found in the communication on the notion of aid of 2016, where the Commission argues that

> There are circumstances in which certain infrastructures do not face direct competition from other infrastructures of the same kind or other infrastructures of a different kind offering services with a significant degree of substitutability, or with such services directly.[24] The absence of direct competition between infrastructures is likely to be the case for comprehensive network infrastructures that are natural monopolies, that is to say for which a replication would be uneconomical. Similarly, there may be sectors where private financing for the construction of infrastructures is insignificant.[25]

Thus, as to the construction of rail infrastructure,

> the Commission considers that an effect on trade between Member States or a distortion of competition is normally excluded … in cases where, at the same time (i) an infrastructure typically faces no direct competition; (ii) private financing is insignificant in the sector and Member State concerned and (iii) the infrastructure is not designed to selectively favour a specific undertaking or sector but provides benefits for society at large.

The construction of a railway infrastructure which is made available to all potential users on equal and non-discriminatory terms "typically fulfils the conditions set out in paragraph 211" and its financing therefore does not distort competition or trade (point 219). The same reasoning, according to the

Commission, applies to "investments in railway bridges, railway tunnels and urban transport infrastructure" (such as tracks for trams or underground public transport).

In order for the entire public funding of a project to fall outside State aid control, Member States must ensure that the funding provided in the above-mentioned situations cannot be used to cross-subsidize or indirectly subsidize other economic activities, including the operation of the infrastructure. This condition can be met either by providing that the infrastructure owner does not engage in any other economic activity or, if this is not the case, that it keeps separate accounts, allocating costs and revenues in an appropriate way and ensuring that any public funding does not benefit other activities. The absence of indirect aid can also be ensured by means of a tender.

For the operation of railway infrastructure, which according to the Commission may be considered an economic activity, it is still possible to exclude the existence of State aid if, for instance, there is a legal monopoly and competition for the market is excluded.[26]

These general statements notwithstanding, in 2016 in its *Scandlines Danmark* judgment, the General Court recalled that the application of Art. 107 must take into account the relevant legal and economic context.[27] In this judgment, the General Court partially annulled a Commission decision of 2015 which approved the public financing of the Fehrmarn tunnel between Danish and German islands. Two ferry operators that would have been directly affected by the project complained against the Commission decision and the General Court argued that the analysis carried out by the Commission in this respect was insufficient. Therefore, in June 2019 the Commission reopened the case in order to carry out a more in-depth analysis. Following discussion with the Commission, the Danish authorities implemented certain changes, limiting the public financing to the minimum necessary to make the investment happen. In its decision of March 2020 the Commission concluded that the aid measure to support this project satisfied the requirements of the State aid rules for important projects of common European interest (IPCEI).[28]

For the sake of completeness, it should be recalled that aid to rail transport service providers has often been considered compatible by the Commission, pursuant to Art. 93 or Art. 107(3) TFEU, on the basis of an expected net positive impact in terms, for instance, of improved transport coordination or reduction of negative externalities associated with road transport.[29]

10.6.2   Some Remarks

The case of public funding of rail infrastructure clearly indicates that, the more remote are competitive pressures, the less State aid control intervenes and the more important becomes the role of regulatory tools aimed at disciplining incumbent undertakings and promoting efficiency. The process whereby the Guidelines should be revised at regular time intervals allows the Commission to assess whether taking into account the developments in transport markets, the traditional approach whereby the rail infrastructure is considered a natural monopoly remains justified.

10.7   PUBLIC TRANSPORT SERVICES

10.7.1   Compensation for Public Service Obligations and State Aid Control

One of the main areas of State aid control concerns compensation for public service obligations for services of general economic interest, including public transport services (ranging from air and maritime links to regional rail and local bus transport services).

The two main issues are the following:

a.   under what conditions compensation for public service obligations (PSO) is not State aid; and
b.   if State aid cannot be excluded, under what conditions compensation for public service obligations can be considered compatible with the Treaty.

For public transport of passengers by rail and road the legal benchmarks for the assessment of compatibility are Art. 93 TFEU and its implementing regulation 1370/2007, whereas for other transport modes the main legal basis is Art. 106(2) TFEU.

10.7.2   Is Compensation for PSO State Aid?

The starting point is the landmark judgment of the Court of Justice in the *Altmark* case, concerning public support to a local public transport operator in Germany. In *Altmark*, the Court indicates that the existence of aid can be excluded if four cumulative conditions are met, which indicate the absence of any advantage:

a.   There is an entrustment act clearly defining the public service obligation.
b.   The parameters for calculating compensation are established in advance.
c.   Compensation does not exceed the net costs incurred in discharging the PSO, taking into account the relevant receipts (which may be affected by regulation) and a reasonable profit.
d.   Either the provider is chosen through a public procurement procedure which allows the choice of the bidder at the least cost for the community or, instead, the level of compensation is determined on the basis of an

analysis of the costs of a typical well-run and adequately equipped undertaking in the sector concerned (an efficient benchmark).

10.7.3 Is Compensation for PSO Compatible with the Treaty?

After the *Altmark* ruling, the Commission used its regulatory and soft law tools to design a package aimed at avoiding overcompensation for alleged public service obligations even when not all the *Altmark* conditions are met. The package, initially adopted in 2005, was revised in 2011–2012. Currently, it includes: (i) a Directive on transparency (2006/111), requiring accounting separation between SGEI and other activities unless compensation is established by means of a public tender; (ii) the SGEI de minimis Regulation 320/2012 (for amounts not exceeding €500,000 over three years); (iii) Decision 2012/21, which exempts from notification aid below given thresholds, subject to a set of conditions;[30] (iv) an SGEI Framework Communication setting further efficiency-enhancing requirements for cases not covered by the previous tools, including periodic checks for overcompensation and recovery of any extra payment.

Neither Decision 2012/21 nor the SGEI Framework applies to public transport services for passengers by rail and road. For these services, the corresponding provisions aimed to ensure no overcompensation for public service obligations are contained in Regulation 1370/2007, which considers both the case of tenders and the case of direct awards of contracts.

The lack of an *ex ante* definition of a properly justified public service obligation has been an issue in several cases in which the Commission considered State aid in the transport sector incompatible with the Treaty, from *Société Nationale Corse Méditérranée (SNCM)*[31] to cases concerning the public transport sector in Italy.[32]

10.7.4 Some Remarks

The EU State aid framework for the compensation of public service obligations is very detailed and has a broad scope of application. In this area, State aid rules constitute a kind of cross-sector regulation, with the only exception of the special rules of Regulation 1370/2007 for public transport by road and rail. At least indirectly, these State aid rules push Member States into adopting efficiency-enhancing solutions aimed at avoiding overcompensation of public service obligations.

Compared with an efficiency-oriented regulation of subsidies, the SGEI package raises a number of issues.

First of all, it remains to be seen for which SGEI it is possible to find the efficient benchmark required by the fourth *Altmark* condition. In the guidelines concerning the application of the *Altmark* case law, the European Commission stresses that, in the absence of an appropriate tendering procedure consistent with EU Directives on public procurement and concessions, neither reference to a single undertaking, nor to undertakings holding artificial advantages, nor to undertakings not meeting the qualitative requirements established by the rules of the relevant Member State to be considered a well-run company, would be considered an appropriate benchmark.

However, the Commission acknowledges that "where a generally accepted remuneration exists for a given service, that market remuneration provides the best benchmark for the compensation in the absence of a tender".[33]

When the requirement for competition in the market is not met and a proper benchmark cannot be found, the Commission requires further measures so as to limit the risk of overcompensation. In particular, according to the general framework for services of general economic interest (2012/C 8/03) the Commission requires accounting separation and regulatory incentives for the efficient provision of the SGEI. For land transport, however, the looser rules of Regulation 1370/2007 apply: it is sufficient that compensation should not exceed the costs of the undertaking concerned, including a reasonable profit.

A further issue is whether the requirement of a regular *ex post* monitoring of overcompensation is consistent with a regulation based on price or subsidy caps incentivizing operators to increase their efficiency and reduce costs, or whether it risks nullifying the efficiency-enhancing incentives.

10.8 CONCLUDING REMARKS

Whenever there is competition between infrastructural facilities of the same or of different types, State aid control aims at limiting distortions resulting from the use of State resources when State aid is not strictly justified by the need to pursue a common interest objective.

The need to comply with State aid rules may increase the effectiveness of national policies and can thus be viewed as an opportunity instead of merely a constraint. For instance, basing infrastructure development on broad national strategies, as suggested by the Commission for airports, fosters the coherence of public measures and leads to priority setting. The relevance given by the Commission to the existence of reliable business plans encourages national authorities to carry out an *ex ante* assessment of the economic sustainability of projects supported by public resources. For SGEI, an accurate *ex ante* identification of public service obligations and the criteria for their compensation is of the utmost importance in order to provide citizens with quality and efficiency. In the same perspective, in the case of direct award of contracts, the compensation for the undertaking in charge of public service obligations should always include incentivizing mechanisms and reference to appropriate benchmarks. Finally, both the *ex post* assessment of whether State aid measures have attained the relevant objectives and discussions of experiences and methodologies with the Commission and other national authorities may provide valuable indications to national authorities on how to improve their policies in the transport sector.

National regulatory authorities can play an important complementary role in the design of national policies and in ensuring compliance with State aid rules. Firstly, regulation affects the profitability of private investment and therefore may have an impact on whether public support is needed or whether market forces are sufficient to pursue a specific public policy objective. Therefore, if the regulatory framework is unclear or unstable, it becomes very difficult to ascertain whether public aid is necessary and proportionate. Secondly, in sectors where effective procompetitive access regulation and accounting separation rules already exist, it may be easier to prove that there will not be distortions of competition in the use of infrastructure financed by public resources. Moreover, regulatory authorities can provide technical support in the design of procompetitive tenders, in benchmarking exercises aiming to assess whether the MEOP test is satisfied, in the elaboration of major State aid schemes in regulated sectors, and in the *ex post* evaluation of the impact of aid measures. This suggests that, as far as policies for SGEI and infrastructures are concerned, regulatory authorities should be properly involved in the governance of the system at the national level.

For benchmarking, which is used both in regulation and in State aid control, the existence of widespread public intervention should be taken into account, as suggested by the Commission in the 2014 Aviation Guidelines, in order to avoid taking biased comparators as benchmarks.

Public funding of rail infrastructure does not fall into the scope of State aid control when, due to a natural monopoly, it is not liable to distort competition. Thus, the task of promoting efficiency must be carried out by other policy tools, mainly regulation.

In respect of compensation for public service obligations, the State aid package sets out a detailed framework aimed at avoiding overcompensation. Some of its requirements (e.g. accounting separation, and efficiency-enhancing mechanisms for the largest cases) can be met by sectoral regulation, pointing at the complementarity between regulation and State aid control. On the other hand, some requirements of the State aid framework, such as the *ex post* recovery of any overcompensation, may clash with efficiency-incentivizing regulatory strategies whereby companies are allowed to appropriate the benefits of cost reductions.

More generally, economic regulation and State aid control play an important role but are not sufficient to ensure an efficient use of public resources in the transport sector. They should be part of a broader policy aimed at creating a legal and administrative environment favourable to investment and ensuring an overall intermodal planning of infrastructure to pursue common interest objectives, as well as a careful definition of any public service obligation which duly takes into account counterfactual scenarios and alternative policy measures.

NOTES

1. Article 107(3) TFEU covers, in particular, aid to facilitate the development of certain economic activities which do not adversely affect trading conditions to an extent contrary to the common interest, and aid to promote the execution of an important project of common European interest. Pursuant to Art. 106(2) TFEU, undertakings entrusted with the operation of services of general economic interest are subject to competition rules in so far as the application of such rules does not obstruct the performance, in law or in fact, of the particular tasks assigned to them. Thus, aid for the compensation of public service obligation, when justified, is compatible with the Treaty. The development of trade must not be affected to such an extent as would be contrary to the interests of the Union. Finally, Art. 93 TFEU provides that aid in the transport sector shall be compatible with the Treaty if needed for the coordination of transport or for the compensation of public service obligations.
2. 2014/C 99/03.
3. 2014/C 92/01.
4. The use of resources of publicly controlled companies is not considered State aid if the decision is not imputable, directly or indirectly, to public authorities. See, for instance, Court of Justice, C-482/99, *France v. Commission*, and C-262/12, *Association Vent de Colère*. On the notion of State aid, see Commission Notice on the notion of State aid as referred to in Article 107(1) of the Treaty on the Functioning of the European Union (NoA Notice), 2016/C 262/01.
5. NoA Notice, footnote 329.
6. Commission XXVth Report on Competition Policy, paragraph 175.
7. General Court, case T-128/98, *Aéroports de Paris* (2000), upheld by the Court of Justice, case C-82/01 P (2002), and joined cases T-443/08 and T-455/08, *Leipzig Halle* (2011) upheld by the Court of Justice, case C-288/11 P (2012).
8. See in particular Court of Justice, case C-280/00, *Altmark Trans*.
9. Decision C(2017) 5049 final of the Commission of 20 July 2017, *Slovenia – Alleged aid in favour of Komunala Izola* (SA.45220).
10. General Court, judgment of 14 May 2019, case T-728/17, *Marinvest and Porting c. Commission*.
11. Directive 2006/111 of the Commission of 16 November 2006.
12. See below, section 10.6.2.
13. That is, the measure does not entail an appreciable distortion of competition or trade. The SGEI de minimis regulation was adopted in 2012 (Commission Regulation (EU) 360/2012), whereas the general more restrictive de minimis regulation was adopted one year later (Commission Regulation (EU) 1407/2013).

14. General Block Exemption Regulation 651/2014, amended in 2017 to include sections on ports and airports; Regulation 1370/2007 for public transport services by road and rail, amended by Regulation (EU) 2016/2338; Commission Decision 2012/21/EU for other SGEI, including airports and ports with average annual traffic not exceeding 200,000 and 300,000 passengers, respectively.
15. On this point, see Court of Justice, case 526/14, *Kotnik*.
16. The Analytical Grids on the application of State aid rules to the financing of infrastructure projects were first published in 2012 and then updated in 2015, 2016 and 2017. They are published as Commission's Staff Working Documents and are available at https://ec.europa.eu/competition/state_aid/modernisation/notice_aid _en.html.
17. The 2014 Guidelines are currently being revised within the fitness check of the State aid modernization initiative.
18. See for instance the Commission decision which considered aid to the Gdynia airport incompatible with the Treaty, (2014) OJ L 357/51.
19. Arts 56a and 56b, Regulation 651/2014. The block exemption for airports has been added by the Commission in 2017, on the basis of the experience resulting from more than 50 State aid cases concerning airports.
20. Commission Decision *Investment aid to the port of Salerno*, SA 38302, 2014.
21. Commission Decision *UK Liverpool City Council Cruise Liner Terminal*, SA 35720, 2014.
22. Art. 56c, Reg. 651/2014. Before introducing the block exemption, the Commission adopted decisions in more than 30 State aid cases concerning ports.
23. This insight has already been anticipated in a letter by DG Comp to DG Regio in 2011: www.wsfondi.lv/upload/00-vadlinijas/note_on_State_aid_for _infrastructure_projects.pdf.
24. E.g. commercial ferry operators can be in competition with a toll bridge or tunnel.
25. 2016/C 262/01, point 211.
26. NoA, point 219. See also Commission Decision of 17 July 2002 on State aid N 356/2002 – *UK Network Rail* and Commission Decision of 2 May 2013, SA. 35948, *Czech Republic – Prolongation of interoperability scheme in railway transport*. Accounting separation is required to prevent cross-subsidization.
27. General Court, judgment of 13 December 2018, case T-630/15.
28. European Commission (2014), Criteria for the analysis of compatibility with the Internal Market of State aid to promote the execution of important projects of common European interest (IPCEI), 2014/C 188/02.
29. For an overview of such cases, see the 2008 Railway Guidelines; see also Woll and Meaney (2017), paragraph 4.2.
30. The thresholds are an average annual traffic not exceeding 300,000 passengers for air and maritime links to islands and for ports and not exceeding 200,000 passengers for airports; the conditions include the duration of the entrustment, accounting separation and regular checks on the absence of overcompensation and, should overcompensation occur, its recovery.
31. T-454/13, *SNCM v. Commission*.
32. T-15/14, *Simet v. Commission*; T-720/16, *Arfea v. Commission*.
33. 2012/C 8/02. The Union courts have accepted some flexibility in the application of this requirement. See, for instance, C-341/06, *Chronopost*; T-289/03, *Bupa Insurance*.

BIBLIOGRAPHY

Bruzzone, G. and M. Boccaccio (2018), "Infrastructure Financing and State Aid Control: The Potential for a Virtuous Relationship", in B. Nascimbene and A. Di Pascale (eds), *The Modernization of State Aid for Economic and Social Development*, Springer.

Bruzzone, G. and M. Boccaccio (2019), "Infrastructures and SGEI: The Scope of State Aid Control and Its Impact on National Policies", in P.L. Parcu, G. Monti and M. Botta (eds), *EU State Aid Law. Emerging Trends at the National and EU Level*, Edward Elgar Publishing.

European Commission (2008), Community Guidelines on State aid for railway undertakings, 2008/C 184/07.

European Commission (2012), Communication on the application of the European Union State aid rules to compensation granted for the provision of services of general economic interest (Framework Communication SGEI), 2012/C 8/02.

European Commission (2014), Guidelines on State aid to airports and airlines, 2014/C 99/03.

European Commission (2014), Guidelines on the Interpretation of Regulation 1370/2007 on public passenger transport services by rail and road, 2014/C 92/01.

European Commission (2014), Criteria for the analysis of compatibility with the Internal Market of State aid to promote the execution of important projects of common European interest (IPCEI), 2014/C 188/02.

European Commission (2016), Notice on the notion of State aid as referred to in Article 107(1) of the Treaty on the Functioning of the European Union (NoA Notice), 2016/C 262/01.

European Commission (2017), Analytical Grids on the application of State aid rules to the financing of infrastructure projects, Staff Working Document available at https://ec.europa.eu/competition/state_aid/modernisation/notice_aid_en.html.

Nicolaides, P. (2018), *State Aid Uncovered. Critical Analysis of Developments in State Aid 2018*, Lexxion.

Papandropoulos, P. and E. Righini (2017), "Infrastructure Aid", in P. Werner and V. Verouden (eds), *EU State Aid Control: Law and Economics*, Wolters Kluwer.

Woll, U. and A. Meaney (2017), "Transport Aid", in P. Werner and V. Verouden (eds), *EU State Aid Control: Law and Economics*, Wolters Kluwer.

11. Benchmarking in EU antitrust law

Ginevra Bruzzone

11.1 INTRODUCTION

Benchmarking also plays a role in the enforcement of antitrust rules. As early as 1978 the European Court of Justice acknowledged that, for determining whether the price charged by a dominant company is unfair within the meaning of Article 102 of the Treaty on the Functioning of the EU (TFEU), competition authorities can compare it with the prices of competing products. Competitive benchmarks can also be used by competition authorities in merger control, for instance when the parties, in order to obtain the approval of a notified merger, propose behavioral remedies such as the commitment to grant access to key infrastructure on competitive terms. However, this chapter will focus on the use of benchmarking in the enforcement of the prohibition of the abuse of dominance and in particular of the prohibition of exploitative abuses, since it is the area in which, in the case law, there has been a more lively debate on methodological issues.

When comparing the task of competition law enforcers with the task of regulators, an important difference has to be kept in mind. Article 102 TFEU on the abuse of dominance is a prohibition rule, based on broadly worded notions, which has to be applied on a case-by-case basis and entails the imposition of sanctions in the case of infringement. Therefore, the application of this rule implies a presumption of innocence: it is for the competition authority or for the party alleging the infringement before national courts to prove by means of appropriate methodologies, according to the standard of proof required by the case law, that the undertaking actually infringed the law by charging prices which are "excessive" or imposing trading conditions which are "unfair".

11.2 THE PROHIBITION OF EXPLOITATIVE ABUSES OF DOMINANCE

In the EU, in contrast to other jurisdictions including the US, competition law includes some provisions which, in principle, may be used as a substitute for economic regulation of dominant undertakings. In particular, Article 102(a)

TFEU prohibits conduct by one or more dominant undertakings "directly or indirectly imposing unfair purchase or selling prices or other unfair trading conditions". This conduct is usually referred to as exploitative abuse of dominance. By contrast to exclusionary abuses, these practices are not harmful to the structure of competition in the relevant market but may be seen as the "abusive" exploitation of the market power held by the dominant company.

A broad consensus exists on the fact that direct control of prices or trading conditions should not be the main task of competition authorities. The best possible intervention against excessive prices or unfair trading conditions is indirect intervention, i.e. enforcement and/or advocacy action to eliminate or rectify the conditions that cause such prices/practices. In most sectors, high profits will normally attract new entrants and the market will in due course correct itself; therefore intervention by competition authorities may distort the process. Moreover, in the presence of structural obstacles to the competitive process (e.g. a natural monopoly on a lasting basis) *ex ante* regulation is more appropriate than antitrust intervention.

Thus, traditionally, the prohibition of exploitative abuses, including the prohibition of excessive pricing, has been applied sparingly by competition authorities and courts. In practice, competition authorities use Article 102 TFEU to prohibit exploitative abuses in specific cases where the protection of users cannot otherwise be adequately ensured. Often, this tool is applied in markets with lasting market power where for some reason regulation is either nonexistent or ineffective.

In recent years, there has been a kind of renewed interest by the European Commission and national competition authorities in cases concerning alleged excessive prices. As Commissioner Vestager put it in a speech of 2016, "The last thing we should be doing is to set ourselves up as a regulator, deciding on the right price. But there can still be times when we need to intervene. ... The best answer is often to adjust regulation .... But, as the recent action by the British and Italian competition authorities shows, there can be times when competition rules need to do their bit do deal with excessive prices."

The exceptional circumstances in which the antitrust prohibition against excessive prices should be used are a matter for lively discussions in the competition policy community. The checklist usually includes the following:

1. The market in which the dominant firm operates is characterized by high and non-transitory barriers to entry, leading to a monopoly or near monopoly.
2. There are no effective ways to eliminate these barriers.
3. The market is not supervised by a sectoral regulator having jurisdiction to solve the matter.
4. Innovation is limited.

5. Prices are far higher than average total costs and may prevent the emergence of competition in adjacent markets.

Taking this general framework into account, within a broader study on the use of benchmarking it may be interesting to provide a brief overview of the approach of the European Court of Justice to the assessment of whether the prices applied by a dominant company are "excessive".

11.3   BENCHMARKING FOR THE ASSESSMENT OF EXCESSIVE PRICES

In its landmark 1978 judgment in the *United Brands* case, the Court of Justice indicated that "charging a price which is excessive because it has no reasonable relation to the economic value of the product supplied ... is an abuse", but at the same time quashed the decision of the European Commission because it failed to make out a clear case finding an excessive price.

The Court suggested that to determine whether a price is abusive, it should be considered "whether the difference between the cost actually incurred and the price is excessive" and, if so, whether the price is "either unfair in itself or when compared with other competing products".[1]

Some more precise indications on how to assess whether prices are excessive were provided in 2018, in a preliminary ruling issued by the Court of Justice in the *Akka Laa* case concerning the rates applied by a collecting society.[2]

First, in *Akka Laa* the Court of Justice acknowledges that there are different methods which can be used to ascertain whether a price is excessive, including methods based on a comparison of the prices applied in different Member States. If the price is appreciably higher than those charged in other Member States and the comparison has been made on a consistent basis, that difference may be regarded as indicative of an abuse of a dominant position.

The Court adds that a comparison cannot be considered to be insufficiently representative merely because it takes a limited number of Member States into account, on condition that such States are selected in accordance with objective, appropriate and verifiable criteria. Those criteria may include, inter alia, consumption habits and other economic and sociocultural factors, such as GDP per capita and cultural and historical heritage. The relevance of the criteria applied in a specific case must be assessed by the competition authority/national court, taking into account all the circumstances of the case. For instance, neglecting the different willingness to pay resulting from divergences in living standards and purchasing power may lead to biased results; it may thus be appropriate, when making the comparison, to take the purchasing power parity (PPP) index into account. A comparison with a larger set of States may be used to check the robustness of the results.

Moreover, the Court indicates that the comparison may be limited to one or several specific user segments, if there are indications that the possibly excessive nature of the price affects those segments.

In order to assess whether the difference in prices is appreciable, and thus presumptively abusive, the Court observes that it would be improper to refer to fixed minimum thresholds, since the circumstances specific to each case are decisive in this regard. A difference may be considered appreciable if it is both significant and persistent on the facts with respect to the market in question, this being a matter for the competition authorities or courts to verify. Indeed, decisions in which the European Commission found excessive pricing cover cases in which the price difference with competing products was around 40 percent (*Deutsche Post II*, 2001/354 EC) and cases in which it was as high as 400–600 percent (*British Leyland*, 1984/379/EEC).

Finally, in *Akka Laa* the Court of Justice said that, when on the basis of the above-mentioned criteria, the difference with respect to the benchmark is regarded as presumptively abusive, it is for the dominant company to show, when feasible, that its prices are fair because there are objective justifications for such difference.

A more detailed discussion of the use of benchmarking in the application of competition law is found in the opinion of Advocate General Wahl in *Akka Laa*.

AG Wahl stresses the potential benefits of combining different methods. In the absence of "an ubiquitous test and given the limitations inherent in all existing methods", he argues that in order to minimize the risk of errors, competition authorities should strive to examine a case by combining several methods among those which are accepted by standard economic thinking and which appear suitable and available in the specific situation. This approach, in fact, has already been followed by a number of antitrust authorities worldwide. For example, the UK Office of Fair Trading (OFT) has done so in the *Napp* decision on abuse of dominance of 2001, in which Napp was found to be supplying sustained release morphine to patients in the community at excessively high prices, while supplying to hospitals at high discount levels, with the effect of eliminating competition; the Competition Appeal Tribunal upheld the judgment. It is also consistent with suggestions made in international discussion forums (OECD, 2012) as well as in economic literature (Röller, 2008; Motta and De Streel, 2007). Admittedly, the combined application of several imprecise methodologies, even where producing mutually consistent results, may not lead to a more reliable conclusion: the weaknesses of one method are not necessarily remedied by applying another equally weak method. Yet,

> if the methods are applied independently of each other, a given limitation inherent to one of them would not affect the results obtained through the use of other methods.

Accordingly, provided that the methodologies used are, in themselves, not flawed, and that they are all applied with rigour and objectivity, the convergence of results may be taken as an indicator of the possible benchmark price in a given case. (Opinion of AG Wahl, *Akka Laa*, para. 53)

That said, AG Wahl acknowledges that there may be cases in which only one of those methods of determining the benchmark price is available or suitable. In those cases, the authority should consider other indicators which may corroborate or, conversely, cast doubt on the result of that method.

First, a price cannot easily be set significantly above the competitive level where the market is not protected by high barriers to entry or expansion. Otherwise, the market should be able to self-correct in the short to medium term: high prices should normally attract new entrants or encourage existing competitors to expand. That is why, according to the Advocate General, unfair prices under Article 102 TFEU can only exist in markets where the scope for free and open competition is reduced, typically in regulated markets. Obviously, the higher and longer-lasting the barriers created by the legislature, the more a dominant undertaking should be able to exercise its market power.

Second, a price significantly in excess of a competitive price is less likely to occur in markets where there is a sectoral regulator whose task is, inter alia, to fix or control prices charged by the undertakings active in that sector. Sectoral authorities are clearly better equipped than competition authorities to oversee prices and, where necessary, act to remedy possible abuses. It would seem, therefore, that antitrust infringements in those situations should be mainly confined to cases of error or, more generally, to regulatory failures: cases where the sectoral authority should have intervened and erroneously failed to do so.

Third, AG Wahl remarks that an undertaking with market power is evidently less able to leverage its position when negotiating with powerful buyers. For instance, in a case concerning licenses for the use of copyrighted musical works, such as *Akka Laa*, the negotiating position of small shops is likely to be different from that of international platforms (such as Spotify) or groups of large and sophisticated undertakings (such as Hollywood majors). The size and financial strength of an undertaking may have a significant weight in the negotiations. However, the extent to which the licensed products constitute an important (or even indispensable) input for the customers' business may also be of great importance in that context. Clearly, depending on the specific circumstances of each case, other factors may also be relevant.

11.4   EXAMPLES IN THE TRANSPORT SECTOR

Although, as anticipated, there are only a small number of cases in which Article 102 TFEU has been applied to alleged exploitative abuses, some of these cases concern the transport sector.

In the early 1990s, there have been some cases in the airport sector in which the Italian competition authority ascertained abuses consisting in requiring, from users of the airport infrastructure, payment for services which they had not requested.[3]

At the EU level, in *Scandlines v. Port of Helsinborg* (2004), notwithstanding a price difference of 360 percent, the European Commission rejected a complaint arguing that the prices applied by the Port of Helsinborg were abusive, since the comparison with other ports was not made on a consistent basis and, moreover, did not properly take into account differences in willingness to pay. In the Commission's view,

> customers are notably willing to pay more for something specific attached to the product/service that they consider valuable. This specific feature does not necessarily imply higher production costs for the provider. However, it is valuable for the customer and also for the provider, and thereby increases the economic value of the product/service.[4]

In Italy, in a decision of 2008 concerning airport fees, the competition authority stressed that actual prices were not in line with regulatory obligations; interestingly, the authority argued that, when available, regulatory models and data should be referred to.[5] A further case concerning air transport (*Veraldi/Alitalia*, 2001), entailing a comparison between the prices applied by Alitalia on different routes, was dismissed because the alleged abuse was not proven to the required standard.[6] In some of these cases the issue of whether one should refer to the cost of the dominant company (which may be inefficient) or to efficient costs was discussed. It was considered inappropriate to include in the comparison nonprofitable situations. If estimates are based on restrictive assumptions, there should be more flexibility in assessing whether a difference in prices is proof of the existence of an abuse.

11.5   SOME CONCLUSIONS

Whenever enforcing the prohibition of exploitative abuse of dominance is appropriate, the issue emerges of how to apply a proper benchmarking methodology for ascertaining whether observed market conditions may be presumptively considered unfair. As stressed by Advocate General Wahl in *Akka Laa,*

> a lack of reliable data or the complexity of the operations involved in the calculation of the benchmark price (or in corroborating it) cannot justify an incomplete, superficial or dubious analysis by a competition authority. In other words, difficulties encountered by an authority when carrying out an assessment cannot be to the detriment of the undertaking being investigated. Regardless of the specific situation in a given case, the method(s) applied and the other indicator(s) examined must give the authority a sufficiently complete and reliable set of elements which point in one and the same direction: the existence of a difference between the (hypothetical) benchmark price and the (actual) price charged by the dominant undertaking in question.

In this respect, the analysis of benchmarking methodologies used in regulation, contained in Chapter 2 of this volume, may also provide useful insights to competition law enforcers.

In any case, when applying a prohibition rule based on broadly worded notions, such as the prohibition of excessive prices by dominant companies, the possibility for the defendant to provide a justification for its conduct should be preserved.

NOTES

1. Court of Justice, judgment of 17 February 1978, case 27/76, *United Brands Company and United Brands Continentaal BV v. Commission.*
2. Court of Justice, judgment of 14 September 2017, case C-177/16, *Akka Laa.*
3. Autorità garante della concorrenza e del mercato (AGCM), A11, *Ibar-Aeroporti di Roma,* 1993; A56, *Ibar-SEA,* 1994.
4. Case COMP/A.36.568/D3, paragraph 227.
5. AGCM, A376 and A377, *Airport Fees,* 2008.
6. AGCM, A306, *Veraldi/Alitalia,* 2001.

BIBLIOGRAPHY

Bruzzone, G. (2015), "Rapporti tra l'Autorità di regolazione dei trasporti e altre autorità dipendenti di vigilanza e garanzia", in Advisory Board of the Autorità di regolazione dei trasporti (ART), *Istituzioni e regolamentazione dei trasporti: temi di riflessione,* September 2015, available at www.autorita-trasporti.it/wp-content/uploads/2015/12/Rapporto-Advisory-Board-2015.pdf.
De Coninck, R. (2018), "Excessive prices: an overview of EU and national case law", *e-Competitions Excessive Prices,* Article no. 86604, www.concurrences.com.
Evans, D. and J.A. Padilla (2005), "Excessive prices: using economics to define administrable legal rules", *Journal of Competition Law and Economics* 1(1), 97–122.
Geradin, D., A. Layne Farrar and N. Petit (2012), *EU Competition Law and Economics,* Oxford University Press, Oxford.

Motta, M. and A. De Streel (2007), "Excessive pricing in competition law: never say never?", in Konkurrensverket Swedish Competition Authority (ed.), *The Pros and Cons of High Prices*, Swedish Competition Authority, Stockholm.

OECD (2011), *Regulated Conduct Defence*, OECD Policy Roundtables on Competition Policy.

OECD (2012), *Excessive Prices*, OECD Policy Roundtables on Competition Policy.

Röller, L. (2008), "Exploitative abuses", in C.-D. Ehlermann and M. Marquis (eds), *European Competition Law Annual 2007: A Reformed Approach to Article 82*, Hart Publishing, Oxford.

Vestager, M., (2016), "Protecting consumers from exploitation", Brussels Chillin' Competition Conference, 21 November.

PART V

Conclusion

12. Conclusion: benchmarking and regulation in transport

Ginevra Bruzzone and Chris Nash

It will be clear from the foregoing chapters that the authors of this volume regard benchmarking as a very valuable tool in the regulator's toolkit.

Incentives for companies to operate efficiently, pursue quality and invest may result either from competitive pressures or from the regulatory environment. In the transport sector, there remain many areas in which one cannot rely on competition in the market and therefore it is necessary to provide the appropriate incentives either through forms of competition for the market or by means of an appropriate regulation. Benchmarking can play an important role in all these situations, across the different transport modes.

Rail infrastructure, in particular, can be considered a natural monopoly, and indeed European rail policy seeks to introduce competition in or for the market for train operations, but to create a publicly owned monopoly provider of infrastructure at one remove from the final market. Hence, a proper regulatory framework is key.

In the public provision of roads, there is similarly a need to promote efficiency in construction, maintenance and renewal. It can be pursued by means of public procurement or, for toll roads, by means of concessions. Even with competition for the market, there is still a role for regulators in promoting a proper design of tenders, concession contracts and remuneration mechanisms.

For ports and airports, the issue of monopoly power is controversial, as there are often strong neighbouring competitors, and the growth of low-cost airlines and shipping companies willing to use secondary ports and airports has increased this competition. Nevertheless, the fact that these are not perfect substitutes for the main ports and airports and that it is usually impossible to produce competitors with all the same advantages of location, leaves open the question of whether some form of regulation is needed and how it should be designed.

For transport operations, competition in the market is common in many parts of the transport sector, but not all. In particular, for subsidised regional or local public transport, competition in the market is not common. Competition for the market is the obvious alternative, but it may also have problems in terms of ensuring that bidding is realistic, that a genuine transfer of risks is achieved and that bidders do not assume they will be able to renegotiate the contract if they get into difficulties.

Benchmarking is most obviously useful in the regulation of the natural monopoly, where a judgement is needed on the degree to which an efficient operator should be able to reduce costs over time in order to ensure that regulated prices are based on the costs of an efficient firm. Where direct awards of contracts for transport operations are made, benchmarking is also important for the same reason. With competition for the market, benchmarking has another important role in identifying the optimal size and length of contracts, as well as the effectiveness of other contract provisions such as financial incentives. In general, competition for the market requires a number of competitors and this will work best where individual contracts cover the minimum size necessary to exploit economies of scale. There is evidence for instance cited above (Chapter 4) that economies of scale in toll road provision are exhausted at a moderate size, permitting a number of different operators to coexist in many countries.

Even where there is competition in the market, benchmarking may play a role in checking whether competition is strong enough to be effective in ensuring the efficiency of all firms. The European Court of Justice has long acknowledged the use of benchmarking in the application of competition law, in particular when ascertaining whether a dominant undertaking is charging excessive prices. At the same time, the Court of Justice has constantly stressed the importance of the benchmarking methodology meeting the required standard of proof.

As to methods for benchmarking, in the early days reliance was based on finding comparable companies so that simple comparisons of unit costs were sufficient. However, of course, companies were never identical and there was always argument about the validity of the comparisons. In some sectors where there was a single national infrastructure provider, as is often the case with road or rail infrastructure, comparisons either had to be with similar companies abroad or in other sectors, which are always more difficult.

With the development of modern techniques, it has become far more possible to allow for differences in the environment (e.g. length of haul, traffic density) and in the nature of the output (intercity transport versus commuter, transport of bulk commodities versus containers) so that finding exactly comparable organisations has become less crucial. However, many difficulties remain, such as allowing for the impact of differing quality of service on costs. There are limits to the extent that differences may be taken into account, partly because the number of observations may not be sufficient, but more often because of lack of data.

The availability of appropriate data, in terms of quantity and quality, is very important for any benchmarking technique. Usually, firms are multi-product, and for effective benchmarking data is needed which disaggregates costs and output into individual products. For regulated companies, regulators need the power to require provision of such data. Similarly, where there is competition for the market, the authorities need to collect such information so as to design public contracts for the management of infrastructure or the provision of public transport services. Where there is competition in the market, it is more difficult to ensure a routine supply of such data, but at the very least, competition authorities need powers to collect it when competition issues arise.

Looking at the challenges related to data collection, if data is based on self-declarations by companies, it must be checked and, whenever necessary, cleaned. Moreover, since public funding is common in the transport sector, the existence of widespread public intervention should be taken into account in order to avoid taking biased comparators as benchmarks.

More generally, an efficiency-enhancing policy strategy requires not only modern economic techniques but also an appropriate institutional design. A worry in both competition for the market and regulation of natural monopoly is regulatory capture. This is particularly a danger when politicians see benefits to themselves from protecting incumbents, as is particularly likely to be the case where they are in the public sector, as is common in the transport sector. The best guard against this is to ensure that regulators are genuinely independent, with clearly defined powers and duties which they can pursue free from day-to-day political intervention.

International cooperation also has an increasing role to play. So far, in those markets where at the national level there is only one company or a very small number of comparable companies, benchmarking with undertakings in other Member States has been discouraged by practical and legal problems. The development of international datasets would strongly benefit from the setting of common standards for the collection of information.

Index